PC NETWORKING
FOR SYSTEMS PROGRAMMERS

WILEY SERIES IN
DATA COMMUNICATIONS AND NETWORKING
FOR COMPUTER PROGRAMMERS

SERIES EDITOR:
Gerald D. Cole, Independent Consultant

David Claiborne • Mathematical Preliminaries for Computer Networking
Gerald D. Cole • Computer Networking for Systems Programmers
Gerald D. Cole • Implementing OSI Networks
Stan Schatt • PC Networking for Systems Programmers

PC NETWORKING
FOR SYSTEMS PROGRAMMERS

Stan Schatt

John Wiley & Sons, Inc.
New York • Chichester • Brisbane • Toronto • Singapore

Copyright © 1992 by John Wiley & Sons, Inc.

Schatt, Stanley.
    PC networking for systems programmers / Stan Schatt.
        p.   cm
        (Wiley series in data communications and networking for computer programmers) Includes bibliographical references (p. 179) and index.
        ISBN 0-471-55268-2 (paper: acid-free paper)
        1. Local area networks (Computer networks) 2. Computer network architectures. 3. Local area networks (Computer networks) - Management.
    I. Title. II. Series
    TK5105.7.S368 1992   91-47969
    004.6'8--dc20   CIP

PRINTED IN THE UNITED STATES OF AMERICA
10 9 8 7 6 5 4 3 2 1
Printed and bound by Malloy Lithographing, Inc.

This book is for my wife, Jane—the world's greatest reading specialist and my very best friend.

BRIEF TABLE OF CONTENTS

PREFACE

1.	Networking and Distributed Processing	1
2.	Communications Basics	11
3.	Local Area Network Hardware	31
4.	Network Architecture	45
5.	Contention and Noncontention Networks	57
6.	Network Software	79
7.	Repeaters, Bridges, Routers, Brouters and Gateways	101
8.	Network Management	125
9.	Network Security and Reliability	141
10.	E-Mail and Fax Servers on the Network	153
11.	Checklists for Network Evaluation and Selection	167
	BIBLIOGRAPHY	179
	GLOSSARY	181
	A GUIDE TO NETWORK VENDORS	189
	INDEX	195

TABLE OF CONTENTS

PREFACE

1. **Networking and Distributed Processing**   1
   The Trend Toward Networking   1
   Distributed Processing and Shared Hardware Resources   2
   Types of Networks   7
   How Network Standards Evolve   8

2. **Communications Basics**   11
   The Basis of a Communications System   11
   Data Representation   11
   Data Encoding   12
   The DTE/DCE Interface   13
   Data Transmission   15
   Cabling   18
   IBM's Cabling System   22
   Universal Wiring Systems   23
   Analog Transmission   25
   Wireless LAN Transmission   28

3. **Local Area Network Hardware**   31
   The File Server   31
   The File Server's Use of Memory   35
   The PC Network Node   39
   The Network Interface Card   42

4.	**Network Architecture**	**45**
	Some Design Approaches	45
	The OSI Model	48
	The IEEE 802.2 Specifications	52
5.	**Contention and Noncontention Networks**	**57**
	Contention Networks	57
	Noncontention Networks	67
	Some Proprietary Networks	74
6.	**Network Software**	**79**
	Operating Systems	79
	DOS 3.1 and Record Locking	80
	Microsoft Networks (MS-NET) and the Network Operating System (NOS)	80
	Limitations of Programs Running Under MS-NET	81
	Proprietary Network Operating Systems	81
	Client Servers	97
	AppleTalk and Macintosh Networks	98
7.	**Repeaters, Bridges, Routers, Brouters and Gateways**	**101**
	Repeaters	101
	Bridges	102
	Routers	110
	Brouters	114
	Gateways	114
8.	**Network Management**	**125**
	What is a Network Management System?	125
9.	**Network Security and Reliability**	**141**
	Preventing Unauthorized Network Access	141
10.	**E-Mail and Fax Servers on the Network**	**153**
	CCITT Fax Standards	154
	Electronic Mail on Local Area Networks	157
11.	**Checklists for Network Evaluation and Selection**	**167**
	The Needs Analysis	167
	Selecting Network Components	173
	Network Software	175
	The Network Procurement Process	177
	BIBLIOGRAPHY	**179**
	GLOSSARY	**181**
	A GUIDE TO NETWORK VENDORS	**189**
	INDEX	**195**

PREFACE

Being suddenly thrown into the world of networking is often a very frustrating experience for computer professionals. From the perspective of someone with years of mainframe experience, networking can seem to be a bewildering world in which international and de facto standards often conflict, key hardware and software components that should be compatible are not, and new products seem to emerge almost daily, casting doubt and confusion.

In such a world, a customer should be able to call a vendor and find out about how to make product A work with product B. Unfortunately, vendors often have myopic views regarding product choices and frequently plead ignorance about how other vendors' products operate with each other.

PC Networking is designed for the computer user who wants a briefing on the current networking landscape and enough unbiased information to evaluate and select a Local Area Network (LAN) intelligently or upgrade a current network configuration.

Chapter 1 explains the major benefits of networking and describes some distributing processing trends. It also describes some of the major standards organizations and indicates how international communications/networking standards are developed.

Chapter 2 provides an overview of communications, including descriptions of different types of transmission and media. In addition to conventional media, the chapter covers some exciting new microwave LANs. Chapter 3 focuses on PC network hardware including different types of memory management and disk drive controllers. It explains the difference between micro channel architecture and EISA, the two leading bus contenders for "muscle" file servers. Also covered are the "super servers" such companies as Compaq and NetFrame have developed.

The next two chapters focus on network architecture. Chapter 4 provides an overview of the OSI model and the IEEE 802.2 specification for local area networks. Chapter 5 looks at a number of real networks using the theory in the previous chapter as a foundation. You'll look at Ethernet, including the new 10BaseT standard, as well as token bus and token ring networks. You'll also observe how an Apple Macintosh network is configured.

The final six chapters look at network management issues. Chapter 6 examines network software, Chapter 7 covers diagnostic tools and day-to-day management control and Chapter 8 looks at network management. Finally, Chapter 9 examines network security and reliability, and Chapters 10 and 11 focus on E-mail, fax servers and network evaluation.

The book includes checklists to help the computer professional ask the right questions and narrow down the network selection process. It also contains a bibliography, a guide to network vendors, and a glossary.

I have tried to write to you, the reader, in much the same way I would talk to a client who has hired me as a consultant. Rather than writing entire chapters on the major network operating systems currently on the market, for example, I have tried to focus on the products' significant features and differences. Why select LAN Manager instead of NetWare? Why purchase an EISA file server rather that a micro channel architecture file server? What kind of protocol analyzer do you need? Should you select token ring or Ethernet? How can you bridge the Macintosh computers in your office? These are some of the frequently asked questions I have tried to answer in this book. I have also tried to provide you with enough communications theory and practical product information to help you make intelligent decisions . . . and perhaps save yourself the price of a consultant. Happy networking!

1

NETWORKING AND DISTRIBUTED PROCESSING

While we will examine the details of how personal computer networks function in later chapters, it is worthwhile spending a few moments first looking at the major benefits that networking offers a company. This chapter examines these benefits and then describes the different types of networks currently available. Because it is virtually impossible to talk about networks without talking about network standards, we'll also take a brief look at the major organizations that establish these standards.

■ THE TREND TOWARD NETWORKING

The 1980s saw the emergence of the "yuppie," Wall Street's fascination with the junk bond, and the rise of the personal computer (PC)*. While today the yuppie is a fading breed and the junk bond is no longer attractive, Apple Corporation cofounder Steve Jobs's vision of a computer on the desk of every information worker is almost a reality.

The linking together, or networking, of these PCs has become a major trend in the 1990s. Here *networking* is defined as the sharing of hardware resources, software resources, and information. As you will see in this chapter, there are many immediate benefits to networking and many, even greater benefits promised in the near future.

The current benefits of networking computers together, as opposed to relying on separate PCs, are these:

- more efficient use of hardware resources;
- more efficient use of software resources;
- the ability to share key information;
- improved information management;
- improved security.

---

* We'll use the term *PC* in the generic sense to describe any personal computer, including the Apple Macintosh, and not limit the term to an IBM microcomputer.

■ DISTRIBUTED PROCESSING AND SHARED HARDWARE RESOURCES

There is no comparison between the raw processing power of a mainframe computer that is designed to serve hundreds of users and the power of a PC designed for a single user. The mainframe computer exemplifies centralized computing. Hundreds of terminals rely on this powerful computer to provide all the processing power required. Networked PCs exemplify distributed processing—each PC has the power to process its own information. As you'll see in later chapters when we examine client servers, future networks might very well distribute processing tasks among mainframe computers, minicomputers, and microcomputers without the end user even being aware of precisely where the information is coming from.

Distributed Processing

The growth of networks has been fueled by the realization by many companies that distributing their processing among hundreds of PCs can often be more efficient than relying upon the mainframe for all their computing needs. While the mainframe handles a company's accounting and manufacturing needs, networked PCs can reduce the processing burden on this expensive machine by handling such applications as word processing, spreadsheets, databases, and project management.

To summarize, then, **distributed processing** means that networked PCs use their own microprocessors to run programs and process data while taking advantage of the network's storage capacity to save and retrieve files. A company already using stand-alone PCs can network these machines for a fraction of the cost of adding a second mainframe.

Shared Hardware Resources

A major advantage of networking microcomputers is that they can share expensive hardware resources such as laser printers, plotters, and optical disks. While a small company with ten employees might not be able to justify more than one Apple LaserWriter or two Hewlett-Packard LaserJet printers, it can optimize this equipment by sharing it with networked PCs. Network software can queue up print jobs so that they will be printed on a first-come, first-served basis. It is even possible to alter this order if a high-priority job must be printed immediately.

In another example, several architects using a computer-aided drawing (CAD) program can share a networked professional-quality plotter and help to justify the cost of this expensive device. Similarly, all network users can access information from an expensive optical disk drive—which can retrieve data from dozens of laser disks containing literally billions of records—attached to one of the networked PCs.

Shared Software Resources

Another major advantage of networking PCs is that it allows them to share software resources. Rather than having to purchase a copy of WordPerfect and dBASE IV for each employee's PC, a company can purchase a single network version of each program. Network software not only saves money, it also increases employee efficiency. A single network copy of a program ensures that all employees are using the same version and that all their data files are compatible.

Running a single network version of a program also makes it much easier to provide employees with training and software support. Programs such as Closeup now make it possible for a corporate software support specialist sitting at a help desk to view a network user's screen and correct a problem remotely.

Shared Information

While networking can save companies substantial amounts of money because of the more efficient use of hardware and software resources, its most significant advantage is that it makes information more accessible. All users can share the same information. Let's say that the XYZ Corporation has a program running on its network that contains both the company inventory and customer order processing. Salespeople can check the inventory file to see the number of widgets in stock before entering an order. If Bob sells the last widget just before Mary checks this item, she will be able to tell her customer that she needs to back-order since her computer screen will have displayed the result of Bob's recorded sale.

In a company with a network electronic spreadsheet program, the network manager trains departmental managers where to store their files on the network so that consolidation can take place. Each department manager submits budget information that is consolidated automatically into a single report. This report totals all departmental figures and calculates whether the company is meeting its budget forecast.

Electronic Mail (E-Mail)

When PCs are networked, it is possible to improve corporate communications by installing electronic mail (E-Mail). Some E-Mail systems permit lengthy files and even graphics to be attached to a message. On cc:Mail, for example, it is possible to send a memo concerning a budget and then attach both a spreadsheet showing the actual figures and a graph displaying the results.

Some E-mail systems incorporate bulletin boards. These electronic bulletin boards serve as a place for users to leave messages on a certain topic, messages that everyone can read just as if they were pinned to a physical bulletin board in city hall.

While E-Mail has not eliminated the need for paper altogether, it has made office communications more efficient. Return receipts can be requested when a memo is sent. A manager scheduling a meeting can use E-Mail and a distribution list to send a notice and an agenda to everyone scheduled to attend. Some E-Mail systems can organize correspondence by topic, date, or sender. An E-Mail user can request all messages from, say, J. J. Hill concerning the Phillips merger between July 15 and September 1 and see them retrieved and displayed far more quickly than if a human were assembling the information. Many E-Mail systems running on PC networks have pop-up menus that enable a user to view a mailbox from within an application program such as Word-Perfect. To examine mail while writing a report, a user can press a couple of "hot keys" and activate this pop-up menu without ever leaving the WordPerfect program.

The standardization of E-Mail specifications in the near future will make it much easier for a user on one computer network to send mail to a user on another across the globe even though the two networks use different E-Mail programs. An IBM PC user on a network in Los Angeles will be able to send an electronic mail message to a Macintosh user on a Japanese computer network in Osaka. Later in this book, we'll return to this topic and examine it in much more depth.

Groupware

One of the newer types of network software is known as groupware. Designed specifically for networks, this type of software improves the ways groups work together. One example of groupware is Broderbund Software's ForComment. This product enables several network users to view the same document and enter their own comments, which can then be viewed by other network users, along with the original document. So, for example, if several programmers do not like the way the rough draft of a software manual describes a particular module, they can enter their comments and the person who wrote the document can see their comments on the relevant pages.

The Coordinator is another example of how groupware running on a network can improve corporate communications. The Coordinator has the ability not only to send and receive E-Mail, but also to organize all communications on a project-by-project basis so they can be retrieved easily. This program encourages users to relate documents to be transmitted to others already stored.

The Coordinator also has scheduling capabilities. So, for example, a manager can schedule a meeting by letting this program search the calendars of all committee members and determine the best available time. Many administrative assistants and secretaries

---

Calendar for Mon 03-Jun-91

Appointments   Subject
  9:00 — 10:00am   Budget meeting with Lois
 10:00 — 1:00pm   Quarterly marketing meeting
  2:00 — 4:00pm   Interview candidates for analyst position

Reminders   Confirm reservations for Tahoe

Conversations
28 May Pwilson to complete request Revised regional sales figures

Carry forward
26 May rjackson to complete request Graphics on International Sales
27 May tnunn to complete request Estimate on 3rd Quarter Domestic Sales

---

Figure 1-1. The Coordinator is groupware that can be used to schedule meetings for network users quickly and efficiently.

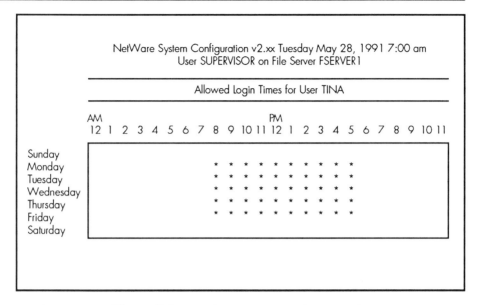

Figure 1-2. A user's access to a network is restricted to
Mondays through Fridays from 8:00 AM to 5:00 PM.

find this particular groupware function particularly appealing. Figure 1-1 shows The
Coordinator's calendar and E-Mail functions.

Improved Information Management

PC users often complain that networking limits their freedom. Suddenly a network
manager appears who sets down certain housekeeping rules—concerning, for example, the types of files that can be stored, when files must be backed up, the types of
programs that can be used, and even when the network can be used. Figure 1-2 illustrates how a network manager on a NetWare network has restricted the access of a network user.

A network manager controls users' rights on the network. Does a user want to place a
certain program on the network? This person must go through the manager, since only
the manager can install a new program and empower users with network rights.
Depending on the network, the network manager can establish when users must
change a password, which directories of files users can see, and even which computers
users are permitted to use.

Stand-alone PC users often procrastinate when it comes to backing up their files, but
network managers safeguard data by determining when files are to be backed up.
Network users must also follow rules and save files in specified directories in much
the same way that clerical workers file papers according to company rules so they can
be easily located.

Because a network forces all users to follow the same information-handling rules, information becomes more accessible within the entire company. Does someone need a spe-

cific budget worksheet created by another department? Assuming that this user has the network rights to the worksheet, enabling him or her to locate, retrieve, and read it, the network filing system will probably make it relatively easy to locate this file.

PC Network filing systems are set up in a hierarchical fashion similar to the way a PC hard disk is organized. The result is a file structure that looks like the organizational chart of a large company. A relatively small number of major or parent directories have several directories (subdirectories) or children directories under them. It is relatively easy to locate files if they are stored in logical fashion in appropriately named directories and subdirectories.

Figure 1-3 illustrates this structure. Users have the rights to use but not change or delete the WordPerfect program. They are given all rights to their own user directories so they can create, modify, and later delete the document files that they create.

Improved Security

Networks offer a company greater security than do stand-alone computers. Users are usually required to use passwords to log onto the network and network software enables the network manager to audit users' activities. If Bob tries repeatedly to gain access to a directory to which he is denied permission, the network notes this activity and records it. If the company owns a single copy of a program, it can use programs such as Sitelock to lock the program at one user. Everyone on the network can use this program, but only one user at a time can gain access. This practice protects companies

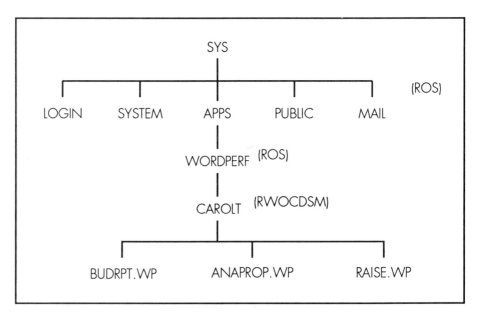

Figure 1-3. A PC network's hierarchical file structure makes it easy to locate files.

from disgruntled employees lodging complaints with software firms that the companies are using illegal copies of a program and breaking software licensing laws.

There is even network software available that enables network managers to monitor PC users' floppy disk drives. If a user attempts to use a copy of a program whose serial number is not on file on the network, the user will be denied access. Of course, users who disconnect from the network and use their own hard drives can still access illegal software they have loaded there, but that's a problem the network manager and corporation can handle by auditing the software on local drives and imposing strict penalties for possession of illegal software.

∎ TYPES OF NETWORKS

So far in this chapter we've been talking about networks in very general terms. There are a number of different types of networks, however, and these differences are usually based on size.

The Local Area Network (LAN)

The local area network (LAN) links together personal computers at a single site. If several buildings are linked together, the LAN is said to exist in a campus environment. LANs generally are limited to a couple of miles in length, depending upon the type of cabling and transmission used, but it is difficult to state absolute maximum values for an industry that changes almost daily. Our primary focus in this book will be on LANs.

Metropolitan Area Networks (MANs)

A Metropolitan Area Network (MAN) encompasses an entire city or metropolitan area. The city of Cambridge, Massachusetts, for example, has been developing a MAN that links together dozens of LANs on college campuses and medical facilities. While LANs are usually owned by the companies that installed them, the MAN is often a service provided by a telecommunications vendor such as a local telephone company.

Wide Area Networks (WANs)

The Wide Area Network (WAN) comprises a large geographical area that can include several states or even the entire world. A WAN can include both private and public networks. We will examine how WANs work in great detail later in this book.

Enterprise Networks

Many companies face the problem of incompatible networks. For example, a firm might have PCs linked together on a network, a Digital Equipment Corporation minicomputer to handle accounting, and an IBM mainframe computer to handle manufacturing. Today, companies are increasingly integrating such components into one *enterprise network*.

A company with several branch offices might envision an enterprise network that includes LANs, MANs, and WANs. The key challenge is to enable users to exchange meaningful information with each other easily. Later in this book we'll examine both the obstacles to achieving network integration and the tools—such as bridges, routers, and gateways—that make it possible.

■ HOW NETWORK STANDARDS EVOLVE

Networks have become more popular in part because several national and international organizations have labored to establish standards. Without these standards, companies would find it virtually impossible to mix and match network components, including the microcomputers that serve as network nodes. While it is still much safer to mix and match stereo components than network circuit cards, the computer industry is making progress in developing network standards. Let's look at some of the key organizations working on this monumental task.

For a standard to be meaningful, it must be accepted both internationally and domestically. New standards are usually developed within national organizations and then move to an international standards organization, where they are debated, refined, and finally adopted.

The Electronics Industry Association (EIA)

The Electronics Industry Association (EIA) is composed of U.S. electronics manufacturers. It has produced several communications standards for the products its members produce, including the RS-232 specification for asynchronous communications associated with "serial" printers. We'll examine this specific standard in Chapter 2.

The American National Standards Institute (ANSI)

The American National Standards Institute (ANSI) acts as a clearinghouse for U.S. standards. It serves as the U.S. representative to the International Standards Organization (ISO), which we'll look at shortly. ANSI has developed a standard for optic fiber networks (FDDI) transmitting data at 100 million bits/second.

The Institute of Electrical and Electronics Engineers (IEEE)

The Institute of Electrical and Electronics Engineers (IEEE) has been instrumental in developing several key network standards. Its 802 Committee has developed specifications for such popular network architectures as the bus (802.3) and the token ring (802.5). It has also developed standards for metropolitan area networks (802.6) and networks that integrate voice and data information (802.9). We'll be looking at these specifications in more detail in later chapters.

The European Computer Manufactuers' Association (ECMA)

The European Computer Manufacturers' Association (ECMA) is the European equivalent of our EIA. It works closely with both the ISO and the IEEE 802 Committee in developing computer-related standards.

The International Consultative Committee for Telephone and Telegraph (CCITT)

The International Consultative Committee for Telephone and Telegraph (CCITT) is affiliated with both the United Nations and a branch of the International Telecommunications Union. The U.S. State Department has a representative on this very important committee that has established international standards for communications equipment, such as modems, which are integral to any wide area network.

The International Standards Organization (ISO)

The International Standards Organization (ISO) contains representatives from the principle standards organizations in participating countries. Perhaps the best known work of the ISO is its Open Systems Interconnection Model (OSI Model). Computer networks that incorporate a variety of hardware and software must share a common set of rules, or protocols, for communicating. We'll look at how the OSI Model provides such protocols in later chapters, but for the moment we'll simply say that when major manufacturers adhere to the OSI Model, companies are not locked into a single company's network hardware and software; they are able to link IBM, DEC, and AT&T as well as other computer networks without much difficulty.

How Network Standards Develop

The ISO's procedure for developing a standard illustrates just how time consuming this process is. An examination of the terminology used to describe different stages of this process is important, because so much of what we will be discussing later in this book is still evolving toward standardization.

The ISO begins by issuing a Working Draft (WD). This working paper is formalized into a Draft Proposal (DP), which is usually implemented on an experimental basis by some leading software developers. An ISO group uses feedback from these early users to modify this proposal into a Draft International Standard (DIS).

This draft is circulated widely among developers, manufacturers, and large end users for comment and corrections. Usually, after some minor corrections, the draft becomes an International Standard (IS). Later, any necessary changes are incorporated into a Draft Addendum (DA), which is circulated for comment. Ultimately, suggested corrections to this draft are incorporated into a formal Addendum (AD) to the international standard.

Knowing this ISO terminology will help you understand just how far along in the process a proposed network standard is. Manufacturers are reluctant to start producing products reflecting a new network standard until it reaches the DIS stage. Sometimes network vendors will announce a new product that reflects a DIS set of specifications and promise that they will provide free updates to their customers if any changes are made before finalization of the international standard.

2

COMMUNICATIONS BASICS

All networks are communications systems. In this chapter, we look at the components of a communications system. We'll follow data as it moves from one computer through an interface to a transmitting device and observe how this data can travel in different forms (digital signals or analog signals) over different types of media, including cabling and air. After noting the advantages and disadvantages of networks utilizing different cabling schemes, we'll examine how infrared and microwave technologies can be used to transmit information over networks.

■ THE BASIS OF A COMMUNICATIONS SYSTEM

Data communications has its own jargon. Standards for LAN and wide area networks frequently refer to data terminal equipment (DTE) and data communications equipment (DCE). **Data terminal equipment** often refers to a computer or terminal. DTEs are connected to **data communications equipment (DCE)**—for example, modems that facilitate transmission over a cable. Figure 2-1 illustrates a typical communications system.

■ DATA REPRESENTATION

Because computers only process information in binary (1s and 0s), data must be translated so that characters, numbers, and even control codes can be converted into the positive 5 volts (binary 1) and negative 5 volts (binary 0) that computers understand. PC LANs tend to use the 7-bit **American Standard Code for Information Interchange (ASCII)**, with an eighth bit included for error checking. Conversely, IBM's mainframe computers utilize the 8-bit **Extended Binary Coded Decimal Interchange Code (EBCDIC)**. These two data formats are incompatible, an obstacle that must be overcome to enable PC LANs to transmit and receive information over gateways from mainframes. We'll examine this topic in a later chapter, when we look at the various types of available LAN gateways.

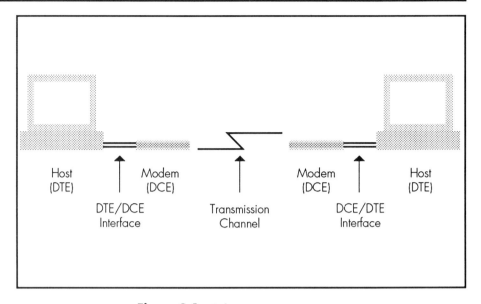

Figure 2-1. A data communications system.

■ DATA ENCODING

Let's assume that a short message is to be sent from one computer (DTE) over a network to a second computer. The message ("A meeting is scheduled today at 2.") is stored in an ASCII file as a string of 1s and 0s. For example, the very first word ("A"), for example, is represented in 7-bit ASCII as 1000001.

The microcomputer contains a special network circuit card (in this case, the DCE) that is capable of converting the data into a voltage pattern and then transmitting this voltage over the network channel or cable. Messages are transmitted over a network in a voltage pattern designed to make it easy for the receiving microcomputer's circuit card (DCE) to interpret. If 1s were transmitted as positive 5 volts, a string of them would be difficult to interpret accurately—it would be hard to determine when one signal ended and the next began, since the discrete bits would not vary. Two commonly used network encoding schemes are Manchester Encoded Binary and Non Return to Zero Inverted (NZRI). As Figure 2-2 illustrates, *Manchester Encoded Binary* provides a signal transition for every bit. This extra overhead is permissible on LANs with plenty of bandwidth to spare.

Non Return to Zero Inverted (NRZI), on the other hand, reduces overhead by providing a transition only on every binary 0. Possible confusion over a long string of 1s is eliminated by "bit stuffing," in which extra 0s are inserted in strings of 1s upon transmission and then removed upon arrival at the destination microcomputer.

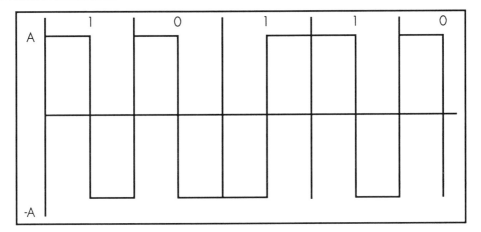

Figure 2-2. Binary data may be encoded to improve accuracy and lower bandwidth requirements. Source: Cole, *Computer Networks for Systems Programmers.*

■ THE DTE/DCE INTERFACE

For meaningful communication between the DTE and DCE to take place in a data communications system, there must be an interface, a connecting point through which electrical signals travel in accordance with rules or specifications that both sending and receiving devices follow. In this section, we'll examine a few of the standard interfaces associated with PC LANs.

The RS-232C Interface

The Electronics Industries Association, discussed in Chapter 1, developed a DTE-to-DCE interface standard a number of years ago known as Recommended Standard #232, or, as it is more commonly known, RS-232C. The *C* refers to the particular version of the standard. The specifications published in 1969 describe a 25-wire interface for transmission of up to 20,000 bits/second at distances of up to 50 feet. It is possible to transmit much farther than 50 feet without losing data, but most manufacturers will not honor maintenance contracts if longer cables are used. Although an RS-232C interface has 25 wires or pins, only a few pins are generally required for communication to take place. In fact, there is also a 9-pin version of this standard.

You might expect that a group of manufacturers would at least agree on which pins should carry specific information. Unfortunately, RS-232C is probably the most non-standardized standard in the data communications industry. It is necessary to keep manuals for all the devices to be linked, since they will probably not all use the same pins to carry the same control information. With the appropriate manuals available, a data communications technician can make what is known as a crossover cable to link two RS-232C interfaces successfully.

Pin	Signal	Source
1	Protective Ground	DTE
2	Transmitted Data (TXD)	DCE
3	Received Data (RXD)	DTE
4	Request to Send (RTS)	DCE
5	Clear to Wend (CTS)	DCE
6	Data Set Ready (DSR)	
7	Signal Ground (GND)	
8	Data Carrier Detect (DCD)	DCE
15	Transmit Signal Element Timing (TSE)	DCE
17	Receive Signal Element Timing (RSE)	
20	Data Terminal Ready (DTR)	DTE
22	Ring Indicator (RI)	DCE

Figure 2-3. The RS-232C standard.

Figure 2-3 describes the information usually carried over specific pins on an RS-232C interface. Because voltages are measured against some reference level, one pin (GND) carries this reference level. Two lines carry data. One (RXD) carries data from the DCE to the DTE, while a second line (TXD) carries data from the DTE to the DCE. For synchronous communications, two clock lines (RSE and TSE) provide the information necessary for the DCE and DTE to synchronize their clocks.

The EIA-232D Interface

The EIA has developed a "D" version of its RS-232 interface standard. RS-232D is upwardly compatible from RS-232C because it does not change any pin designations. It does, however, add some new signals. Pins 9 and 10 are reserved for testing. The major changes reflected in this interface are associated with modems, the devices used for data transmission over phone lines. We'll look at the world of modems later in this book.

The RS-449 Interface

The EIA developed its RS-449 standard to try to overcome many of the limitations found in RS-232C. RS-449 describes a 37-pin connector that includes diagnostic circuits. The RS-449 interface provides mechanical, functional, and electrical specifications (under EIA 422 and 423) for data communications up to 40 feet at transmission speeds of 10 million bits/second or up to 4,000 feet at speeds of 100 kilobits/second. RS-449 includes a loopback capability that enables a DTE operator to determine whether or not the interface and DCE are operating properly by observing whether or not the data transmitted matches the data looped back. The Apple Macintosh family of computers utilizes an RS-449 interface.

The EIA-530 Interface

In 1987 the EIA adopted its EIA-530 standard, which it called "High Speed 25 Position Interface for Data Terminal Equipment and Data Circuit Terminating Equipment." This standard tries to consolidate the features the public seemed to like best about RS-232 (a 25-pin interface) and RS-449 (specifically, speed and distance), but it has not become popular, probably in part because European and the international standards organizations have been adopting their own comparable sets of specifications. Many vendors and customers alike have chosen to stay with the conventional RS-232C or even RS-449 interface while they wait to see what happens in an industry that seems to change from day to day. RS-232C is still the DTE/DCE interface of choice on most PC LANs.

Let's return to the scenario we have been describing regarding the transmission of a simple message over a network. We have encoded the message and now have an RS232-C DTE/DCE interface. The next step is to transmit the data over a network channel or cable.

■ DATA TRANSMISSION

The data communications system we have been describing has now generated data (in this case, a message) that it has encoded into a specific voltage pattern for transmission over a network cable. The two most common methods of transmitting data over a network are asynchronous transmission and synchronous transmission. The voltage must now be packaged for network transmission. As an analogy, think of the way the post office treats the same information that is stamped two different ways: "overnight delivery" and "third class." Different procedures govern the routes these packages will take as well as how they will be delivered.

Asynchronous Transmission

Asynchronous (standing for "not timed") transmission consists of a start bit indicating that a message is to follow, eight bits of information, and then a stop bit signifying the end of the transmission. Known also as start-stop transmission, the line in its idle state maintains a negative voltage. A start bit consists of a change to a positive voltage. Under this scheme, 1 bits are represented by negative voltage and 0 bits by positive voltage. The stop bit consists of one bit time of negative voltage.

This type of transmission might be adequate on some very small PC networks with minimal data traffic, but asynchronous transmission is inexpensive but highly inefficient. A full 20 percent of the traffic pattern (2 of the 10 bits) consist of overhead. The significant amount of time that the channel remains idle awaiting the next transmission also makes this transmission type inefficient.

The RS-232 Zero Slot LAN

Many very small companies have simple networking needs; such firms want to be able to transfer files occasionally and share an office printer. One solution is the **zero slot LAN**, a small network that uses asynchronous transmission to link PCs via their RS-232 interfaces. Figure 2-4 illustrates a typical zero slot LAN. Notice that in this case cables

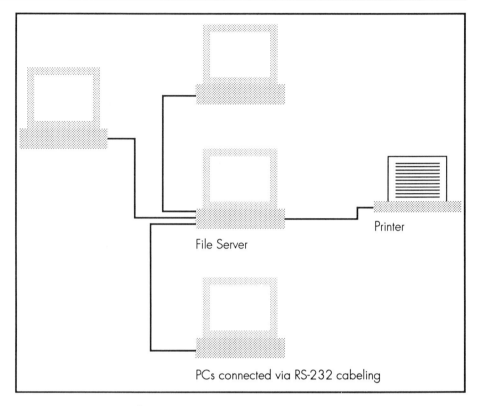

Figure 2-4. A zero slot LAN with a file server.

extend from the RS-232 ports in each PC to RS-232C ports in a PC designated as the file server. This file server controls a printer linked directly to it via cable.

Some companies might not have any one PC that is fast enough or contains a large enough hard disk drive to serve as a network file server. As an alternative, some zero

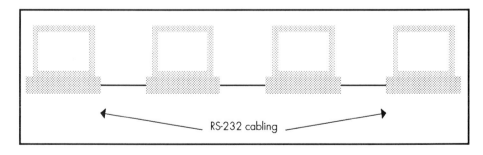

Figure 2-5. A zero slot LAN with PCs daisy-chained together.

slot LANs have PCs linked to each other without a file server. As Figure 2-5 illustrates, each PC has two RS-232 interface cards and each PC is daisy-chained to the next PC. The slow transmission speed as well as the distance limitations of RS-232 transmission mean that only a few PCs can be linked together in this type of network.

Data can travel along such a LAN asynchronously at speeds ranging from 9,600 bps for a 1,000-foot distance to 115,000 bps for a distance of 50 feet. Zero slot LANs can usually support a maximum of 8 to 12 users because of the processing strain on the file server and the bottlenecks caused by the low speed of data transmission.

Zero slot LANs often come with software that includes file or record locking as well as electronic mail. Printer spooling software is also standard, since a major reason people install a network is to share a printer. Popular zero slot LANs include NetCommander, EasyLAN, and ZeroNet. These low-cost networks typically come with menu driven software, which often make it unecessary to have a full-time network administrator.

Synchronous Transmission

Synchronous transmission is based on the ability of the sending and receiving computers to synchronize their internal clocks in order to communicate via large blocks of data. This type of transmission is highly efficient, because a large bit stream—control information plus data—is sent with a minimum of overhead. As Figure 2-6 illustrates, a frame of synchronous information consists of discrete fields, each consisting of a predetermined number of bits. Synchronizing bits at the beginning of the frame ensure that the bit stream can be interpreted accurately. An error checking field enables the receiving computer to determine whether or not data has been lost during transmission. Some of the newer network architectures include very large data fields—upwards of 6,000 bits. Conventional Ethernet, which we'll examine in a later chapter, has a maximum data field length of 1,500 bits. Under synchronous transmission, up to 95 percent of the total bits transmitted can be data.

Let's assume that we now have transmitted data onto the network and turn our attention to the network channel—that is, the cabling. As you'll discover in the next section, cabling can take many different forms.

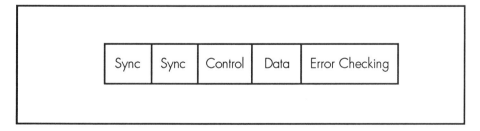

Figure 2-6. A frame to be transmitted via synchronous transmission.

■ CABLING

At industry seminars network cabling does not usually receive the same degree of attention as network software, but network managers have learned the hard way that wiring problems can cause crippling traffic congestion or even bring down the entire network. In this section, we'll look at the cabling options available for PC LANs as well as at the criteria network managers should use when selecting media.

To select the appropriate cabling for a PC network, the network manager must balance two factors: company needs that cannot be compromised versus the real possibility that up to 50 percent of the network budget might be required for cabling purchase and installation.

Speed

Not all media can handle top network transmission speeds. While thin coaxial cabling might be adequate for 10 Mbs Ethernet transmission over short distances, it is inadequate for high-speed networks such as an FDDI fiber optic network, a topic we'll return to in a later chapter.

Bandwidth

The amount of data a medium can handle is known as as its bandwidth. While baseband twisted-pair and coaxial cable can transmit limited amounts of information, fiber has the bandwidth to handle millions of bits/second of information. Broadband coaxial cabling also has enormous capacity, since it can carry several different channels of information simultaneously.

Reliability

How important is it that the data carried over a network arrive error-free? Even though only a few computers are networked, the amount of electrical interference in a factory environment, for example, might require the protection against electrical interference offered by optic fiber or heavy coaxial cabling.

Security

Ever heard how easy it is to "tap" a phone conversation? Twisted-pair wiring is not very secure against it; nor is coaxial cabling. Optic fiber offers the greatest security but at a hefty price.

Cost

Beware of the fire inspectors. What might seem to have been very inexpensive unshielded twisted-pair (UTP) might prove expensive if shielded is required. Similarly, a fire inspector might require that already installed coaxial cabling be replaced with a fire-resistant type—which could amount to three times the cost of the original cabling.

Twisted Pair

The most common type of cabling around the office is likely to be twisted-pair wire, since it is used for telephone system transmission. Each twisted pair consists of one wire used to send information and a second to receive signals. The wires are twisted into a

Color A	Color B	Pair #	Wire Colors	Body Stripe
White	Blue	1	White-blue	Blue-white
Red	Orange	2	White-orange	Orange-white
Black	Green	3	White-green	Green-white
Yellow	Brown	4	White-brown	Brown-white
Violet	Slate	5	White-slate	Slate-white
		6	Red-blue	Blue-white
		7	Red-orange	Orange-white
		8	Red-green	Green-red
		9	Red-brown	Brown-red
		10	Red-slate	Slate-red
		11	Black-blue	Blue-black
		12	Black-orange	Orange-black
		13	Black-green	Green-black
		14	Black-brown	Brown-black
		15	Black-slate	Slate-black
		16	Yellow-blue	Blue-yellow
		17	Yellow-orange	Orange-Yellow
		18	Yellow-green	Green-yellow
		19	Yellow-brown	Brown-yellow
		20	Yellow-slate	Slate-yellow
		21	Violet-blue	Blue-violet
		22	Violet-orange	Orange-violet
		23	Violet-green	Green-violet
		24	Violet-brown	Brown-violet
		25	Violet-slate	Slate-violet

Table 2-1. Color coding twisted-pair wire.

spiral pattern to prevent the mutual inductance of a wire from developing a secondary signal in its neighbor ("crosstalk"). Each wire is covered with a layer of insulation to prevent it from touching the other and making electrical contact.

A cable can consist of from 4 to 3,000 twisted pairs bound together. Twisted-pair wire can vary in diameter from 16 AMG (American Wire Gauge; 0.05062 inches) to 26 AMG (0.1594 inches).

Cables often consist of 25 twisted pairs. To make it easy to identify and trace wires, twisted pair is color coded. Ten different colors are used, with one wire in a color from a Color Group A and the other wire in a color from Color Group B. Table 2-1 gives the color coding scheme for twisted-pair wire used by the telecommunications industry. Usually only 25 combinations of colors are used in a cable of 25 twisted pairs. In cables containing more than 25 pairs, the first 25 pairs are wrapped in a blue ribbon within the cable while the second 25 pairs are wrapped in an orange ribbon. In such a case, the color code is repeated in the binding ribbons.

Shielded Twisted Pair

Both shielded twisted-pair (STP) and unshielded twisted-pair (UTP) wire are available. The more expensive shielded variety includes a protective insulated jacket that provides it with greater protection against electrical interference.

STP consists of 24 AWG solid, thermoplastic insulated conductors formed into 4 individually twisted pairs. IBM, the originators of STP, have indicated it will support up to 260 users per ring on its Token Ring LAN, while UTP will only support 72 users per ring. This vendor only supports STP on its 16 Mbs Token Ring LAN.

Unshielded Twisted Pair

Recently UTP has been growing in popularity at the expense of STP and coaxial cabling, because vendors have found ways to minimize electrical interference and optimize speed. As will become clear in later chapters, several vendors have UTP-based LANs transmitting data at 10 million bits/second (Mbs). There is even a 100-Mbs product known as FDDI over UTP.

UTP is about half the cost of its major competitor, coaxial cabling, and it is much easier to install. In addition to having the greatest bend radius (the easiest to bend), it is the lightest in weight. UTP's modular jacks and the patch panels that are usually used to manage the wiring make it easy to change cabling configurations.

With all these wonderful features going for it, why doesn't everyone use UTP? A major disadvantage is that in many instances where UTP cabling has been used there is little or no documentation to trace pairs and determine which ones are still good. A poorly labeled patch panel can be an invitation to disaster, since it is almost impossible to determine which wires to connect. Another disadvantage of twisted pair is its limited bandwidth. Both the amount of data and the distance (around 300 feet) that this type of channel can carry are limited. As companies begin to transmit more video images over their networks, bandwidth will become an increasingly important consideration in the selection of media.

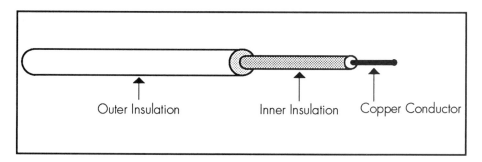

Figure 2-7. Coaxial cable.

We'll return to twisted-pair wiring in later chapters when we look at the most exciting new application of this medium—the new IEEE standard known as 10BaseT, which provides the specifications for 10 Mbs baseband twisted-pair LAN cabling.

Coaxial Cable

Coaxial cabling contains an inner conductor, or wire, surrounded by an outer conductor very much like a hollow tube. As illustrated in Figure 2-7, insulation material occupies the space between the inner and outer conductors, while the entire cable is wrapped in a protective jacket or shield. This type of cabling is known as coaxial, or "coax," because both conductors run along the same line or axis of the cable. Coaxial cabling can be either broadband or baseband. We'll look at the baseband variety now and defer our discussion of broadband to later in this chapter when we look at analog transmission.

Baseband Coaxial Cable

You can think of baseband coaxial cable as a single channel very much like a large garden hose capable of carrying large amounts of information. As if on a single-lane highway, information can only travel in one direction at a time. When it first appeared, baseband coax was thick and offered great protection from electrical interference but was expensive and difficult to install. The thin baseband coaxial cabling known as "cheapernet" cannot transmit information as far as the thick variety can (around 100 feet to the 300 feet of thick cable) and does not offer the same degree of protection against electrical interference, but it is easier to install and far less expensive.

Optic Fiber Cable

Optic fiber cable consists of a core composed of very thin glass or plastic and an outer jacket or sheath separated by a layer of cladding. The cladding, made of glass or plastic packing material, has a different refractive index from that of the other parts, so any light that strays from the core is reflected back to it.

Unlike twisted pair or coax, optic fiber transmission is immune to electrical interference, because it uses light rather than electrical energy. A light-emitting diode or laser converts a computer's digital information into light photons. Data travels in the form of light waves through the optic fiber cable until it reaches its destination, where a photodiode converts the light energy back into electrical impulses.

Multimode Fiber

Multimode was the first type of optic fiber available. It is available in four primary core sizes: 50/123, 62.5/125, 85/125, and 100/140, with the first number representing the core size and the second number representing the fiber's outside diameter. The unit of measurement used here is the micron, which is 1/1000 of a millimeter. Multimode fiber has a bandwidth that ranges from 200 MHz to 3 GHz/km.

Single-Mode Optic Fiber

Since approximately 1984, single-mode optic fiber has dominated the market. The core radius of the more expensive single-mode optical fiber is smaller than that of multimode fiber, reduced so light flowing through it can only travel at a single angle. Because the photons travel in a straight line, transmission is superior to that on multimode fiber and can achieve a bandwidth of between 3 GHz and 50 GHz/km.

Optic fiber is much more expensive by far than twisted pair or coax, but it offers the greatest bandwidth, the greatest security, and the longest transmission distance. Table 2-2 summarizes major features of the different cabling options.

■ IBM'S CABLING SYSTEM

Because IBM plays such an important role in the PC industry, its cabling system is often used as a reference point by vendors describing their own products. For example, a vendor might note that a LAN uses IBM Type 1 cabling. Variations of IBM cabling systems are briefly described below.

Type 1 Data Cable

This type of cabling uses two solid, 2 AWG twisted-pair wire. The cable is shielded with a polyester-aluminum foil shield. Often used for connecting microcomputers to wiring closets or for linking wiring closets together, Type 1 cable supports up to to 16 Mbs transmission with a maximum distance of 330 feet. It will support an asynchronous terminal at speeds up to 19.2 Kbs.

Cabling type	Advantages	Disadvantages
Unshielded Twisted Pair	• Inexpensive • Often already installed • Easy to install	• Limited distance • Subject to intererence • Limited bandwidth
Coaxial Cabling	• Relatively inexpensive • Greater distance than UTP • Proven technology • Provides protection against interference	• Bandwidth better than UTP but still limited • More expensive to install than UTP • Distance more limited than optic fiber
Optic Fiber Cabling	• Greatest bandwidth • Greates protection against interference	• Very expensive • Difficult to install

Table 2-2. Cabling options available for LANs.

Type 1 Plenum Data Cable

This cabling is virtually identical to Type 1 data cable except that it has a fire-retardant teflon jacket.

Type 1 Outdoor Data Cable

This cabling is distinguished from other Type 1 media by its corrugated metallic cable shield, which suits it for outdoor installations.

Type 2 Data and Telephone Cable

This cabling consists of two twisted-wire pairs with a braided shield for data transmission and four unshielded twisted pairs for voice transmission. Voice and data can be transmitted over the same cable from a work area to a wiring closet. Performance characteristics are the same as with Type 1 cabling.

Type 2 Data and Telephone Plenum Cable

This variation has a fire-retardant teflon jacket.

Type 5 Fiber Optics Cable

IBM uses two 100/140 micron optical fibers inside a PVC jacket. The typical bandwidth range is up to 500 MHz.

Type 6 Data Cable

This cabling consists of two twisted pairs of #26 AWG with a braided cable shield and PVC jacket. Performance is virtually identical with Type 1 cabling. Often it forms the patch cables used for linking longer lengths of Type 1 and Type 2 cabling.

Type 8 Under Carpet Cable

Type 8 cabling consists of two parallel pairs of #26 AWG with a PVC jacket. The maximum distance from floor connector to wall box is 148 feet. The performance characteristics are the same as Type 1 cabling.

Type 9 Plenum Data Cable

This medium consists of two twisted pairs of #26 AWG with a braided cable shield and teflon jacket. This cable does not have to be placed in a conduit and has the same performance characteristics as Type 1 cabling.

■ UNIVERSAL WIRING SYSTEMS

Network managers planning new installations might be wise to plan for a future in which voice, data, and video information will flow through the same network. The key to a universal wiring system is to provide the maximum amount of wiring capacity and flexibility both at the networked microcomputer's site and in the wiring room. When an employee moves to another office and another LAN, the required cabling changes should be held to the absolute minimum.

A universal wiring scheme includes both horizontal and vertical components, so that users on the tenth floor can enjoy the same connectivity as those on the ground floor. Similarly, users in different buildings—in a campus environment—also need to be linked to the network. Figure 2-8 illustrates one possible wiring plan.

Notice that the wiring room contains housing for the main and intermediate distribution frames as well as termination points for the rise and horizontal wiring subsystems. The main distribution frame (MDF) connects a private branch exchange (PBX) telephone system and a central processing unit (CPU) to a riser subsystem. The MDF includes termination blocks, patch panels, and patch cords. In many ways it resembles the control panel found in a telephone office during the era when operators had to manually connect two callers.

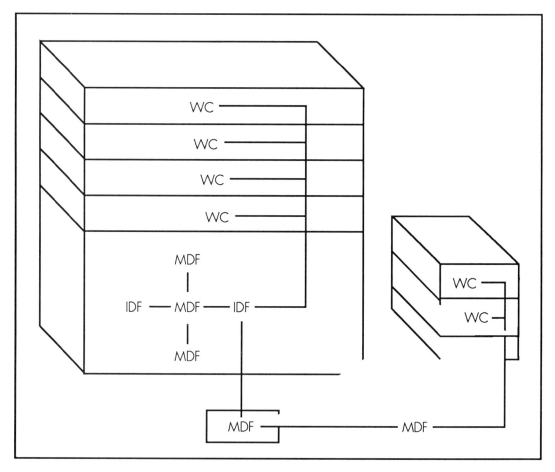

Figure 2-8. A universal wiring plan.

Under a universal wiring scheme, each floor has its own wiring closet (WC) serving the horizontal wiring subsystem on that floor. All networked computers on a floor can be connected via a star cabling arrangement with the IDF. Often two four-pair twisted-pair cables can be connected to each computer. One pair is used for voice and the remaining cables are used to carry data. Outlets can be installed to handle both voice and data needs on each floor. Notice that in a campus environment, buildings are linked together via a backbone.

◀ ANALOG TRANSMISSION

So far we have been looking primarily at how digital information is transmitted as voltage pulses over cabling. Analog transmission is built around the analog sine wave. The analog sine wave illustrated in Figure 2-9 has certain features—a specific height (amplitude), a frequency (period), and a phase (its starting point relative to its ending point).

Modems

A continuing, unchanging analog sine wave is known as a carrier signal; it has the potential to carry information, but does not carry specific information as long as it continues without any change or modulation. A **modem (Modulation/Demodulation)** modulates or converts a digital data signal into tones that take the form of an analog signal that changes to reflect the information it is conveying. When this signal reaches its destination, a second modem demodulates this signal back into digital information.

Modems alter one of an analog sine wave's characteristics—either the frequency (frequency modulation), the amplitude (amplitude modulation), or the phase (phase modulation)—in order to convey information.

Frequency modulation is the most common form of modulation. A modem can change the number of cycles per second (or frequency) of a sine wave just as humans can change the pitch of their voices. Yodeling is an example of human pitch modulation

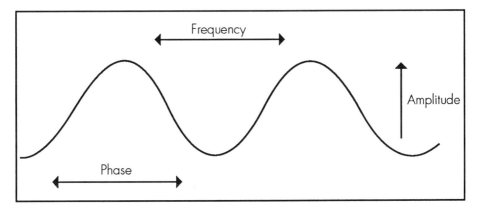

Figure 2-9. An analog sine wave has certain characteristics.

that approximates the frequency modulation approach of many modems. A modem might transmit 0 bits at 2,025 cycles per second and 1 bits at 2,225 cycles per second.

In **amplitude modulation** the power of a signal's transmission is varied. This approach is not used very much, because it is too susceptible to variations in line conditions, especially noise.

Phase modulation is far more complex than amplitude modulation. In effect, the entire sine wave is shifted a certain number of degrees, with a complete shift representing 360 degrees. Several bits can be depicted in a phase change so that the amount of information transmitted over a phone line can be doubled, tripled, or even quadrupled. We'll return to this topic in a later chapter when we look at PC LAN communications servers and the roles that modems play.

Analog Transmission Over Broadband Coaxial Cable

Undoubtedly you've already seen broadband coaxial cabling even if you've never seen a network. This is the medium used by cable television companies. Broadband coax provides a number of channels, each of which broadcasts at a different frequency, ranging from 5 MHz to 300 MHz. These channels can carry a variety of signals,

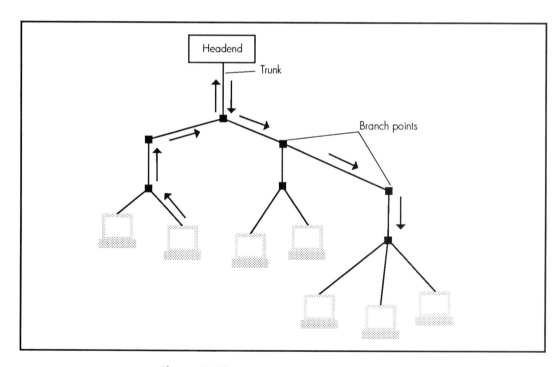

Figure 2-10. The structure of a broadband network.

including voice, video, and computer data. To minimize interference among the channels, **guardbands,** or safety bands, separate the assigned frequency bandwidths.

A major advantage of broadband networks is that they can transmit signals for far greater distances than those using digital transmission. A baseband Ethernet network is limited to 500 meters while a broadband Ethernet network can transmit for 3.5 kilometers. Also, the shielding that protects against electrical interference on broadband cabling makes it an ideal medium for factory environments.

Broadband networks utilize a treelike structure. The headend is connected to a trunk, which has feeder cables leading to drop cables, as illustrated in Figure 2-10.

IBM's first local area network, PC LAN, utilized broadband coaxial cabling. Each networked computer transmitted its message to a head station using a modem to broadcast at a specifically assigned frequency. The head station then rebroadcast this message to the destination microcomputer using a different frequency.

Analog transmission over a LAN is expensive, since each workstation must have its own broadcasting facility, usually in the form of a modem. The advantage of a network with broadband cabling is that it can carry a lot of information for greater distances than is possible with baseband transmission. As networks expand to carry video, voice, and computer data, broadband networks might become more popular. Figure 2-11 illustrates a broadband LAN's transmission channels.

Broadband coaxial transmission has some disadvantages worth noting, however. It is important to estimate a broadband network's potential growth carefully, because even with increments of only 6 MHz there are a finite number of frequencies and therefore a finite number of channels available. Major changes in the types of information carried on such a network might require a complete reassignment of all frequencies, a time-consuming job that disrupts network operations while it is being implemented. The complexity of a broadband network requires highly skilled technicians on staff. And finally, the technology is expensive compared to baseband technology.

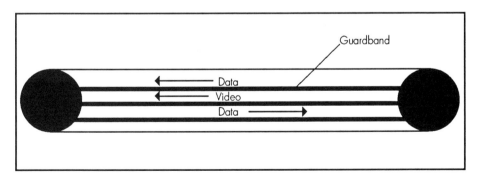

Figure 2-11. A broadband LAN in action.

■ WIRELESS LAN TRANSMISSION

Analog transmission over LANs can take many different forms besides modems using broadband coaxial cabling. A new approach uses the air itself as a medium for transmitting light or radio waves. While wireless LANs are not intended for the average network installation, this technology does have significant advantages. No wiring expense or problems are associated with wiring. Most industry polls reveal that a significant portion of network problems are related to cabling. Finally, wireless LANs are easy to install and very easy to relocate. This technology is ideal for a mobile, quickly changing network, a task force environment consisting of rapidly changing personnel, or a location where wiring is simply not permitted.

The major types of wireless communications we'll consider in this chapter include infrared light, infrared laser beams, and radio frequency. The latter includes microwave transmission.

Infrared Light

It is possible to link microcomputers on a network via infrared light. Using the same technology that enables you to control your television set by remote control, infrared systems from Photonics Corporation transmit light beams across the ceiling of an office and use devices attached to each networked microcomputer to transmit and receive these transmissions.

Photonics' Photolink device can transmit data within a 70-foot-diameter circle without repeaters, devices that retransmit signals to increase the size of a network. While more expensive than conventional network transmission components, this infrared network can transmit at the same speeds as the conventional network.

Infrared transmission does not require any FCC licensing, which is a decided advantage. It's bandwidth is limited, however, which eliminates it from consideration if video or graphics are to be a large part of the network traffic. Also, infrared transmission can be used only in line-of-sight situations, which eliminates locations with enclosed offices. Infrared transducers (an LED and some photo cells) can be mounted on extensions to reach above cubicles and provide the necessary line of sight for communication. Unfortunately, though, infrared technology is very susceptible to interference. Placing something in the path of the light beams can disrupt network transmission.

Laser Transmission

There are a number of advantages to replacing infrared light with laser transmission and a single but significant disadvantage. A laser beam is much tighter and less likely to be interrupted than infrared light. Infrared laser installations must also have line-of-sight transmission paths. The major obstacle to infrared lasers are their expense. The current cost makes them a better candidate for linking LANs together than for linking together microcomputers in a single network. Laser Communications, Inc., currently offers a product known as Laser Atmospheric Communications Equipment (LACE), which has a 3,300-foot transmission distance maximum.

Radio LANs

We'll look at two current types of wireless LANs that use radio signals—spread spectrum and broadcast-type radio transmission. **Spread spectrum** technology spreads a data signal across a wide range of radio frequencies. This type of transmission does not require a line of sight between sending and receiving networked computers. Also, it does not require any FCC licensing.

Performance can be more than adequate for many situations. NCR's WaveLAN, for example, transmits at 2.5 Mbs. Its distance is limited to a maximum of 800 feet indoors with an omnidirectional antenna. Outdoors, however, it can transmit up to 5 miles with a directional antenna. One serious limitation is that this technology cannot transmit through concrete or steel walls.

The Local Area Wireless Network (LAWN) of O'Neill Communications Inc. is another example of spread spectrum technology. Its network device attaches to the RS-232 port of a network microcomputer. Designed for between 2 and 20 users, LAWN can transmit up to 100 feet within a building (300 feet with two repeaters) and up to 500 feet between buildings.

LAWN spreads its signal over several frequencies between 902 and 928 MHz, which minimizes interference and enhances security. It transmits up to 38,400 bits per second over each of four channels.

Narrow-band or broadcast radio wireless LANs transmit with more power than spread spectrum technology but do so over a very narrow frequency. Such a LAN can transmit up to 15 miles, but has a very high cost and requires an FCC license. Apple has

18 GHz	Motorola's Microwave LAN, Radar, Satellite Control Link
5.8 GHz	Frequency for Radio LANs
2.7 GHz	Police Radar
2.4 GHz	Frequency for Radio LANs
1.2 GHz	Police Radar
.90 GHz	Radio LANs
.80 GHz	Cellular Telephone

Figure 2-12. The range of frequencies for radio wireless LANs.

approached the FCC with a proposal for reserving the 1.8–1.9 GHz range of radio frequencies specifically for narrow-band radio LANs. A wireless network transmitting at this frequency range could provide speeds of 10 Mbs over distances up to 150 feet. Other companies have developed products that utilize different frequencies. Megadata offers a narrow-band system at approximately $2,500 for a single circuit board that includes the radio transmitter.

The largest radio communications equipment vendor, Motorola, offers an 18-GHz narrow-cast LAN known as the Wireless-in-Building Network (WIN). WIN is capable of supporting speeds of more than 14 Mbs. One of Motorola's first WIN products is known as Altair, a wireless network consistent with Ethernet, a major network architecture discussed later in this book. An FCC license is required, but it does give the owner actual ownership of a channel broadcasting over an area 35 miles in diameter. Figure 2-12 illustrates the range of frequencies associated with radio wireless LAN communications.

3

LOCAL AREA
NETWORK HARDWARE

Let's pay a visit to the network hardware store. In this chapter, we'll examine the basic building blocks of a LAN, including the file server and network node. We'll look at the different types of file servers available and examine the controversy over the merits of Extended Industry Standard Architecture versus Micro Channel Architecture. We'll also view some of the different disk drive and RAM technologies. It can prove very confusing when a vendor extols the virtues of one brand and criticizes all others. In the network world, unexplained acronyms can be detrimental to your economic health.

◾ THE FILE SERVER

The **file server** is the single most important component in most local area networks. It should be the network's fastest computer. Generally, it will have several megabytes of memory (RAM) as well as a large hard disk drive with literally hundreds of megabytes of memory or even billions of bytes of memory (gigabytes), depending on the number of network users.

Typical Functions

On most networks the file server is dedicated to such key functions as the following:

- managing the network's file structure, including its directories and subdirectories;

- retrieving files requested by network users;

- saving files for network users;

- managing security (who gets to see which files);

- managing print queues (who gets to print first);

- monitoring network efficiency.

When a file server fails, unless there is a backup unit, the entire network goes down. We'll return to this topic later in the chapter devoted to network security.

The File Server's Microprocessing Chip

A file server's microprocessor has an enormous work load to handle. Generally, i must perform tens of thousands of tasks each second in order to maintain network efficiency. To keep up with this workload, a microprocessing chip has its own clock which issues pulses a specific number of million of times per second. The microprocessor can schedule certain tasks based on this internal clock. The faster the clock speed of the microprocessor, the more tasks it can schedule.

The original IBM PC, based on the Intel 8088 microprocessor, had a clock speed of 4.77 Megahertz (MHz), which meant that its internal clock issued 4.77 million pulses each second. The next generation of PCs including the IBM PC AT (Advanced Technology) were built around the Intel 80286.

The Intel 80286 Microprocessor

The IBM PC AT was a vast improvement over the original PC. Its 80286 microprocessor was able to process 16 bits of information at a time. Also, it had a 16-bit data path to maintain smooth operation. For various marketing reasons, IBM originally crippled this computer's clock so that it ran at around 6 MHz. Later, pressure from manufacturers of lookalikes (clones) that ran faster forced IBM to adjust the AT's clock. Today, many 80286-based machines run at 10 MHz.

Companies with larger LANs have gravitated to models with Intel 80386 or even Intel 80486 microprocessors. It's worth taking a few moments to note the differences in these chips.

Intel 80386SX-Based File Servers

This microprocessor features a 32-bit processor and a 16-bit data path. Some companies have been attracted to these models because they offer a relatively inexpensive migration to a 32-bit processor. In addition to the speed a 32-bit processor offers, another reason companies are migrating their file servers up to the 80386SX is its ability to run software designed for the standard 80386.

Intel 80386SX-based file servers generally have clock speeds ranging from 16 MHz to 20 MHz and 24-bit data buses. For very heavy processing, this smaller data bus can cause the same kind of traffic congestion we saw with the original PC's 16-bit processor and 8-bit data bus (the Intel 8088).

File Servers with Standard Intel 80386 Microprocessors

File servers with the standard Intel 80386 microprocessor (sometimes referred to as an 80386D) can provide clock speeds ranging from 20 to 33 MHz. They also offer a full 32-bit data bus. There usually also is a significant difference in the size of the "footprint" of these standard 80386 models compared to the scaled-down SX models. The "footprint" refers to the size of the microcomputer. These top-of-the-line models offer more expansion slots for adding circuit cards than the scaled-down models and more built-in features, such as a built-in graphics adapter.

File Servers with Intel 80486 Microprocessors

Currently, the ultimate "muscle machine" for a PC file server without going to a nonstandard design would include an Intel 80486 microprocessor. Models using this chip run at 33 MHz, but it is the new architecture sported by these models that makes a difference in overall power and efficiency.

Some of these 80486-based computers offer Extended Industry Standard Architecture (EISA). To make EISA clear, however, we're going to have to backtrack and look at ISA.

Industry Standard Architecture (ISA)

When IBM introduced the IBM PC in August 1981, it pointed up the advantage of this 16-bit computer over the current microcomputer king-of-the-hill, the 8-bit Apple IIe. We now use the term **Industry Standard Architecture (ISA)** to describe the architecture of this 16-bit machine. It is true that the IBM PC had a 16-bit microprocessor (the Intel 8088), but its data bus was only 8 bits wide. This meant that while the PC could process data 16 bits at a time, it could only send the data to disk or RAM 8 bits at a time. This situation is analogous to a subway station at rush hour where passengers move through 16 different turnstiles to a platform where they must line up to load into a train's 8 open doors. Obviously, the approach was pretty inefficient, but the 8088 was a very inexpensive chip.

An ISA file machine can only address 16 bits of data directly, which means that it might not be able to address sufficient memory to run some of the new application programs efficiently. Both the newer bus architectures, EISA and Micro Channel Architecture, to be discussed shortly, can address 32 bits.

A major limitation of ISA is its inability to share hardware interrupts—the signals that let the CPU know it needs to perform a certain task immediately—with other peripherals. One way of overcoming this obstacle is to purchase a bus mastering card for an AT machine. While not compatible with the PC and XT versions of ISA, bus mastering does work on AT machines.

Speeding Up AT Class File Servers with Bus Mastering

Some companies have managed to continue chugging along with ISA machines as file servers. While the obvious way of speeding up operations and improving file server efficiency on these AT class machines is to replace this old timer with a faster 80386-based machine, there is one interim solution worth considering: a bus mastering network interface card. Such an adapter takes control of the network node's bus for short periods of time and transfers data directly between the LAN and the node's system memory. These circuit cards bypass the file server's CPU and thus eliminate several memory-to-memory data transfers. The result is increased network I/O performance and better response time for all network users.

Extended Industry Standard Architecture (EISA)

In 1988 a group of IBM compatible microcomputer manufacturers (Compaq, Olivetti, Hewlett-Packard, AST, Epson, Tandy, NEC, Wyse, and Zenith) gathered together to develop plans for a 32-bit version of the ISA bus. These computer manufacturers were countering IBM's announcement of Micro Channel Architecture and its statement that this technology would only be available for licensing to companies that retroactively paid license fees for their previous use of ISA technology. This "group of nine," as they became known, later released the specifications for **Extended Industry Standard Architecture (EISA)**, a new 32-bit bus architecture backward-compatible with ISA machines and, even more important, open and not proprietary technology. EISA machines can use most of the peripherals and add-in cards developed for an ISA machine.

As noted, bus mastering is a technique in which a bus master takes control of a system bus and transfers data directly to and from system memory at very high speeds. EISA supports two different bus mastering schemes, one for ISA machines and one for a 32-bit bus.

While ISA machines still dominate the market, the real benefits of EISA are expected to be seen when 80486-based machines become more popular along with the development of programs designed to utilize this blinding speed.

Micro Channel Architecture

IBM's Intel 80386 and 80486-based microcomputers use the company's own proprietary **Micro Channel Architecture**, a new type of microcomputer bus architecture that is incompatible with older PC and AT designs. This new architecture permits up to 15 different processors on 7 add-in cards to access its bus. Each processor can control private resources, such as the memory on its own add-in card, while also accessing the public resources of the file server—for example, its memory, disk storage, and external communications.

Unlike conventional bus architectures, in which the user must install cards and set them to avoid interrupt conflicts, Micro Channel's Program Option Select (POS) handles this process automatically. POS identifies a card when it is installed in a slot and resolves any resource-assignment conflicts without requiring the user to set any switches.

This approach is a major advantage for network managers, because historically they have had to resolve conflicts created among cards from several different vendors all demanding the same interrupt or slot on the motherboard. POS provides an autoconfiguration option that eliminates this problem for network managers.

Micro Channel also offers level-sensitive interrupt signaling. This means that signals remain active in a queue until they are serviced. This technique cuts down on the chances of losing a request when two interrupts occur at the same time.

IBM claims that, for a number of reasons, Micro Channel is far more efficient than conventional bus architectures. Rather than being character-oriented when it transfers data, it is block-oriented, moving 128 bytes in a continuous block. Also, Micro Channel uses hardware-mediated channel arbitration. This means that the system sets the terms and conditions under which a subsystem or processor can obtain access to system assets. It also limits how long any one subsystem can maintain control.

ISA Versus Micro Channel Architecture

At this time, EISA and Micro Channel Architecture are competitive. Both architectures offer blinding speed and bus mastering. From a network management perspective, Micro Channel Architecture does offer easier installation of circuit cards, but it assumes that all vendors have created products that are "well behaved" when it comes to the ways they issue interrupts. Some network managers are reluctant to commit entirely to IBM's proprietary architecture, because such a decision will force them to follow IBM's drumbeat in the future, wherever it leads. EISA's open architecture holds open the possibility that there will be a number of third-party products available in the future.

■ THE FILE SERVER'S USE OF MEMORY

One of the most important file server considerations besides its microprocessor and bus architecture is the amount and type of memory it can hold. To reduce the frequency of retrieving data from disk, file servers use memory to cache (store in RAM) information. While a file server can retrieve data from RAM in millionths of a second, it can only retrieve information from disk in thousandths of a second.

Novell's file server software (NetWare) exemplifies why a file server capable of holding 16 Mb of RAM is usually preferable to a model with a maximum capacity of 5 to 8 Mb of RAM. NetWare uses **directory hashing**, a technique in which it maps all directory files and keeps this information in RAM as a kind of super index. When a network user requests a file, the file server need only examine a few directory entries to locate the particular file. Since this information is in RAM, the process is lightning fast.

NetWare also uses file server memory to perform **disk caching**. Using this technique, the file server anticipates future user file requests based on a frequency chart of previously requested files. It keeps an image of these frequently requested files in RAM. Once the file server has responded to a request requiring it to retrieve information from disk, the file server keeps an image of this file in RAM anticipating a second request. When this second request comes, the file server is able to respond 100 times faster than if it had to go out to its disk drive and locate the file.

The Different Types of RAM

A large amount of RAM is not the only requirement for file server efficiency; the RAM must be of the right kind. Before a file server (or any PC) can write information to specific locations in RAM, it must refresh or clear those memory locations of information already there. Each period of time that a PC must wait for the RAM to be cleared before writing to it is known as a **wait state**. Most of the newer file servers on the market will feature no wait states or one at most.

The file server's RAM can be organized in different ways, and these can have significant effects on the RAM's speed. Some high-end models offer **Cache memory**, a very-high-speed RAM requiring special software and hardware (a chip such as the Intel 82835 32-bit cache controller chip) to hold information with the expectation that it will soon be requested again.

Interleaved memory is another approach taken by some PC manufacturers. Using this technique, memory is divided into two or four portions that process information alternatively. This arrangement enables portions of RAM to be refreshing themselves while other portions are processing information. Compaq computers are the best examples of **Static Column Page-Mode RAM**. A chip's address is broken into two parts, the column and row address. This approach usually eliminates the need to send out the complete address of the chip, which means that read/write access time is shortened significantly.

Multiprocessor File Servers

If a file server's single microprocessor is taxed to the limit, why not add additional processors? In effect, why not blur the distinction even further between a super microcomputer and the traditional minicomputer that used extra processors to off-load its work?

Recently, several companies have begun to offer file servers complete with multiple processors. Vendors have taken two basic design approaches—enhancing existing technology or developing machines featuring new, proprietary (nonstandard) architecture. Compaq's Systempro takes the conventional approach. It is an EISA machine that features two Intel 80386 or 80486 microprocessors, depending upon the model selected. The Systempro uses a symmetrical design, which means that ideally each processor can handle the same tasks so that they simply divide the workload and double the throughput. This machine also has seven 32-bit EISA slots, a maximum of 256 Mb of RAM. A Systempro with its internal drive positions and its Intelligent Array Expansion System filled can support almost 20 gigabytes of storage. One of the slots can also be used for a 1.3- or 2.0-gigabyte digital audio tape drive or 320- or 525-megabyte tape drive.

Conventional NetWare and VINES network operating systems can be run on the Systempro, but they only use one of the two microprocessors. The Systempro requires its own version of a network operating system such as NetWare or VINES in order to optimize its performance and use both its processors.

Banyan has released a version of VINES for the Systempro. Known as VINES Symmetric Multiprocessing (SMP), this network operating system permits the Systempro to optimize its architecture. This combination of hardware and software is worth considering for companies with many users and very heavy processing loads. While the file server is expensive, its performance might mean that a second file server could be deferred or even eliminated.

Microsoft also offers a multiprocessor addition to its LAN Manager software. Known as Microsoft's Multiprocessing Server Pak, this software assigns LAN Manager and file I/O tasks to one of the Systempro's processors while the second processor performs OS/2 operating system tasks. We call this approach asymmetrical, since the two processors do not perform the same tasks.

NetFrame Corporation's NetFrame represents a more radical break from conventional file servers. This multiprocessing machine uses its own proprietary architecture based on some mainframe principles. It uses a number of techniques, including a hierarchical bus structure, to speed up operations. Data can be sent out via one network interface while a query is being read in via another. Internal bus speed often approaches mainframe proportions, and this machine features a distinctly asymmetrical design, in which different microprocessors have distinctly different functions.

With NetFrame, it is possible to run different network operating systems on the different microprocessors. In effect, the machine could provide the processing as well as the internal bridging between a NetWare and a LAN Manager network.

NetFrame is a completely proprietary design. This means not only that network software companies must write special versions of their programs for this machine, but also that any hardware additions will probably have to come from this company itself rather than from third-party vendors. The speed offered by NetFrame is very appealing, but being locked into the proprietary hardware of a small company is a bit frightening to seasoned network managers who have seen the rise and fall of many companies the past few years.

A File Server's Disk Drives

A file server's disk drives must be fast and reliable. To complicate matters, there are several different kinds of disk drives on the market, and vendors are likely to extol the virtues of their drives and castigate their competitors. Let's examine some of these drives objectively. As with virtually everything else in the computer industry, you'll probably have to balance performance against price.

Enhanced Small Device Interface (ESDI)

The Enhanced Small Device Interface (ESDI) evolved as a higher priced but much faster alternative to Seagate's ST-506 standard hard drive interface. ESDI drives can attain a transfer rate of about three times the speed of an ST-506 drive. Firmware built into the ESDI controller and into its drive supply each with the information needed to communicate. Most systems support a maximum of two ESDI devices at once with cables directly connected from each drive to the computer.

Small Computer System Interface (SCSI) Drives

One of the newer star players in the file server drive industry is the Small Computer System Interface (SCSI) drive. SCSI drives adhere to an ANSI standard. While slightly more expensive than ESDI drives, SCSI models have independent controller logic; this means that the controllers monitor operations on several different drives (up to seven devices), which frees up the computer to perform other tasks.

SCSI drives do have high overhead; when a computer requests data through a SCSI interface, it must acknowledge each SCSI command as it is received. Currently, there are two major advantages to using SCSI drives. One advantage is that up to seven drives can be linked together over a bus. A second major advantage to a SCSI interface is that it is standard for all kinds of peripherals, including scanners, optical disks, and so on. Companies can go with the SCSI standard and not have to worry about specialized drivers for their peripherals.

The SCSI interface has another advantage that could become far more important in the future. A new SCSI-2 standard can be used with EISA computers to virtually double throughput.

The Emerging SCSI-2 Standard

The ANSI committee debating SCSI-2 standards has not finalized this set of specifications yet, but whatever cannot be resolved will be left for a newly formed committee that will begin debating a SCSI-3 standard. Among the features many people expect to come from SCSI-2 are the following: disk drives up to 25 meters from their host, data transfer up to a possible 40 Mb/second, and a certified set of commands. SCSI-2 is also expected to add scanning devices and optical memory devices as well as CD-ROM and network interfaces to the list of devices it supports.

Intelligent Disk Array (IDS)

Computers from Compaq Computer Corporation use the company's own Intelligent Drive Array (IDS) controller chip, which can synchronize several hard drives to function as a single, large hard disk array. The Systempro model, for example, can synchronize four disk drives to address a total of 840 Mb. The Compaq drives and controller are reliable, fast, and proprietary (nonstandard).

Optical Disk Drives for File Servers

While most companies will not select an optical disk drive ("laser disk") as its primary file server drive, this new technology is making significant inroads and staking out a place as one of the drives attached to a file server. Novell now certifies optical drives for its NetWare operating system. Microsoft's High Sierra format (ISO-9660) makes an optical disk look like a standard MS-DOS drive, with standard DOS directory and subdirectory structure.

While optical drives used to be read-only, new technology provides the ability to erase old information and write over it, just as on a conventional drive. Sony's new erasable disk drive includes a SCSI interface.

Optical drives are still far more expensive than conventional drives. Their access times have inched closer toward those of conventional drives, but their major attraction is still their removability. A network manager can insert a new cartridge from a library and provide network users with more than 600 Mb of information. As the "library" component of a network, these drives provide a very valuable service.

To summarize, the following is a checklist for file server selection:

1. Does the file server have the raw processing speed to keep the network operating efficiently?

2. What kind of RAM does the file server use? What is the maximum amount of RAM this model can use?

3. How compatible is the machine to be used as a file server with the network operating software to be installed? Is there special software (network drivers) in the network operating system for this particular machine?

4. How many expansion slots does the file server offer? File servers need more and more slots as a network grows.

5. What kind of documentation is offered with this machine? Is there an index? Is there a troubleshooting section?

6. How easy is the file server to set up? How easy is it to acccess the system RAM and math coprocessor sockets? Are there labels inside the case that describe switch settings? Is automatic I/O configuration offered?

7. What kind of service policies are available? Is there toll-free support? Is one-year service and on-site service available?

8. Is an adequate sized power supply available? Today's file servers require at least a 200-watt power supply and probably even more, depending upon what is running on the machine.

■ THE PC NETWORK NODE

By its very nature, distributed processing will succeed or fail based upon the success or failure of its network nodes, or networked microcomputers, to operate efficiently. Since local area networks evolve over a period of time, it is typical to see a wide range of PC models—including, XTs, ATs, and the newer class of IBM PS/2s and "gang of nine" EISA models—as network nodes. The Macintosh can also be part of this group, but AppleTalk nodes are treated later.

Network Node Memory

The network software required on each network node can require upwards of 40 Kb of RAM. The PC's own disk operating system can double this RAM requirement. Users who want to add convenient desk accessory programs such as Side Kick must realize that these terminate and stay resident (TSR) programs also require RAM. The result is that network nodes might require additional RAM to run sophisticated network application programs such as Revelation or WordPerfect. There are a couple of ways to expand network node memory.

Expanded Memory

Some networked PCs have expanded memory. An Intel 8088-based PC can use a special circuit board and software to swap extra RAM in and out of its 1 Mb memory address. Unfortunately, this technique only works with application software that recognizes and utilizes the specific expanded memory board. In 1985, Lotus, Intel, and Microsoft devel-oped the Expanded Memory Specification (EMS), which is also referred to as LIM (in honor of the three companies that developed it). EMS is a bank-switching approach that uses four potentially overlapping strips of RAM rather than one. PC nodes with extended memory hardware and software can pose problems for the network manager, who must ensure there are no conflicts with other network programs that use these areas.

Extended Memory

Intel 80286 and 80386-based network nodes can use extended memory. Their 16-bit and 32-bit processors can address large chunks of memory beyond 1 Mb. Because the PC operating system was written to address a maximum of 640 K of RAM, the solution is to use a different operating system to address this memory. We'll return to this topic when we look at network software, but at this point we'll note that the OS/2 operating system is an example of a PC environment designed to use far more than 1 MB of RAM; in fact, it can address up to 16 MB of RAM. At least two major network software packages (NetWare and LAN Manager) can incorporate PC nodes running OS/2.

There are a number of memory manager programs, including QUEMM and 386MAX, designed to manage extended memory on stand-alone PCs. On a network, though, there is a need for a networkwide memory management program. Net Room now seems to have the lead in this new category of software. The program is capable of handling a variety of conflicts arising from TSRs that are loaded locally and via net-work on a network node.

Diskless Network Nodes

One popular type of network node is the diskless microcomputer. This machine is an Intel 80286, 80386SX, or 80386D microcomputer specifically designed for its network role. Usually, to take up less room on a desk, it has a very small footprint. It has a built-in network interface as well as necessary interfaces for its monitor and a possible printer. More importantly, though, is the lack of a disk drive.

Diskless network nodes are ideal for work areas where there is public access, since, owing to the lack of disk drive, users cannot download files. A special Read-Only Memory (ROM) chip causes the machine to "boot" from the network's file server, which in turn loads the necessary network software into this machine. These nodes are generally packed with network features and provide good value if they are never intended to do stand-alone work requiring a disk drive.

There are some negatives concerning diskless computers worth pondering. Every time a diskless computer needs to retrieve an application from the file server, the machine's performance decreases and network traffic increases. Since many network applications support virtual memory, when a diskless node runs out of RAM the additional data is paged to disk, in this case the file server. Once again, the result is an increase in net-work traffic. So purchasers should address the kinds of applications to be run on the diskless network node before purchasing one.

Different Graphics Standards

When IBM first issued its PC, there were really only two graphics choices—a mono-chrome or a low-resolution color monitor. The number of picture elements, or pixels, that can be addressed and the speed with which the screen can be "refreshed" and redrawn determine resolution. Since the release of the IBM PC, the numbers of both graphic interface choices and potential problems for network managers have increased. Let's examine some of the major standards.

Color Graphics Adapter (CGA)

The first color adapter card IBM sold was known as the Color Graphics Adapter (CGA). This circuit card provided 640 × 200 pixel resolution along with a choice of 16 colors, any four of which could be used on the same screen. Many "muscle" users were unhappy with the limited color choices and the problems the relatively low resolution presented for reading text. Help in the form of a higher quality and more expensive graphics interface was on its way. Keep in mind, though, that there are still tens of thousands of network users with CGA cards in their computers. A network manager buying network software must still be careful to ensure that the program comes with CGA drivers.

Extended Graphics Adapter (EGA)

Extended Graphics Adapter (EGA) is capable of providing 640 × 350 pixel resolution along with the ability to display 64 colors, 16 at any given time. EGA provides enough resolution to read text comfortably as well as much improved graphics capabilities. It has been the standard on most newer network nodes until recently. Virtually all major network software has EGA drivers.

Video Graphics Array (VGA)

Video Graphics Array (VGA) was released by IBM along with its PS/2 family of computers. VGA features 640 x 480 pixel resolution as well as a color palette of 4,096 colors, 256 of which can appear on a screen at any given time. VGA is currently the video standard of choice on most new 80386 and 80486 microcomputers.

XGA

Extended Graphics Array (XGA) is a new graphics interface promoted by IBM and currently limited to microcomputers that have Micro Channel Architecture. It provides 1,024 × 768 pixel resolution and a 256 color palette. While the resolution is superb, XGA could present a number of network compatibility problems with existing software. This graphics adapter will require its own drivers for applications. If a network user needs this level of resolution to run a computer-aided drawing program on the network, make sure that the software company has a set of drivers available for this adapter card before moving to XGA.

The following is a checklist for network node selection:

1. What is the node's footprint? There is a distinct tradeoff between a small footprint and the number of expansion slots and disk drive bays available. Before

selecting a node, be sure to consider what future expansion might be necessary and whether sufficient slots are available.

2. The type of memory used is important. Some memory caching schemes present problems when the node is networked. Be sure to let your vendor know what type of networking you'll be doing and get some technical support.

3. Be wary of unusual and/or proprietary graphics adapters. Some high-powered computer-assisted drawing workstations might have very high resolution adapters that are so unusual that network software will not work with them. It is critical to ask what kinds of drivers are available.

4. How much RAM can the node hold? If there is any likelihood of moving to OS/2 on the network, this could be a significant question. Also, what kinds of RAM does the computer hold and how much of it can be placed directly on the motherboard? Eight Mb of RAM might seem like a lot now, but some day you might really need the full 16 Mb of RAM that some models offer.

5. What kind of microprocessor do you need? The 80286-based nodes are very inexpensive, but they are probably at the tail end of their useful product life. An 80386SX model is now priced very competively and has the ability to run 32-bit programs. The major options will probably be an 80386SX and a standard 80386 microprocessor. The type of programs to be run by the user as well as the price you are willing to pay will probably be the determining factors.

■ THE NETWORK INTERFACE CARD

It is very hard to generalize about LANs. Some networks are cabled directly to each other without the need for network circuit cards, but these are generally very small. We'll look at this type of LAN in the next chapter. Here we'll look at a basic network component for PCs residing on most LANs—the network interface card (NIC).

The network interface card, sometimes known as the network adapter, provides the key to network transmission on a LAN. Each networked PC has a NIC that contains the software as well as hardware required to package data into an acceptable network frame format and then transmit it in a voltage pattern that can be interpreted by a destination NIC.

NICs are LAN-specific. In the next chapter, we'll examine the major types of LANs. At this point, though, note that an Ethernet network that uses twisted-pair wire must have a NIC designed for this specific type of network and cabling. An Ethernet LAN with thin coaxial cabling would require an entirely different NIC.

NICs must be intelligent enough to determine if there has been a collision on the LAN and to know what to do in this instance. They also must have enough RAM on them to hold a message for transmission or a message that has been received.

The following is a checklist for selecting a network interface card:

1. If a network seems to be slowing down, it might be because of slugglish NICs.

A NIC with its own coprocessor and additional RAM can speed up operations.

2. Can your network node use a 16-bit NIC? While some 8-bit NICs, such as the Western Digital Ethernet card, are lightning fast, the substitution of a 16-bit card can often make a significant difference in speed.

3. Reliability is a key issue. Who will service your NICs? 3Com's cards are so reliable that the company recently announced a lifetime warranty.

4. Compatibility is a key issue. Does your network software provide drivers for this particular NIC? Are there interrupt conflicts that are difficult to pin down and resolve?

5. Documentation is also important. Some NICs come with a thin pamphlet that looks as though it has been translated from a foreign language by someone who does not understand English. Look for clear descriptions of pin settings and a troubleshooting section.

6. What kind of technical support is available? Is there a toll-free number?

4

NETWORK ARCHITECTURE

This chapter on network architecture looks first at various ways networks can be physically laid out and then at some international standards that specify, on a layer-by-layer basis, which tasks must be performed by which network elements. We'll observe how the International Standards Organization's Open Systems Interconnect model (OSI model) operates and look at the IEEE 802 committee's specifications for a common network architecture or topology.

■ SOME DESIGN APPROACHES

Sometimes the term **topology** is used to describe a network's structure or architecture. It is absolutely critical to remember that the topology you choose for a network will determine the media access control method, or how data is actually transmitted onto the network.

A Small Network of Daisy-Chained PCs

A number of relatively low priced LANs use a very simple daisy-chaining structure to exceed the transmission speed of RS-232 "Zero Slot LANs" while offering a number of additional services. AT&T's Starlan is an example of a LAN that can be designed as a small, daisy-chained network of up to 10 PCs (we'll examine a far different, far more complex Starlan topology in Chapter 5). Starlan's daisy-chain design has a maximum length for its connecting cords of 400 feet (122 meters). Each computer in this daisy chain must have a NIC, AT&T's Network Access Unit. The first PC in the AT&T daisy chain needs a loopback plug that sends data traveling through the network back toward the transmitting device. Starlan in this daisy-chain arrangement transmits data at up to 1 Mbs over standard twisted-pair telephone wire.

The Bus Topology

The bus topology is a data highway. Drop cables tap into this cable and lead to the network nodes. As evident in Figure 4-1, when a node has a message to transmit to another node, it broadcasts its message in both directions on the bus so that each node is aware of this transmission even though only the destination node actually reads it. An obvious limitation of a bus network is that only one message can travel down this highway at a time, and there are bound to be collisions, since all nodes contend for the right to use the highway.

The network interface card (NIC) in each node is programmed to recognize its own network address. If it sees that the frame transmitted down the bus contains a destination address that differs from its own, then it ignores this frame and does not attempt to read the contents. While a signal weakens as it moves down a bus channel, it can be strengthened by use of a repeater.

The bus is an attractive network topology because it represents a mature, reliable technology that offers inexpensive components. It can be easily expanded simply by adding additional taps and drop cables to new nodes. Bus networks are well suited for most office buildings. A central cable or backbone can be run through the office with drop cables leading to each desk.

A major disadvantage of bus topology is that a break in the bus disrupts the entire network. Another common problem is a malfunctioning NIC. Sometimes these NICs will "jabber," which means that they will constantly transmit frames over the bus. Such a situation can soon cause massive congestion on the network and slow throughput to unacceptable levels. As we'll see when we examine network management in a later chapter, there are management tools to diagnose and help solve these problems.

The Star Topology

One of the oldest network topologies is the star. Nodes are cabled directly to a central computer or file server. Since each node has its own connection with the central computer or hub, a break in cabling does not bring down the entire network, only the node

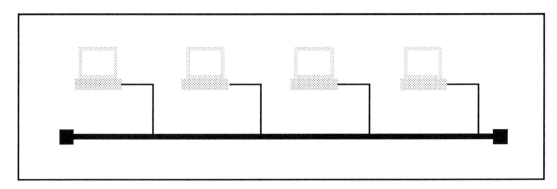

Figure 4-1. A bus network.

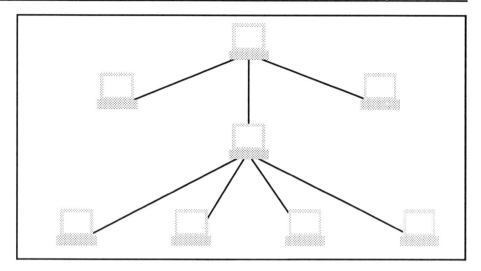

Figure 4-2. A distributed star topology. Courtesy of Learning Tree International.

on this particular cable is affected. Another advantage of star topology is that network management is facilitated, since all network traffic goes through a central computer.

A major disadvantage of a star topology is that the entire network fails if the central computer malfunctions. This particular limitation has led to the development of distributed stars.

Distributed Star Topology

The distributed star, or tree, topology permits several stars to be linked together, as illustrated in Figure 4-2. The disruption of the central computer on one star does not bring down the other networks. In Chapter 5 we'll examine a couple of proprietary networks (Arcnet and ProNET-10) that utilize this network architecture.

The Ring Topology

While IBM did not originate the ring topology, it has certainly helped popularize it with its Token Ring Network. Wire centers known as Multistation Access Units (MAUs) are linked to each other in a ring. Each MAU resembles a multiple outlet. Nodes are cabled to the MAU, which contains its own bypass circuitry. If a node's NIC becomes defective or its cabling goes bad, the MAU can bypass this node and retain the network's electrical integrity.

Unlike a bus, where a signal soon loses its strength and must be amplified with a repeater, the token ring's nodes have NICs that regenerate each signal that travels around the network. So, in effect, each NIC acts as a repeater. This means that the signal is just as clear and strong when it reaches the most distant node as when it is first generated.

Ring topology is complex and the components are more expensive than those of a bus, but there are advantages to this approach. Signals remain strong without repeaters and, as you'll discover shortly, these networks have remarkably good throughput, since there are no data collisions. Nodes usually take turns using the network rather than battling for control of the network as they do on a bus network.

■ THE OSI MODEL

The International Standards Organization (ISO) has developed a model for communications between computers known as the Open Systems Interconnect model (OSI model). Virtually all major computer vendors, including IBM, AT&T, and DEC, have agreed to develop products that are OSI compatible. We are still a few years away from a major shift toward OSI compliance, especially since a lot of OSI-compliant software has yet to be written. Still, the government has even begun to require vendors to provide it with products that meet the specifications for a Government OSI Profile (GOSIP). The OSI model is a set of layered protocols that govern the ways that computers communicate such key information as how they will frame data, how they will provide error checking and flow control, and even which computer will communicate first.

By looking at the OSI model's set of layered protocols, you'll begin to see the major issues that must be resolved to handle such common problems as communicating between a DEC VAX running Ethernet on its network and an IBM PS/2 running Token Ring Network on its LAN. The OSI model will also provide a good introduction to the major software network compatibility issues we'll consider in Chapter 6. The purpose of this section, then, is to help you understand the general functions of the various layers of the OSI model without necessarily understanding specifically how this complex model works. Gerald Cole covers the theory behind the OSI model admirably in Chapters 3 through 7 of *Computer Networking for Systems Programmers* (John Wiley & Sons, 1990), the first book in the Wiley series in Data Communications and Networking for Computer Programmers.

Layered Protocols

The OSI model is a layered set of protocols or software programs. Each OSI model is concerned with particular functions, and the software specifications found at that layer deal with these specific functions. There is some overlap, owing to the compromising nature of international standard making. The Data Link layer, for example, offers several different types of protocols for framing bits for transmission. Different computer manufacturers will prefer different protocols, but computers running OSI software will be able to make the necessary conversion from one protocol to another.

Overhead is the price paid for using an international standard such as the OSI model. Instead of a single protocol for connecting networks, for example, there are three types of connections supported. For companies that need this type of connectivity, the benefits of internetwork compatiblity far outweigh the disadvantages. Companies that have a proprietary network of homogenous computers have no need to switch their particular types of hardware and probably have much more efficiency.

A major advantage of layered protocols is that a particular layer can be modified as technology changes without disrupting the entire model. For example, there have been a number of changes in electronic mail standards over the past few years, but these changes need only be incorporated in one OSI layer; the other layers remain untouched.

When two computers using OSI-model software establish communications, they negotiate the terms of data transmission by sending packets of data and control information back and forth. Each layer of software will communicate information for the corresponding software layer on the other network. As illustrated in Figure 4-3, Network A builds a packet containing all this information and transmits it over a channel to Net-

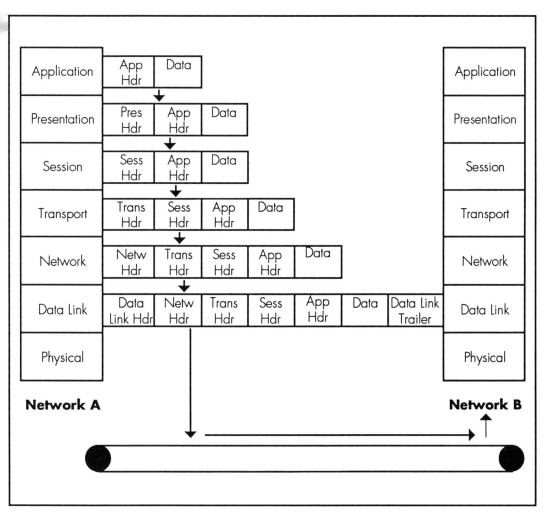

Figure 4-3. The OSI model in action.

work B. Each OSI layer of the receiving computer in Network B strips the packet of the information designated for it by its corresponding peer on Network A. This process continues in both directions until communications are terminated.

What kind of issues must be negotiated and communicated between networks? The two networks must agree on such basics as how the data will be represented—for example, do they both understand IBM's EBCDIC coding scheme or should they use ASCII coding? Are the cable or line conditions bad enough to require extra error checking? Does one network expect an acknowledgment every time a packet is received? As you can see, quite a bit of information must be exchanged to prepare for meaningful communications.

As we look at the seven layers of the OSI model, you might want to remember that one way to keep functions straight is to categorize the top four layers as the managers, which decide what needs to be done. The first three layers are the workers, which ensure that the tasks are actually accomplished.

The Application Layer

A program (application) requires certain key information from a computer on another network. It issues a command to software residing in the Application layer of the OSI model suite of protocols. The Application layer software will provide the next lower layer (the Presentation layer) with control information designed for its peer layer on the other network. It will also include commands to program processes running in the Presentation layer, since each layer services the layer directly above.

The Application layer is concerned with such key issues as terminal emulation, file transfers, and electronic mail. It contains the specifications for a virtual terminal (VT protocol) and goes a long way toward resolving the differences between terminals by defining a generic type of terminal in terms of the number of characters per line, lines per screen, and so on.

File Transfer Access and Management (FTAM) is a protocol for exchanging files between different networks. The CCITT X.400 recommendations for electronic mail are also a concern of the Application layer. We will return to this topic in Chapter 10 when we look more closely at E-mail on the network.

The Presentation Layer

The primary concern of the Presentation layer is how information is represented. Peer Presentation layer entities on both networks must negotiate the common syntax to be used during communications. How will data be represented? Will floating point numbers be used? What about ASCII? What about encryption for security purposes? The Presentation layer is also responsible for requesting the establishment of a communications session. It provides the Session layer with this request.

The Session Layer

The Session layer is responsible for actually establishing and maintaining a connection with a certain level of service. It must organize and synchronize the dialogues that will take place between corresponding entities of the Presentation layer on both networks. Such questions that must be resolved include, Which network will begin communications? Will both network computers communicate simultaneously? How will the bit streams be synchronized so they can be deciphered? Finally, how will the Session layer ensure that meaningful communications are really taking place? How will communications be reestablished should they break off? Will they have to begin all over again, or can they resume at the point they ended? These are the types of issues that concern the Session layer.

The Transport Layer

The Transport layer is concerned with the quality of service agreed upon for the communications. What type of error rates are acceptable? Does the other network require acknowledgments? What happens when errors are detected? The Transport layer offers five different classes of service, from a very simple, "quick and dirty" basic error-recovery service to a service that provides both error detection and error recovery. If a network is highly reliable, then the basic transport service is desirable, since it requires less overhead.

The Network Layer

The Network layer is responsible for routing and relaying information. It determines the path a packet must travel to reach its destination node, even if this involves transversing several different networks. The LAN routers we'll look at in Chapter 7 function at this level of the OSI model.

The Network layer is capable of creating a virtual circuit, which means that it can route information through several different physical connections that change from time to time. The upper layers of the OSI model are concerned not with these details but only with the results. The Network layer must be able to resequence packets that travel out of sequence. Because the Network layer creates virtual circuits that are subject to frequent change, sequenced packets are likely to arrive out of sequence, since they might take several different paths. The Network layer provides sequence numbers so that these packets can be reassembled in the appropriate order upon reception. When the Network layer receives an acknowledgment that all packets have been received without error and have been sequenced correctly, it notifies the Transport layer.

The Data Link Layer

When we look at LANs in the next chapter, much of what we will be examining will be taking place at the Data Link layer of the OSI model. This key layer is concerned with segmenting a bit stream into a frame for transmission over a network. It coordinates data flow, handles error detection and correction, and handles the actual mechanics of sequencing per the directions of the Network layer.

The Data Link layer is vitally concerned with communications protocols, which determine how it creates the fields that make up the packets that will be transmitted. It packages bits into frames that are designed for specific types of network protocols. It will use one protocol to send data over an Ethernet network, for example, and quite a different protocol to send data over a token ring network. It will use still another protocol to send data over a broadband rather than a baseband network.

The Data Link layer is the key network layer concerned with bridges that link two networks together. When we look at bridges in Chapter 7, we will really be looking at one of Data Link layer's most critical responsibilities.

The Physical Layer

The Physical layer of the OSI model is concerned with communications protocols for physically transmitting data over media. It concerns itself with synchronizing data flow and physical transmission. Most major asynchronous and synchronous interface protocols have been included in the OSI Physical layer. It can, for example, handle analog signals through a modem using RS-232 or RS-449 communications. And it can handle full-duplex and half-duplex transmission as well as various types of error checking protocols.

■ THE IEEE 802.2 SPECIFICATIONS

The IEEE 802.2 committee developed specifications for how the NIC within a network node packages information to be transmitted over the network and how these nodes access the specific network media. The Logical Link Control (LLC) sublayer and the Medium Access Control (MAC) sublayer correspond to the Data Link layer of the OSI model.

The IEEE 802.2 committee also defined a Physical Signaling sublayer that resides in the network node (PLS) and handles the actual encoding and de-encoding of data. It encodes the bit stream of data it receives from the MAC layer before transmitting it on the network. Conversely, the PLS will de-encode an encoded transmission it receives before forwarding the bit stream to the MAC sublayer.

The IEEE 802.2 committee has defined specifications for how the PLS is linked to the medium attachment unit (MAU) by an interface known as the attachment unit interface (AUI). The AUI is responsible for transmitting the physical signals between the PLS and the MAU. The AUI is medium-independent. This explains why a baseband and a broadband Ethernet LAN can use the same AUI even though the media they use differs.

As Figure 4-4 illustrates, the MAU in the 802.2 committee's model has two sublayers—the Physical Medium Attachment (PMA) and the Medium Dependent Interface (MDI). The PMA contains the MAU's functional circuitry, and the MDI is the mechanical/electrical interface between the physical medium (coaxial cable, for example) and the MAU. In this section, we'll examine what occurs when a message must be transmitted from a node over the network.

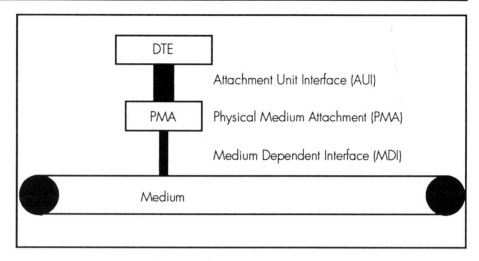

Figure 4-4. The IEEE 802.2 model.

The Logical Link Control (LLC) Layer

The LLC layer establishes, maintains, and terminates a communications path between two network nodes. It also handles such tasks as flow control, error checking and recovery, and the sequencing of frames. It offers both an unacknowledged connectionless service and a connection-oriented service. The 802.2 committee compromised on the type of LLC service because of a major difference of opinion between Ethernet and Token Ring advocates. Ethernet advocates argued that the LLC should make a "best effort" to deliver a frame and rely on higher OSI layers to provide additional support. IBM Token Ring advocates argued that connection-oriented service was the responsibility of the Data Link layer and, specifically the LLC sublayer. The 802.2 committee compromised by requiring the connectionless service and making the connection-oriented service optional.

Unacknowledged Connectionless Service (Type 1)

All IEEE 802 networks must provide specifications for Type 1, or **Unacknowledged Connectionless Service**. This Type 1 service means that the LLC and MAC layers do not provide any acknowledgment (ACK) that data has been received; nor are flow control or error recovery services offered. Often, these functions are performed by software or protocols that exist at higher levels of the network architecture such as the Transport layer.

Connectionless service is fast and efficient. On networks where there is heavy traffic and high throughput, this type of service might be preferable, especially for such tasks as data collection from sensors or database inquiries where the application program clearly indicates to the user whether or not data has been transmitted successfully.

Connection-Oriented Service (Type 2)

The IEEE 802 specifications also call for a **Connection-Oriented**, or Type 2, service. This service incorporates flow control, error recovery, and acknowledgments into the

LLC and MAC layers. This type of service is preferable if no higher level protocols running on the network handle these tasks and/or where transmission errors are highly likely.

With a connection-oriented service, a node's LLC layer generates a connection request to the destination address of the node to receive the transmission. Once the destination node replies affirmatively, the source node begins transmitting data. The receiving node keeps track of the data sequence numbers to ensure that no data units have been lost. Assuming no losses have occurred, the transmitting node sends a disconnect request when it has finished sending data units; the receiving node replies with what amounts to an acknowledgment of ths disconnect condition.

Acknowledged Connectionless Service (Type 3)

Type 3 LLC service permits a network user to send a data unit and receive an acknowledgment of data delivery without having to set up a connection. One practical use of this type of service is to handle alarm signals that must be acknowledged so the originator knows that the destination node is aware of this problem. Under such conditions, there is no desire to take the time to establish a formal connection. Also, this service proves perfectly adequate for polling operations where acknowledgment is required but no formal connection is really necessary.

The LLC's Error Control Function

The LLC is responsible for error control. Two types of automatic repeat request (ARQ) error control techniques are commonly used. Under **Stop-and-Wait ARQ**, a node waits for an acknowledgment that a data unit was received correctly before beginning to transmit again. This approach is simple, but it can slow down network transmission.

The **Go-Back-N ARQ** technique uses the data unit sequence numbers provided by the LLC. Both source and destination nodes keep track of the sequence number of the data unit being transmitted. The receiving node can indicate that a specific number of data units has to be transmitted. It might request, for example, that only the last three of a sequence of seven data units be retransmitted owing to an error it has identified. This technique is network efficient, but it does require buffer space to hold information regarding a sequence of data units. Once the requested three data units are transmitted and successfully received, then the receiving node can process the entire sequence of seven data units.

The LLC Layer's Flow Control

A source network node's LLC layer controls flow control while communicating with the corresponding LLC layer on the destination node. The two LLCs layers agree on a window size, which determines the number of data units that will be exchanged before a response must be sent. The destination node's LLC layer can also provide flow control by issuing a Receive Not Ready (RNR) command to indicate that it is not ready for additional data units.

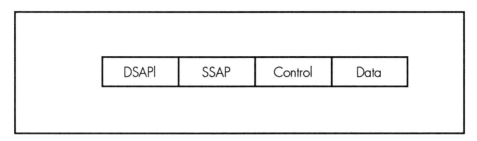

Figure 4-5 The LLC data unit.

The LLC Data Unit

As Figure 4-5 illustrates, the LLC layer places data to be transmitted into an LLC data unit. This data unit will travel down to the MAC, where additional control information is added before transmission over the network. Before looking at the MAC, though, let's examine what is found in an LLC layer data unit.

A network node's LLC layer is responsible for exchanging data units with the corresponding LLC layer on the node receiving a transmission. A data unit can consist of different types of control information, including positive and negative acknowledgments. Some data units contain both control information and data, while others consist entirely of control information. Sometimes an application may require several nodes to communicate with a single node. The 802 committee identifies a **service access point** (**SAP**) as the specific element in a node involved in a data exchange.

An LLC data unit contains a Destination Service Access Point (DSAP) field that contains the address of the destination SAP. The Source Service Access Point (SSAP) field contains the address of the source SAP initiating the message. A Control field reveals what type of information is contained in the data unit. A data unit might contain any one of eight different types of control information, including whether it is a test command that tests the LLC to LLC connection, a disconnect command, or perhaps a frame reject response. The Data field contains user data, which varies depending upon the type of control field that proceeds it.

The Media Access Control (MAC) Layer

The Media Access Control (MAC) layer is responsible for taking the LLC layer's data units, adding the control information necessary for accessing the specific type of LAN hardware involved, and successfully transmitting frames over this network. The MAC layer adds header and trailer fields to the LLC data unit to indicate the beginning and ending of a frame, synchronization bits to ensure that the two nodes' clocks are synchronized to transmit and receive frames, destination and source network node addresses, and error checking information. The IEEE 802 committee developed specific standards for accessing a bus network (802.3), a token bus network (802.4), and a token ring network (802.5). We will examine each of these types of networks in Chapter 5.

The Physical Layer

The 802 committee also developed specifications for different types of media accept-able for these different types of networks. The committee keeps adding specifications to a list that now includes twisted-pair wire, coaxial cabling, and fiber optic cable. Each network node's NIC contains the necessary firmware to provide such Physical layer information as the type of transmission, the type of media, the transmission speed, and so on. This is one reason why it is necessary to buy a media-specific NIC. A twisted-pair wire NIC for a token ring network may not be arbitrarily swapped for a coaxial cable or fiber optic model.

5

CONTENTION AND NONCONTENTION NETWORKS

While we examined some basic principles of network architecture in Chapter 4, in this chapter we will look at a number of real-world networks, including Ethernet, AppleTalk, and Token Ring Network. We'll catagorize networks by whether they use contention or noncontention means to access media.

■ CONTENTION NETWORKS

Many LANs are **contention networks**, which means that nodes must contend or compete for network access. The process is analogous to a group of neighbors who live on a very narrow one-lane street. Because the street is so narrow, these neighbors must battle (or "contend") for exclusive access to the street on a first-come, first-served basis. To drive anywhere, they must look (and listen) in both directions to determine if anyone else is using the street. If the street is idle, the neighbor drives down the street as quickly as possible.

Network nodes on a contention network listen to ensure that another node is not transmitting over the network; then they transmit very rapidly. If two nodes attempt to use the network simultaneously, the result is a data collision that prevents both transmissions from being received. In this chapter, we'll look at two popular contention schemes used on bus networks, CSMA/CD and CSMA, to see how both approaches handle data collisions. The major contention networks we will examine in this chapter are Ethernet, generic IEEE 802.3 LANs, and the 802.3-compliant AppleTalk LAN.

Carrier Sense Multiple Access with Collision Detection (CSMA/CD)

For medium access control, bus networks such as Ethernet and those that are 802.3 compliant use a technique known as **carrier sense multiple access with collision detection (CSMA/CD)**. Network nodes listen to the network medium to identify any transmissions taking place. If the network is idle, the node transmits its information in the form of frames. If the network is busy, the node waits a random amount of time before trying again.

Unfortunately, this approach is not collision-proof, nor was it ever intended to be. Two nodes can each listen, sense no network transmission, and then transmit frames that will collide. CSMA/CD networks have an efficient algorithm to handle data collsions.

When a collision is detected on a network utilizing CSMA/CD, a node broadcasts a jam signal indicating that there has been a collision. Network nodes then wait a random amount of time specified by firmware on their network interface cards before trying to transmit again.

Because even with this random back-off technique CSMA/CD networks still experience collisions, they add a binary exponential back-off technique. While nodes aware of a network collision do continue to try to transmit after waiting a random amount of time, the mean value of the random delay is doubled after each collision. The network will report an error condition after a specified number of failed attempts to resolve this data-collision condition. CSMA/CD does impose a limitation on the physical size of a network based on the roundtrip propagation delay for collision detection. This limitation translates in 802.3 baseband networks to a 500-meter maximum sized segment or a maximum of 2,800 meters for several segments linked together by baseband repeaters.

CSMA/CD operates slightly differently on 802.3 broadband LANs. All stations transmit and receive on different channels, each of which has a specific bandwidth of 6 MHz. Each station broadcasts to the headend station, which, in turn, rebroadcasts the signal to the destination node. A 10 MHz 802.3 channel requires 18 MHz of bandwidth—12 MHz to handle its 10 Mbs data rate and 6 MHz to carry the collision signal.

The CSMA/CD Frame Format

As mentioned earlier in our discussion of the MAC layer, CSMA/CD takes the LLC layer's information and encapsulates it in a frame format. As illustrated in Figure 5-1, the CSMA/CD frame begins with a Start Frame Delimiter field, a bit pattern that indicates the beginning of a frame. The Destination Address and Source Address fields follow; these addresses can be either two bytes for a local network or six bytes for universal addressing. A Length field follows, which indicates the size of the data field and thus whether or not a

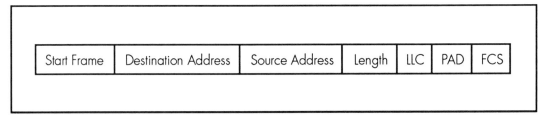

Figure 5-1. The CSMA/CD frame format.

pad field has been included. The LLC information field follows. The frame then contains a Pad field (if necessary) and a a Frame Check Sequence field for error checking.

Ethernet and the Bus Network

It must have seemed like a marriage made in heaven. In 1972, a computer manufacturer (DEC), a chip manufacturer (Intel), and a software company (Xerox) jointly announced specifications for a new local area network known as **Ethernet**, which would be "open" to products developed from third-party vendors. Of course, companies were welcome (and likely) to buy their network computers from DEC, their network interface cards from Intel, and their network software from Xerox. Within a few years there were thousands of Ethernet networks, and Ethernet moved rapidly toward the status of a de facto standard.

Configuring an Ethernet LAN

As Figure 5-2 illustrates, Ethernet utilized thick 75-ohm (later changed to 50-ohm) coaxial cabling and permitted cable segments up to 1,500 feet in length. Segments had to have terminators at both ends. Several segments could be joined together by repeaters. Up to 100 transceivers, or taps, can be placed on a cable segment, but they must be no closer together than 2.5 meters.

The role of the transceiver was to encode data on the cable using Manchester encoding. Cabling from the transceiver ran directly to the network node. With its 10 Mbs transmission speed, Ethernet was designed to handle up to 1,024 nodes on a single LAN; unfortunately, the heavier the network traffic, the more likely it was that data

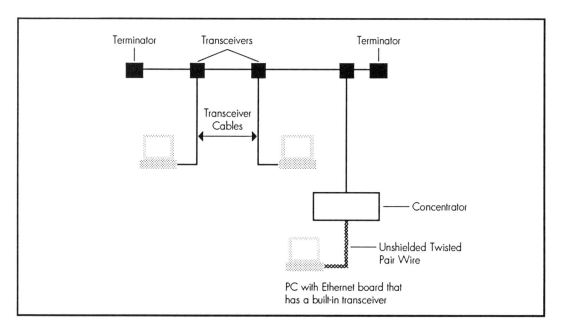

Figure 5-2. An Ethernet LAN.

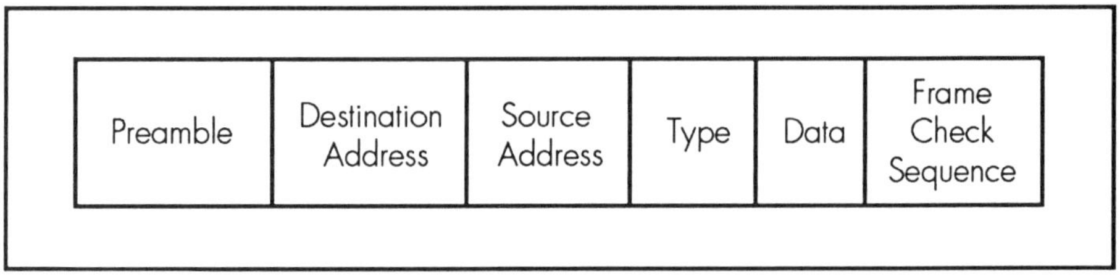

Preamble	Destination Address	Source Address	Type	Data	Frame Check Sequence

Figure 5-3. An Ethernet frame.

collisions would occur and the slower was the network throughput. In other words, while you could have 1,024 nodes on a single Ethernet LAN, you probably would not have designed a network in this fashion. We'll return to this issue later, when we examine the role of bridges connecting Ethernet LANs.

The Ethernet Frame

Ethernet specified a frame illustrated in Figure 5-3. This frame's maximum size was 1,526 bytes, assuming 1,500 data bytes, an 8-byte preamble for synchronization, and a 4-byte CRC for error checking. The preamble consisted of a 64-bit synchronization pattern containing alternating 1s and 0s that ended with two consecutive 1s. The Ethernet frame's Destination Address was a 48-bit field with the first bit indicating the type of address. A 1 bit in this first position indicated that it was a group address, while all 1 bits indicated that it was a broadcast message designed for all network nodes.

The 48-bit Source Address indicates the node transmitting the Ethernet frame. The 16-bit Type field reveals what high-level protocol such as TCP/IP is associated with the frame. TCP/IP (Transmission Control Protocol/Internet Protocol) is the protocol associated with the government internet that links computers across this country. The Data field is followed by an error checking 32-bit CRC field.

The IEEE 802.3 10Base5 Standard

When the IEEE 802.3 committee first began meeting to develop a standard for bus networks using CSMA/CD, it had a serious problem. Ethernet was already well on its way toward becoming a de facto standard. Companies such as Hewlett-Packard, IBM, and AT&T were not about to endorse a standard that gave any kind of edge to their competitors. The result was an IEEE 802.3 standard that is very close to but not identical with Ethernet. Changes included Ethernet's Type field being replaced with a Length field, a slight change in cabling, the addition of a "heartbeat" to determine the network's health, and some changes in terminology. Ethernet's transceiver was replaced with the 802.3 Media Access Unit.

The first of several 802.3 specifications emerging from this committee is known as 10Base5, which is a shorthand industry term for a baseband network capable of transmitting at 10 Mbs for 500 meters. The standard supported a maximum segment distance of 500 meters (1,640 feet), a drop cable (Attachment Unit Interface) with a maximum length of 50 meters (164 feet), and a maximum of 100 nodes per segment.

10Base5 is expensive to install because the NICs and cabling are expensive. The thick coax is difficult to install because it is cumbersome and inflexible. On a positive note, this cabling provides great protection against electrical interference.

It is worth noting that networks containing both Ethernet and 802.3 nodes might experience trouble if the network manager is not careful. Using an Ethernet cable with an 802.3 transceiver could introduce noise that corrupts data.

The IEEE 802.3 10Base2 ("Cheapernet" or Thin Ethernet) Standard

The IEEE 802.3 committee released a standard for an 802.3 LAN that used thin coaxial cabling. This specification is known as 10Base2, or "Cheapernet," because the network is capable of transmitting at 10 Mbs for a distance of approximately 200 meters (185 meters) over inexpensive, thin RG-58 coaxial cabling. Each segment can have a maximum of 30 nodes attached, and the entire network can support 1,024 nodes, the same upper limit found with the 10Base5 specification.

Quite often, 10Base2 LANs are designed with a device known as a **fan out**. As illustrated in Figure 5-4, a fan out acts as a transceiver multiplexer to provide the full LAN data rate to all attached nodes. A fan out supporting eight nodes could also support up to eight other fan outs, so that up to 64 PC nodes could be attached to a single cable segment.

The 802.3 1Base5 (Starlan) Standard

The IEEE 802.3 committee also developed a standard known as 1Base5 to describe a bus network using CSMA/CD that is capable of transmitting data at 1 Mbs over baseband cabling for a maximum distance of 500 meters. Since this standard is also known

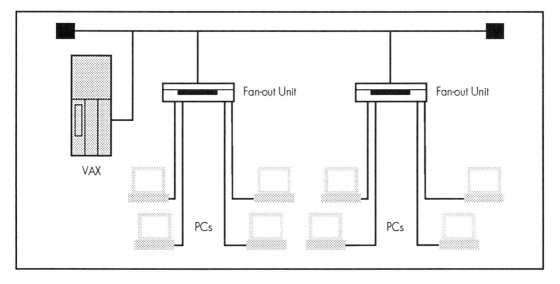

Figure 5-4. An 802.3 LAN with a fan out.

as the "Starlan Specification," we'll illustrate how it is configured by looking at AT&T's Starlan network. AT&T's network uses two pair of 24-gauge twisted-pair unshielded wire. This network follows the standard IEEE 802.3 bus CSMA/CD specifications known as 1Base5.

Each PC node on a Starlan network contains a NIC known as a Network Access Unit (NAU). The NAU senses network traffic and times transmission accordingly, using a CSMA approach. When it receives a "collision present" signal generated by the centralized hub (wire center) known as the Network Hub Unit (NHU), it responds by delaying and then retransmitting a frame. Starlan's NHU can have up to 11 directly

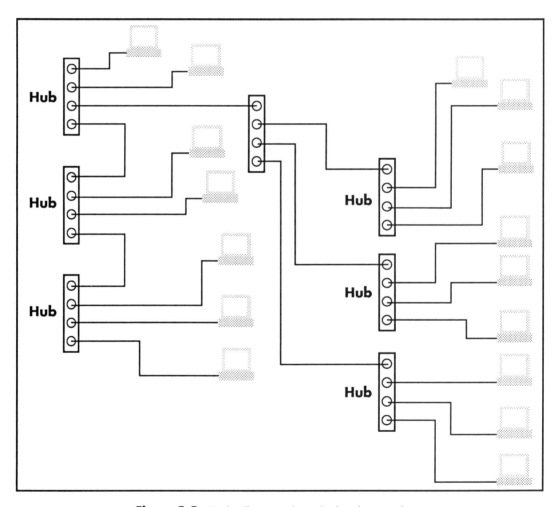

Figure 5-5. Starlan illustrates a large distributed star topology.

connected PC nodes or 11 chains of up to 10 PC nodes, each via single NHU. Up to five levels of hub units can be interconnected, which means that the LAN could cover an 8,000-foot diameter. Figure 5-5 illustrates a distributed star configuration for a Starlan network.

AT&T's NHUs are very sophisticated. They amplify and retime network signals before rebroadcasting them; this accounts for the large geographical area a Starlan can cover. The NHUs are also capable of detecting and isolating jabber conditions caused by a faulty device or connection. A light-emitting diode at the appropriate jack lights up to help isolate trouble and speed repair. Once the problem has been corrected, the connection is reactivated automatically.

AT&T's Starlan 10 Network

AT&T offers another LAN known as Starlan 10. This network is an 802.3-based distributed star capable of transmitting data at 10 Mbs over 24-gauge unshielded twisted-pair wire or 62.5/125 optic fiber wire using special adapters. The NAUs and NHUs found on this network are not compatible with those on the 1 Mbs Starlan network as might be expected. One major advantage (besides the 10 Mbs speed) of using Starlan 10 is that its NHUs can be connected to AUI adapters, which provide network access for devices equipped with Ethernet controller cards including Ethernet version 2.0 and IEEE 802.3 LANs. The AUI connects directly to an Ethernet node while a wire side jack connects to a Starlan 10 NHU via a modular cord.

The AUI converts signals between the media, detects collision conditions, detects jabber and disables the jabbering device, and echos data to the node as well as optionally performing the IEEE 802.3 and Ethernet 2.0 heartbeat function.

Ethernet 2.0

Almost every successful product has a sequel. In order to remain competitive with the IEEE 802.3 standards, in 1982 Ethernet evolved into Ethernet 2.0. Like its IEEE 802.3 competitor, Ethernet 2.0 contained a "heartbeat," a signal enabling a workstation to determine that a frame was actually sent without a collision.

Ethernet 2.0's frame format retained the traditional Ethernet-type field and did not include the 802.3 Length field. Ethernet 2.0 permits the use of thin coaxial cabling and contains a number of significant technical changes, including a change in the line-idle state from .7 volts idle to zero volts idle. A controller designed for Ethernet 1.0 will probably not work with a transceiver designed for Ethernet 2.0.

802.3 10BaseT

Just when it looked as if IBM's Token Ring Network was about to overtake Ethernet and 802.3 bus networks as the most popular topology, the IEEE 802 committee issued its long-awaited standard for 10 Mbs baseband transmission on a bus network using twisted-pair wire.

The 10BaseT specification describes a logical 802.3 CSMA/CD bus that is physically configured as a distributed star. Nodes are connected to wire concentrators, or hubs on a network in which the maximum length of cabling permitted is 100 meters (384 feet).

Thinner, more flexible UTP can be installed faster and costs less than thin coaxial cabling. Some companies are attracted to 10BaseT because they can use extra UTP already installed. With its modular approach, it is possible to move a network node simply by unplugging it from one hub and then plugging it into another hub, much in the way a telephone can be switched from one location to another.

Troubleshooting with 10BaseT's distributed star topology is much easier than with conventional buses, and this is a major advantage. Some hubs will pinpoint the location of a cable break or node failure and then disable that port without affecting the performance of the rest of the network.

A 10BaseT hub acts like a repeater on a standard bus network. When it receives a frame, it broadcasts the frame to all connected nodes. One convenient approach is to attach a hub to a cable with eight twisted-pair cables known as an RJ octopus cable with RJ-45 connectors. Each cable, in turn, can be connected to a transceiver attached to a node with a 10BaseT NIC.

A number of management functions have been established with the 10BaseT specification. The MAU is automatically disabled after it has transmitted for a specified period of time greater than its allowable maximum. This prevents a jabbering node from filling the bandwidth and disrupting traffic. A link-integrity test means that hubs periodically send a signal to a MAU to ensure that it is functioning. If there is no response within a specified period of time, the loopback of data is disabled and the MAU enters a failed test state. When the MAU is functioning once again, it reverts to the link test pass state. On some MAUs, a green light indicates the MAU's status.

The "heartbeat" of each MAU is determined by the signal quality error (SQE) message test. The MAU's SQE tells the hub that this node is capable of detecting collisions and transmitting frames.

10BaseT is very appealing to LAN managers, because it offers a distributed star topology with the ability to quickly diagnose which node is malfunctioning. The faulty node can be disabled easily without disrupting the rest of the network. Owing to its low cost, flexibility, and ease of installation, 10BaseT's use of UTP is also very appealing. While not all previously installed UTP might be usable, network managers often find that there are enough good unused twisted pair in most 25-pair cables to spare themselves the need to pull additional cable.

The IEEE 802.3 10Broad36 Specification

The IEEE 802.3 10Broad36 specification describes an 802.3 broadband network that uses 75-ohm coaxial cabling to provide 10 Mbs transmission speeds for a maximum distance of 3,600 meters (around 2.2 miles). Since the maximum distance of any one segment is 1,800 meters, two 1,800-meter segments radiating from the headend would represent the largest possible 10Broad36 LAN.

Transceivers are responsible for the transmission, reception, and collision detection functions on a 10Broad36 network. A node's NIC contains three two-wire circuit connections to a transceiver, two circuits handle transmitting and receiving Manchester encoded data, and a third circuit is reserved for collision detection information. A 10-MHz square wave is used to indicate a network collision.

For an Ethernet (or 802.3) frame to travel over a 10Broad36 network, it must undergo some profound changes that reflect the differences between baseband and broadband transmission. The baseband frame must be converted from Manchester encoding to NRZ encoding to lower the bandwidth requirements. The frame's signal is "scrambled" in order to improve its uniform power distribution.

Once a 10Broad36 frame is scrambled and ready to be transmitted, it is modulated by a modem from its digital form into an analog wave using a technique known as differential phase-shift keying (DPSK). Using this technique, every zero is represented by a change of phase, while no change of phase takes place when a 1-bit is represented. The receiving modem demodulates this analog signal back into digital form.

The 10Broad36 Frame

In addition to transforming a Manchester encoded frame to one with NRZ encoding and scrambling the frame's signal, some additional fields are added to the frame that reflect the nature of broadband transmission. The Preamble consists of 20 bits transmitted unscrambled as alternating 1s and 0s just as they occur in an Ethernet or 802.3 frame. The Unscrambled Mode Delimiter (UMD) field signifies that the scrambled part of the frame now follows. A 23-bit Seed field helps the receiving transceiver to unscramble the frame. The scrambled fields associated with baseband Ethernet or 802.3 frames follow. A 23-bit Postamble field consists of a carrier phase change after the last bit of the frame followed by a constant-phase carrier for 22 bits. The carrier is turned off at the end of this frame followed by a collision detect self-test.

AppleTalk LANs

Apple Computer Corporation refers to its suite of network protocols as **AppleTalk** and the network's shielded twisted-pair cabling system as **LocalTalk.** The AppleTalk Phase 2 protocol has an LLC layer that contains drivers for a LocalTalk network (LLAP), an 802.3 CSMA/CD contention bus network (ELAP), and an 802.5 token ring network (TLAB).

LocalTalk

A LocalTalk interface is built into every Macintosh computer and Apple laser printer. LocalTalk is a bus network that uses RS-422 signaling for transmission of data at 230.4 Kbs over shielded twisted-pair wire. It requires repeaters for distances greater than 1,000 feet. Because of the limited bandwidth found with STP, most larger LocalTalk networks consist of smaller subnetworks that are bridged together to reduce traffic on any one network segment. In Chapter 7 we'll look at how bridges function.

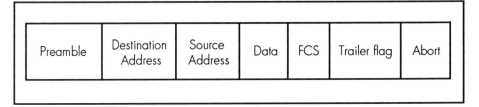

Figure 5-6. The LocalTalk Link Access Protocol (LLAP).

LocalTalk uses a media access method known as carrier sense multiple access with collision avoidance (CSMA/CA). A node that wishes to transmit on the network first listens for any activity. If a collision occurs, all nodes wait a specified period of time plus an additional amount of random time that varies from node to node. Rather than receive an actual signal indicating a collision has taken place, nodes under CSMA/CA assume a collision has taken place when the receiving node fails to respond to a transmission with a "handshake" or control packet with an acknowledgment. When a node fails to receive this acknowledgment, it begins the process of requesting the right to transmit all over again.

LocalTalk's Link Access Protocol (LLAP)

Figure 5-6 illustrates the LocalTalk Link Access Protocol (LLAP). A Preamble is followed by Destination and Source address fields, which in AppleTalk Phase 1 are limited to 8 bits or addresses ranging from 1 to 127 for user nodes and 128 to 254 for server nodes. Address 255 is used for a broadcast address. The data field can hold up to 600 bytes of information. The Frame Check Sequence (FCS) field is used for error checking. It is followed by a trailer flag field and an Abort field that indicate the end of a frame.

LocalTalk nodes send a request-to-send packet to a destination node that replies with a clear-to-send packet. The source node then transmits its data packet. This process continues until another node seizes control during an idle period.

EtherTalk

AppleTalk Phase 1 included an EtherTalk Link Access Protocol (ELAP) that enables AppleTalk to run at 10 Mbs on coaxial cabling as a standard 802.3 CSMA/CD LAN. Because of AppleTalk Phase 1's 8-bit addressing scheme, however, EtherTalk LANs were limited to a maximum of 254 nodes despite the greater speed.

AppleTalk Phase 2 replaced the 8-bit address field with a 24-bit field that provides a theoretical limit of 16 million addresses. Unfortunately, the different frame structure means that AppleTalk Phase 1 and Phase 2 LANs are incompatible. Virtually all hardware and software must be upgraded to move to Phase 2, a reality that has severely hindered the migration of networks to this new standard.

TokenTalk Link Access Protocol (TLAP)

AppleTalk Phase 2's improvements included a TokenTalk Link Access Protocol (TLAP) that enables Macintosh computers to run AppleTalk protocol on a token ring network. The token ring adapter cards are quite a bit more expensive than their EtherTalk counterparts, but prices are likely to drop in the future.

■ NONCONTENTION NETWORKS

Nodes on a **noncontention** network do not have to contend or fight for network access. Instead, they have a certain specified amount of time allocated to them for transmitting over the network. Often the node issues a certain bit pattern or token to indicate that the network's channel is in use. Until the node's time runs out or it no longer has information to transmit and so relinquishes the token, it has uncontested use of the network.

While the transmission speeds of some noncontention networks fall well below that of contention networks such as Ethernet, the throughput, or actual speed in transmitting data that makes it to its destination, is comparable or even superior. However, as you'll discover in the next few chapters, throughput often takes a backseat to other issues, such as price, security, and interconnectivity needs when a company determines whether it wants a contention or noncontention network.

The IEEE 802.4 Specification (The Token Bus)

The IEEE 802.4 LAN is a token bus network, which means that it is physically configured as a bus but functions as a logical ring. It provides 10 Mbs transmission speed when configured as a broadband network and 5 Mbs when configured as a **carrierband** network. Carrierband is a term used to describe a baseband network that includes some modulation to reduce noise. Both broadband and carrierband configurations use 75 ohm coaxial cabling. Token bus is a noncontention LAN that uses a MAC frame with a unique bit pattern as a token to signify that a particular node has control of the network. This token is passed sequentially from the node with the lowest network address to a node with a higher address until it comes full circle back to the node with the lowest network address. Each node knows the address of the node it receives the token from as well as the address of the node it gives the token to when it relinquishes it.

Nodes are assigned a specific amount of network time. In addition, four levels of priority can be assigned to a node's network jobs. A node will usually use its token time

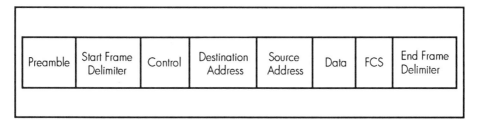

Preamble	Start Frame Delimiter	Control	Destination Address	Source Address	Data	FCS	End Frame Delimiter

Figure 5-7. The token bus frame.

to transmit all Class 6 (highest priority) jobs before beginning to transmit Class 4 jobs. Class 2 and Class 0 jobs have correspondingly lower network priorities.

The Token Bus Frame

Figure 5-7 illustrates a token bus frame. The Preamble field provides a "wakeup" to a node and indicates that a frame is being transmitted. The Start Delimiter (SD) indicates that the Preamble is over and data is to follow. The SD pattern consists of a series of 0-bit signals and N signals, with N signifying nondata. The Frame Control (FC) field reveals whether the frame contains MAC control information or actual data. There are seven different type of frame control patterns. A node on a token bus network might need to claim a token (Claim—Token) or add another node to the network (Solicit—Successor—1 or Solicit—Successor—2). A conflict among several nodes

Token Bus Control Frames	Purpose
Claim-Token	A new token is generated to replace a lost token
Solicit-sucessor-1	Stations with addresses between the token holder and its current successor are invited to join the network
Solicit-sucessor-2	Stations whose addresses are not between the token holder and its current successor are invited to join the network
Who-follows	Helps determine the successor of the successor of a station on the network
Resolve-contention	Several stations use this to resolve contention based on the stations' addresses
Token	The station asks permission to transmit
Set-successor	Requests a station to change the identity of its successor

Figure 5-8. Token bus frame control patterns.

that wish to join the network is resolved by the issuing of a Resolve—Contention frame. The first new node responding receives a Set—Successor frame, which enables it to join the network. Sometimes a node needs to find out which node should receive its token, since the next designated node has failed, so it issues a Who—Follows frame. Figure 5-8 illustrates the possible token bus frame control patterns.

Addressing on a token bus network can consist of 16-bit addressing for a local address and 48-bits for a network with global addresses, which is consistent with the IEEE 802.2 standard. The token bus frame contains a 16-bit or 48-bit Destination Address (DA) field and a corresponding 16-bit or 48-bit Source Address (SA) field follow. IEEE 802 networks must be consistent with the addressing, which means that all network nodes must use the same addressing scheme—local or global. The Data field in an 802.4 LAN can be up to 8,174 bytes, about 5.5 times the size of an 802.3 data field. This significant difference in the size of frames makes it difficult for 802.3 and 802.4 LANs to communicate, since the MAC and LLC layers of the 802.2 specification do not have the ability to segment large packets into smaller packets. Special software must be provided at higher levels of the OSI model to negotiate acceptable packet sizes for transmission during a particular session between these two very different networks. Sometimes routers are used where this segmentation takes place at the Network layer of the OSI model.

A four-byte Frame Check Sequence field provides a cyclical redundancy check (CRC) for any errors that might have occurred during transmission. Finally, an End Delimiter (ED) signifies the end of the frame.

Token Bus Operation

As mentioned earlier, a token bus network passes a token from node to node in ascending address order. During its designated token time, each node must provide time to see if a new node is attempting to become part of the logical ring. It issues a solicit—successor frame and waits a designated amount of time to see if there is a response. If no node responds, it hands the token (and control of the network) to the next higher addressed network node. A new node might respond to the solicit—successor frame by issuing its own set—successor frame. In this situation, the node currently holding the token will designate this new node as the next node to receive the token and then hand the token on.

Finally, where two nodes wish to be added to the network, the node currently with the token will detect a garbled response owing to the conflict between the nodes competing for entrance. The node currently with the token will issue a resolve_contention frame. Each competing node responds based on the first two bits in its address. The node with the lowest address is permitted to issue its set—successor frame and is added to the logical ring. This process is repeated until all nodes attempting to enter the network have the opportunity to issue their set—successor frames and become part of the logical ring.

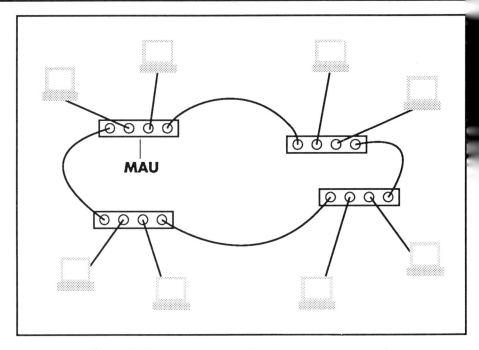

Figure 5-9. MAUs are connected together to form a ring network.

The token bus LAN offers excellent throughput even under heavy loads. It is particularly useful for networks where individual nodes might have very different workloads and priorities. A node can be given both extra token time and higher priorities to ensure that its jobs are transmitted—on a CSMA/CD LAN under heavy traffic conditions, there is no assurance that this will happen. Since all token times are assigned, the network manager can also calculate the worst possible scenario, the upper limit for the time a node will have to wait for network access.

On the negative side, token bus is more expensive to install and technologically more complex than an 802.3 LAN, which could make technical maintenance more challenging.

Manufacturing Automation Protocol (MAP)

One variation of the IEEE 802.4 token bus is a standard developed specifically for a manufacturing environment. General Motors helped develop and push Manufacturing Automation Protocol (MAP) as a standard. The current version (MAP 3.0) is administered by a users group (the MAP/TOP User's Group). MAP is a 10 Mbs broadband network built on a foundation of the IEEE 802.4 standard that includes upper-level protocols appropriate for a factory environment.

One feature of MAP's custom design for factory use is the Manufacturing Message Standard (MMS), an OSI Application layer protocol for formatting and transmitting commands between controlling programs and machines.

A General Motors assembly plant in East Pontiac, Michigan was the first all-MAP plant. Its more than 2,000 taps support more than 2,000 intelligent devices on the factory floor. Each device is attached via a splitter to two independent cabling systems, so if one cable is cut, the other remains functional. By forcing all vendors to provide it with products that are MAP-compliant, General Motors has been able to mix and match vendor products on the MAP network. This network includes DEC VAX minicomputers, IBM 4341 mainframes, and more than 700 asynchronous devices, including terminals, printers, PCs, and robots. The new GM Saturn automobile is being built in an all-MAP plant in Spring Hill, Kentucky.

The IEEE 802.5 Token Ring Specification

The IEEE 802.5 token ring specification describes a ring linking together wiring hubs known as **multistation access units (MAUs)**. Each MAU can have up to eight nodes attached to a node via duplex cabling. Data flows in one direction through each node in a ring through the MAUs. Each MAU has a Ring In (RI) and a Ring Out (RO) connection. The RI and RO ports are used for connecting to other MAUs, as illustrated in Figure 5-9.

Each node has a NIC that generates a +5 volt signal, which opens a relay on the MAU. The adapter card then generates a token or unique bit pattern that travels around the ring and back to it, ensuring that the network is valid. The node can then begin transmitting data. If a node is defective, the MAU can use its bypass circuitry to route network traffic around it without affecting the rest of the network.

Token ring networks are often cabled with standard telephone unshielded twisted-pair wire (Type 3), but they can also be cabled with the IBM cabling system, including shielded cable Types 1 and 2. As a general guideline, the total length of the main ring should not exceed 366 meters (1,200 feet). The maximum number of nodes one main ring can support is 255 (72 with Type 3 cabling), while the maximum lobe distance (the distance between an MAU and a node) is 101 meters (330 feet).

Special extended distance MAUs permit lobe lengths up to 305 meters (1,000 feet) using standard telephone wire (Type 3) and 610 meters (2,000 feet) using shielded twisted-pair wire (Types 1 and 2). Using these enhanced MAUs, network managers can place all MAUs in a centralized wiring closet, which makes network troubleshooting and maintenance much easier.

Token ring networks can transmit at 4 Mbs or 16 Mbs. The 16 Mbs version requires new NICs and (IBM insists) shielded rather than unshielded twisted-pair wire. Some vendors, such as Andrew and Ungermann-Bass, have their own 802.5 LANs running on unshielded twisted-pair cabling. The 16 Mbs version supports a much larger frame size (an increase from 4,501 bytes to 17,997 bytes). Since fewer acknowledgments are required, the larger frame size means higher throughput.

The 16-Mbs token ring networks also feature early token release. Using this technique, a network node transmits its frame and then releases its token (the symbol of

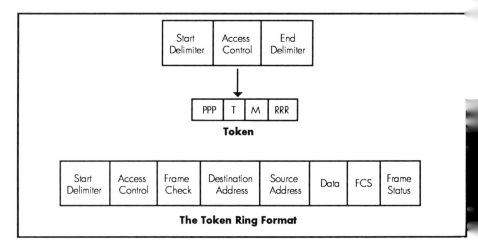

Figure 5-10. The token ring frame and token formats.

its exclusive access to the network) to the next node without waiting for the return acknowledgment of its frame.

Basic Token Ring Operation

A node that needs to transmit seizes a free token. It sets a bit in the token indicating that it now is "busy" and follows the token with a frame it generates that contains both data and control and addressing information. This frame is read by each node on the ring. A node that does not recognize itself as the destination address retransmits the frame to the next network node. Because each node acts as a repeater, the token ring network transmission maintains its strength despite the size of the LAN. The destination node copies the frame's contents to its own RAM, sets bits to indicate that it has received the frame without errors and copied it successfully, and then retransmits the token back to the node originating the broadcast.

Nodes that have a high-priority message to be transmitted can set reservation bits to indicate message priority and their addresses. Assuming no node has a higher priority reservation, the node making this reservation will receive the token when the current token holder times out. Each node has a specific amount of token time during which it controls the network.

A CSMA/CD network such as Ethernet will outperform a token ring network under low traffic conditions, because nodes on the token ring network must wait their turn. Under heavier conditions, however, the token ring network is superior for several reasons. Since this is a noncontention network, there are no collisions and therefore the throughput remains high. Also, no matter how heavy the traffic, nodes are guaranteed network access. Even nodes with large files to transmit will be able to complete this task without having to keep retransmitting the same frames owing to collisions.

A node is designated as the network Monitor and it keeps track of the token time. If a node times out and no token appears for a period of time greater than the time required to transverse the network, then the Monitor will issue a new token. If the Monitor node fails, another node that has been a passive Monitor assumes the role of active Monitor.

The Token Ring Frame

Figure 5-10 illustrates the token or bit pattern used for medium access control on a token ring network. It also illustrates the format of the token ring frame. The Start Delimiter (SD) field consists of a unique 8-bit pattern used to designate the beginning of a frame. The Access Control (AC) field has the format PPPTMRRR, where PPP and RRR are 3-bit priority and reservation variables. M is the monitor bit, while T indicates whether this is a token or a data frame. A token would only add the ED field, while a data frame would require several additional fields.

The Priority field indicates the priority of this specific token. It is possible to establish different priorities for particular nodes so that only certain nodes can use a high-priority token. Similarly, a particular priority code can be limited to certain messages to ensure their immediate transmission.

The Reservation field permits nodes with high-priority messages to indicate that the next frame should be issued with that priority so that they will receive it. The Monitor bit indicates if there is a central ring monitor being deployed.

The Frame Control (FC) field describes the data frame type. If the frame is not a standard IEEE 802.2 data frame, bits indicate what kind of MAC protocol is required. The Destination Address (DA) and Source Address (SA) fields are standard IEEE 802.2 addressing fields that can be local (16 bits) or global (48 bits) as long as the entire network follows the same scheme. The LLC fields contain the LLC information that has been encapsulated into this frame. The Data field can be approximately 4 K for a 4 Mbs token ring network and up to 8 K for a 16 Mbs network. The Frame Check Sequence (FCS) field is used for error checking and is identical with the 802.3 and 802.4 versions. The Ending Delimiter (ED) field contains the error detection bit and intermediate frame bit. The former is set when an error is detected, while the latter is set to indicate that a frame is part of a multiple-frame transmission. Finally, the Frame Status (FS) field contains bits that are set to indicate that the destination-addressed node has recognized its own address and has copied the frame bits to its own RAM before retransmitting the frame back to the source node.

Fiber Distributed Data Interface (FDDI)

The ANSI X3T.9 committee has developed the **Fiber Distributed Data Interface (FDDI)** standard, a counter rotating token ring able to transmit data at 100 Mbs over fiber optic cabling for distances up to 200 kilometers. The FDDI frame's format is identical with that of an 802.5 frame except that it may carry up to 4,500 bytes of data, so it is ideal for large data transfers. Nodes release tokens as soon as they complete a transmission (and before they receive a reply) so that there are multiple tokens on an FDDI network. FDDI differs considerably from 802.5 networks in the specifications for an FDDI network's Physical layer. The FDDI Physical layer contains a Physical Layer Protocol (PHY) sublayer, concerned with the actual data encoding schemes, and a Physical Medium Dependent Layer (PMD), which contains the actual optical specifications. The Media Access Control layer contains token-passing protocols as well as specifications for packet formation and addressing.

FDDI is still extremely expensive technology. Initially it will probably be used for backbones connecting different networks together and for critical points on very large, heavily congested networks.

The FDDI specifications call for a dual ring, one primary ring to carry information and a secondary ring to carry control signals. It is also possible to use both rings for data and achieve a transmission rate of 200 MBs. Should one ring break, the network can bypass the break, isolate the failed station with the broken cabling, and wrap around the second cable to keep functioning.

FDDI is able to handle a maximum of 1,000 connections over a fiber optic path of 200 kilometers. FDDI specifies 62.5/125 micron multimode optic fiber with light generated from LEDs transmitting at 1,300 nm. Each station on an FDDI network functions as an active repeater, so signals are not degraded.

■ SOME PROPRIETARY NETWORKS

The Arcnet Specification

Attached Resource Computer Network (Arcnet) was developed by Datapoint Corporation in 1977. While it is not an IEEE standard, thanks to Datapoint it is a de facto standard. This company has licensed the technology to vendors such as Thomas Conrad and SMC, but it has prevented others from splintering Arcnet into different versions. All Arcnet equipment, regardless of vendor, will probably work together. This includes the new ArcnetPlus technology, discussed further on.

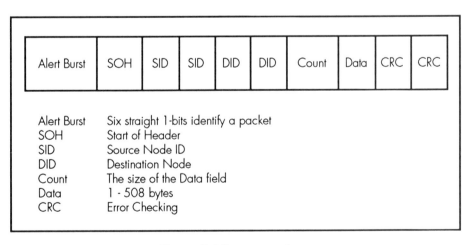

Figure 5-11. An Arcnet frame.

Arcnet is a token bus network that transmits small frames at speeds up to 2.5 Mbs. At low traffic levels, it will not perform as well as an 802.3 LAN, but at high traffic levels, owing to the lack of degradation found in a noncontention network, it might very well exceed its rival's performance. Because Arcnet is mature technology, the cost of its components is remarkably low while its reliability is high.

Arcnet's Token Bus

While Arcnet is a logical ring, its physical structure or topology can take many different forms, as we'll see shortly. Each node's NIC has a unique address between 1 and 255, depending upon how its eight-position DIP switch is set. Each NIC knows both its own address and that of the node to which it will hand over the token when it is finished transmitting. The node with the highest address closes the "ring" by passing the token back to the node with the lowest address.

The Arcnet Frame

There are actually five different types of Arcnet frame formats, depending upon their functions. An Invitation to Transmit frame passes the token from one node to another, while a Free Buffer Enquiry (FBE) is used to inquire whether the next node can accept a data frame. The Data frame itself can be up to 507 bytes, about a third the size of an Ethernet frame. An Acknowledgment (ACK) frame indicates that a frame has been received without errors, while a Negative Acknowledgment (NAK) frame is used to decline a Free Buffer Enquiry.

Let's assume that a user at node 50 needs to send a message to a user at node 100. When node 50 receives the token, it sends an FBE to node 100 to inquire whether this node is able to receive a message. When node 100 acknowledges with an ACK frame, node 50 transmits its frame. When node 100 receives this frame, it checks the CRC field for any errors and then responds with an ACK, indicating successful reception. If node 50 receives no response from node 100, it assumes that the frame was not received and retransmits. Once node 50 has completed its transmission successfully, it issues an FBE to node 51 to see if it is able to use the token.

Fields in an Arcnet Frame

An Arcnet frame contains fields with control information as well as a data field. Figure 5-11 illustrates an Arcnet frame containing data. An Alert Burst field consists of six straight 1 bits, which announces an Arcnet frame to follow. The 1-byte Start of Header (SOH) field indicates the nature of the frame to follow. The 1-byte Source Node ID (SID) field contains the address of the node originating this transmission while the 2-byte Destination Node ID (DID) field indicates the address of the node to receive this frame. Note that these address fields are much smaller than those in the IEEE standard. While this fact is irrelevant for companies planning office LANs, it becomes a considerable factor for companies planning enterprise networks where networks with very large IEEE address fields must exchange information.

The 1-byte Count field indicates whether the frame's data field is 1 or 2 bytes in length. The Data field can be a maximum of 507 bytes, about a third the size of an Ethernet frame. Arcnet's frame size is ideal for small bursts of network traffic such as a database inquiry, and poorly suited to the exchange of large-sized graphics files.

Finally, the 2-byte CRC field is used by the receiving node as an error check to ensure that the frame was not garbled during transmission.

Arcnet's Flexible Topology

Arcnet can be configured in a number of different ways, and this flexibility has added to its popularity. Once limited only to RG-62 thin coax cabling, it now runs on unshielded twisted-pair as well as optic fiber cabling and IBM Types 6, 8, and 9 cabling. Arcnet's popularity in some companies with mainframe operations is explained in part because it uses the same coaxial cabling as IBM's 3270 terminals; many of these companies already had surplus cabling in place and available to build an Arcnet LAN. Today, it is the twisted-pair scheme that is likely to be more attractive to most companies because of its flexibility and low cost.

Up to ten Arcnet nodes can be configured as a bus. This bus can be linked to a star configuration via an Arcnet Active or Passive Hub. Active Hubs (maximum 2,000 feet) and Passive Hubs (maximum 100 feet) are distinguished by the maximum distance permitted between them, since the Active Hub acts as a repeater. Several Active Hubs can be connected to build a LAN up to the 255-node maximum imposed by the NIC's 255-node-address limit. Both 8-bit and 16-bit NICs are available. A node able to utilize the 16-bit card can boost network efficiency signficantly. An Arcnet file server should have the fastest NIC available to help prevent network bottlenecks.

Arcnet's low cost, reliability, and compatibility with coax, twisted pair, and optic fiber media make it very popular with systems integrators. The twisted-pair components are no more expensive than the coaxial components—a far cry from the current Ethernet situation, in which 10BaseT components cost more than their thin Ethernet counterparts.

ArcnetPlus

Datapoint, NCR, and Standard Microsystems have jointly developed a new 20 Mbs version of Arcnet known as ArcnetPlus. This new version supports frame sizes from 12.5 to 4,224 bytes and a maximum of 2,047 nodes per network segment. The NICs adjust to the speed of the card to which they are communicating, so that a 20 Mbs card will slow down transmission to 2.5 Mbs if necessary so it can communicate with an older style Arcnet NIC.

ArcnetPlus adds a 48-bit addressing scheme to match the IEEE 802.2 addressing standard. It also supports the IEEE 802 MAC interface. For a network where traffic is expected to be heavy, network managers might want to select an ArcnetPlus turbo driver from SMC or Thomas-Conrad. These drivers exchange frames up to 4,000 bytes in size. These frames are divided into the standard Arcnet 507-sized frames, but a network operating system such as NetWare will send acknowledgments only after the full 4,000 bytes have been transmitted rather than after each 507-byte transfer. This scheme can make a tremendous difference in throughput.

Thomas Conrad's 100 Mbps Network System

Thomas Conrad Corporation's TCNS is a 100-Mbs proprietary LAN based on Arcnet. The network's distributed star topology and fiber optic cabling permits a total network span of 6,096 meters (20,000 feet). TCNS supports up to 255 nodes at distances up to .8 km (2,600 feet) from a hub. Each frame carries a maximum of 512 bytes, but high-speed drivers permit a packet size of up to 4,096 bytes. TCNS gains its speed by use of specialized NICs, hubs, and software. The NICs support EISA and provide extra speed because of accelerated drivers and the use of 16K of RAM designed for address space. The hubs provide eight-port dual-fiber connections and some handy troubleshooting features, such as an enable/disable button and two LEDs at each port to indicate status and activity. These hubs support network management software known as HubTalk. TCNS's HubTalk provides out-of-band diagnostics, enabling a network supervisor to manage the network's hubs from a network node. HubTalk is capable of managing up to 32 daisy-chained hubs and providing mapping and displaying of each active node. What is interesting about TCNS besides its speed is Thomas Conrad's ability to retain compatiblity with existing Arcnet networks. TCNS can be easily bridged to existing Arcnet networks, so a company could elect to upgrade only a portion of its existing Arcnet LAN. While the company would have to upgrade the Arcnet NICs and hubs to TCNS to gain the 100-Mbs transmission speed, it could retain existing network software and even twisted-pair wire, since TCNS is compatible with these network components.

Proteon's ProNET-10 Network

Proteon's ProNET-10 LAN is a proprietary network in a distributed star topology based on passive wire hubs. Each PC network node has a ProNET-10 NIC capable of transmitting data at 10 Mbs. Because Proteon's own proprietary token-passing scheme uses a noncontention approach to network access, the throughput on this network really can approach 10 Mbs. Nodes can be a maximum of 792 feet from a wire center. Nodes less than 66 feet from a wire center can be connected to the wire center with IBM Type 6 or Type 1 cable. If the node is more than 66 feet from a wire center, then it must be connected to the wire center with IBM Type 1 cabling.

We refer to the wire centers on a ProNET-10 LAN as "passive hubs," because they do not require their own power nor do they repeat signals. Proteon offers other LANs with active hubs that can be used to build a much larger network capable of handling nodes.

802.6 Metropolitan Networks

The IEEE 802.6 committee has been hammering out specifications for a city-wide metropolitan area network (MAN) that would link together local area networks throughout the area. While LANs are usually owned and run by private companies, MANs are more likely to be owned and run by local telephone companies. In Cambridge, Massachusetts, for example, the New England Telephone company has supplied a MAN to link Ethernet LANs at the Harvard Observatory, the Harvard Medical School, the Aiken Computational Laboratory, and Massachusetts General Hospital. A MAN can cover a range of 50 kilometers using fiber optic cabling and sophisticated 802.6 network architecture.

The IEEE 802.6 committee has proposed a dual bus architecture, with each bus carrying traffic in an opposite direction. Nodes send information on one bus and receive it on the second bus using a new Queued Packet and Synchronous Switch (QPSX) medium access control protocol. Nodes keep a record of the number of packet segments awaiting network access. A node that wants to transmit a packet notes its position in the queue; if there are no other packets in the queue, it immediately transmits its packet. The beauty of this approach is that the network traffic is optimized; it never sits idle and there are no collisions. Only two bits of control overhead are needed in the access control field of each packet. A Busy bit indicates that a packet is filled, while a Request Counter bit indicates that a node needs to transmit a packet. Each node has a counter that is decremented every time an empty packet passes it. When its counter reaches 0, this node is free to access the network using the next nonbusy packet that arrives.

As we'll see in later chapters, the MAN is a critical component for an enterprise network. Local area networks might link to MANs, which in turn could be linked to wide area networks. Telephone companies hope that new technology (ISDN) to provide high-speed transmission lines to virtually every company in the near future will make MANs easy to access and economical to use. Companies will be able to interconnect LANs on demand through MANs without having to construct their own fiber optic networks.

6

NETWORK SOFTWARE

Companies evaluating prospective networks are likely to spend far more time examining the software than the hardware. The operating system, network operating system, and file server software selected will determine what features the network will offer. Will the company require separate database servers and E-Mail servers? Will it be necessary to link together Macintosh and PC networks? What levels of security will be required?

These questions raise issues that can only be resolved by looking at the software that will run on a network. In this chapter, we'll examine network software designed to run under DOS, OS/2, Unix, and the Macintosh system software. The leading network operating systems are all powerful and feature-rich, and this chapter will provide information that will help you differentiate among them. While prices change almost as often as the weather, this chapter gives late-1991 prices as a basis for comparison.

One type of network software that is becoming increasingly popular is known as client-server software. We'll examine how these programs work and why they might be beneficial on a network.

■ OPERATING SYSTEMS

Operating systems are sets of programs designed to manage and control the hardware resources of a particular computer. When the Intel 8088-based IBM PC first appeared in 1981, it required a new operating system. The Control Program for Microcomputers (CP/M) operating system that had controlled and managed microcomputers based on the 8-bit Z-80 microprocessor, was soon eclipsed in popularity by MS-DOS and PC-DOS, operating systems designed specifically for the IBM PC and compatibles.

Microsoft's Disk Operating System (MS-DOS) and IBM's version (PC-DOS) are both single-user, single-tasking operating systems. The major functions they perform are examples of the tasks performed by virtually all operating systems. An operating system concerns itself with such tasks as intercepting keyboard commands and check ing their syntax (keyboard processing), storing and retrieving files from disk (file management), and ensuring that a computer's print commands are received and understood by a linked printer (I/O management). DOS ensures that files stored on a microcomputer's hard disk or floppy disks are reflected in a file allocation table (FAT), so that the separately stored portions of a file can be reassembled in the proper sequential order and retrieved.

■ DOS 3.1 AND RECORD LOCKING

Because DOS was designed specifically as a single-user operating system, early versions did not contain **record locking**. This meant that there was no practical way for the operating system to prevent users from trying to view or change a particular record. Consequently, early DOS-based networks created disk servers, microcomputers with their hard disks partitioned into volumes specifically created for different users. The disk server would contain copies of each program in its volumes so that users would not corrupt each other's files by overwriting information.

Disk servers were inefficient because of the redundant software required, and they did not permit what many companies expect from network software today—the ability for several users to share a common program, such as a database, and view the same information.

The network environment changed with the release of Microsoft's MS-DOS 3.1. This version had record and file locking. This meant that DOS 3.1, in conjunction with a Redirector program and a NetBIOS program designed for transport services, could have file servers rather than disk servers. Now it was necessary to keep only one copy of software; the file server would keep the file allocation table and provide file service for all network users. The era of the clumsy disk server was over.

■ MICROSOFT NETWORKS (MS-NET) AND THE NETWORK OPERATING SYSTEM (NOS)

Microsoft developed a "plain vanilla" network operating system called Microsoft Networks (MS-NET) for computer original equipment manufacturers (OEMs). The OEMs, which included companies such as 3Com, Ungermann-Bass, IBM, and AT&T, modified MS-NET by adding key selling features and customizing the product for their hardware. MS-NET provided OEMs with basic file server software, Redirector software, and DOS 3.1.

With MS-NET running as a network operating system (NOS), DOS examines commands to see if they utilize local or network resources. It performs any tasks involving local resources and passes on to the Redirector any commands involving network resources. The Redirector passes on these network requests to the network application program interface, or NetBIOS.

NetBIOS was released originally by IBM as part of its PC LAN network; its specifications were released and soon became a de facto standard. Programs written for IBM's own network that utilized calls to the Redirector and NetBIOS generally worked on OEM networks utilizing MS-NET.

The Redirector occupies a position in the OSI model roughly equivalent to the Presentation layer. It forwards network information to the NetBIOS via server message blocks (SMBs). The position of NetBIOS corresponds to the Session layer in the OSI model. It performs a number of tasks corresponding roughly with those associated with OSI model Session, Transport, and Network layers. It implements the transmission mode to be used (simplex, half-duplex, or full-duplex), which determines whether data will be transmitted in one direction, both directions alternatively, or both directions simultaneously. It also concerns itself with error detection and recovery, and routes messages using IBM's source routing approach, a topic discussed in Chapter 7.

A number of operating systems—including Microsoft's LAN Manager, IBM's PC LAN, and its LAN Server—require a NetBIOS interface to communicate with their underlying transport layer protocols. Both Novell's NetWare and Banyan's VINES offer a NetBIOS interface even though their operating systems do not require it.

◼ LIMITATIONS OF PROGRAMS RUNNING UNDER MS-NET

Several vendors produced their "value-added" versions of MS-NET for a public eager for local area networks. IBM's PC LAN enabled the network manager to set up different nodes offering distinct services, such as network server, messenger, receiver, or redirector. A redirector, for example, was restricted to sending messages and using network disks, directories, and printers. A server, on the other hand, could share its disks, directories, and printers and receive messages for other nodes.

AT&T's StarLAN and 3Com's Ethershare were also MS-NET products. Owing to its solid reputation for hardware and its innovative "value-added" features, 3Com became Novell's leading competitor. Ethershare featured a naming service, excellent E-Mail, and relatively sophisticated network printing. This product also became one of the earliest network operating systems to be offered in a Macintosh version and a version to communicate with IBM mainframe computers.

Despite the relative success of several of these MS-NET products, they all suffered from the basic limitations of any network operating system running under MS-DOS. Network nodes struggled with the 640K RAM limitation while file servers had to work around the 32 MB maximum-size DOS limitation for addressing disk space. Also, as networks became larger, they struggled with an operating system designed for 16-bit microprocessors. We'll return to this issue when we look at the development of OS/2 and OS/2-based network operating systems.

■ PROPRIETARY NETWORK OPERATING SYSTEMS

NetWare

Novell's NetWare occupies an enviable spot in the NOS world, having captured approximately 60 to 70 percent of the market, depending upon which survey you

believe. The company has stated that it is moving toward a product that will be truly
hardware and protocol independent.

The NetWare File Server

NetWare is a proprietary network operating system that is optimized for network operations. A number of techniques are used to speed up file operations, including directory
hashing, file caching, and elevator seeking. In **directory hashing**, the file server keeps
a copy of the directories' contents in RAM. When a user requests a specific file, the file
server knows precisely where to go to retrieve this data and thus saves time.

In **file caching**, the file server keeps frequently requested files cached in RAM so it
does not have to go to disk to retrieve them when they are requested.

In **elevator seeking**, the file server retrieves files that are physically located in the
same area of the hard disk rather than blindly retrieving files in strict sequential order.

NetWare products now also feature a Name Service (the NetWare Name Service, or
NNS), which enables managers to update users' access rights and create and delete
user accounts on multiple servers concurrently. However, this ability to simplify network management is not a true global naming service. VINES's StreetTalk product,
discussed later in this chapter is far more sophisticated than either Novell's NNS or
the product Microsoft offers for LAN Manager.

NetWare 2.2

Novell has consolidated three different products (NetWare ELS, Advanced, and SFT
NetWare) into a single product called NetWare 2.2, which is offered in 5-, 10-, 50-,
and 100-user licenses. NetWare 2.2 can handle a maximum of 100 users on a file server. It offers network security through password protection and the ability to hide and
restrict directories. Each user can be assigned specific rights to directories and files.
NetWare provides network management functions through its SYSCON (system configuration) utility.

NetWare utilizes **Value Added Processes (VAPs)**, programs that permit the server to
host additional applications. They function as interfaces to third-party developers so
they can write programs to these interfaces. VAPs appear to NetWare as if they are
logical users. As users, these VAPs can make requests for operating system services.
For example, they can request that a particular process be scheduled and run, order a
report generated, or request a printer to empty its queue. One example of how a VAP
can work is as a database management system. Such a system could function as a VAP
on a server without requiring a dedicated server for database management. NetWare
for the Macintosh is actually a VAP, as is the NetWare printing program.

Novell currently offers 5-user licenses for $895, 10-user licenses for $1,995, 50-user
licenses for $3,495, and 100-user licenses for $5,495.

NetWare 3.11

NetWare 3.11 can handle up to 250 logical users. When Novell's NetWare Requester program is added, it supports DOS nodes, nodes running Windows, and nodes running OS/2 and OS/2 EE. It also supports Macintosh nodes running Macintosh OS 6.0 or later. This operating system supports very large volumes (32 TB) and very large files (4 GB).

The key to NetWare 3.11 is its use of **NetWare Loadable Modules (NLMs)**, which are software modules that link dynamically to the operating system and enable server-based applications to be added while the server is running. Figure 6-1 illustrates the modular approach used by NetWare 3.11. NLMs include printing functions, various utilities, and protocol stacks. Among the protocol stacks currently available or projected are Xerox Networking System (XNS), Transport Control Protocol/Internet Protocol (TCP/IP), Open Systems Interconnect's File Transfer Access Method (FTAM), Systems Network Architecture (SNA), Apple Filing Protocol (AFP), and Sun Microsystem's Network File System (NFS).

With the protocol support supplied by these NLMs, Unix clients can attach to a NetWare server by using the "Mount" command. They will see the NetWare file system as an extension of the distributed Unix file systems. They will be able to use NetWare print queues via the Unix "lpr" command and transfer files to and from the NetWare server via File Transfer Protocol. Novell's OSI FTAM implementation is in compliance with the Government OSI Profile (GOSIP). While this fact doesn't mean much right now, it will become increasingly important in the future as GOSIP gains momentum.

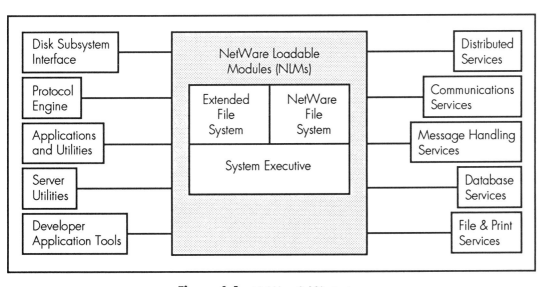

Figure 6-1. NetWare 3.11's structure.

NetWare 3.11's NLMs are loaded only on demand and can be unloaded withou rebooting the system. On NetWare 2.2 file servers, VAPs are loaded automatically an cannot be unloaded while the file server is running. While VAPs running on NetWare 2.2 must log onto the system as a user, which reduces the number of user slots stil available on the network, NLMs can log on to the network as a user and thus use a connection or they can use NetWare Connection 0, which allows multiple NLM connections and does not reduce the number of available connections for network users.

NetWare 3.11 uses memory in a completely different way from NetWare 2.2. It dynamically allocates file server memory based on need and then enlarges or shrinks this memory as needs change. Memory reserved for file caching is used as a pool to handle this dynamic memory allocation. There is another significant difference between this operating system's handling of memory and that of NetWare 2.2. NetWare 2.2 hashes all directories (keeps all directories in RAM) so it can retrieve files quickly. NetWare 3.11 hashes directories as they are used. If a directory item is used once and then not again for a period of time, this entry is purged and the memory reallocated.

Novell has significantly changed its pricing policies by breaking down its NetWare 3.11 product by number of users and unbundling various options. Novell currently prices NetWare 3.11 20-user licenses at $3,495 per server, 100-user licenses at $6,995, and 250-user licenses at $12,495. NetWare for the Macintosh ranges from $895 per server for a 20-user license to $1,995 for a 100-user license. NetWare NFS and NetWare FTAM are priced at $4,995 each. This pricing policy is advantageous to companies that need only certain services, because they can buy just what they need; it hurts companies that need virtually all options for their large networks.

Recently Novell has developed a 1,000-user version of NetWare 3.11 for large corporate customers. It is a desirable solution for companies wanting to centralize E-Mail or databases on one server. Prices are not yet available.

Novell's Open Data-Link Interface (ODI)

Novell and Apple have developed a new standard for device drivers. The **Open Data-Link Interface (ODI)** enables NIC manufacturers to write one device driver for as many protocol stacks as they want to address rather than having to write a different driver for each protocol stack. Ethernet is a prime example of where ODI can make life easier for everyone, from the network manager to the NIC vendor. Without ODI, vendors might have to write separate drivers for TCP/IP, IPX, and AppleTalk protocol stacks. Novell indicates that if ODI becomes a standard, users will not have to worry about protocol-specific NICs or whether or not they have the right driver for that card. All they will have to do is ensure that the NIC they purchase has drivers that are ODI compliant. Another advantage of ODI is that network nodes that utilize multiple protocol stacks will not have to reboot when they switch between applications.

The Open Data-Link Interface (ODI) includes Multiple Link Interface Drivers (MLIDs), the Link Support Layer (LSL), and the various protocol stacks to be supported. The LSL communicates with protocol stacks via the Multiple Protocol Inter-

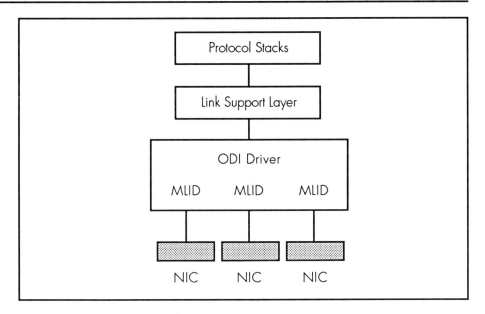

Figure 6-2. How ODI works.

face (MPI) while it communicates with MLIDs through the Multiple Protocol Interface (MPI). Figure 6-2 illustrates how ODI works.

Novell has linked up a number of companies that have pledged support for ODI. Among the leading vendors who have indicated they will develop ODI-compliant products are Retix, Advanced Micro Devices, Compaq, Proteon, Thomas Conrad, Western Digital, and The Wollongong Group. Once again the public will vote with their dollars to decide which proposed standard (Novell's ODI or Microsoft's NDIS, which we will look at shortly) becomes a de facto standard.

NetWare and OS/2

Novell offers the NetWare Requester for OS/2. In addition to providing NetWare to OS/2 file service, this program now supports diskless OS/2 workstations, OS/2's high-speed file systems (HPFS), long-name and extended-attribute-aware utilities, and up to 255 Named Pipes connections. We will examine the concept of Named Pipes when we look at OS/2, but for the moment think of it as a way that processes running within programs can communicate directly with each other.

An OS/2 workstation running NetWare's Requester can act as a client to the NetWare network and provide access to OS/2 distributed applications, including such applications as Sybase's SQL Server and Lotus Notes.

Figure 6-3 illustrates how NetWare's OS/2 Requester works. An OS/2 client opens a Named Pipe to the NetWare network, a process that creates a pipe or connection, gives it a name, and thus becomes the pipe's server. Other processes can then communicate

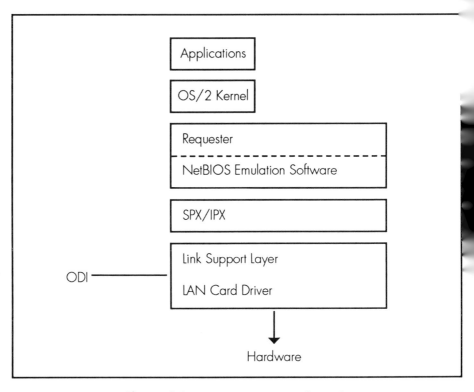

Figure 6-3. The NetWare Requester for OS/2.

with this process by name. With NetWare Requester, whenever a Named Pipe connection is established, there is a corresponding SPX (NetWare's Sequenced Packet Exchange protocol) connection established. The NetWare network communicates internally via SPX and IPX protocols while still preserving the Named Pipe interface. The Requester takes the OS/2 workstation's requests to its OS/2 Kernel (the "brains" of this operating system) and reroutes these commands for input/output services to the NetWare server via IPX/SPX.

NetWare and Enterprise Networking

Because NetWare controls such a large part of the NOS market, it is not surprising that third-party vendors have come forward to develop products, including several that enhance communications. Novell itself has been active in this area. Its own SNA Gateway provides support for the Service Advertising Protocol (SAP), enchanced CICS support, and support for the AS/400. It can provide up to 128 Token Ring or SDLC remote sessions and up to 40 CoaxMux sessions. The NetWare 3270 LAN Workstation program provides support for Systems Application Architecture (SAA) specifications as well as a transfer program that supports file transfers with PS/CICS and OfficeVision/MVS.

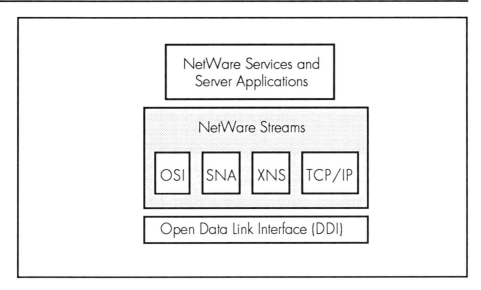

Figure 6-4. NetWare's future open architecture.

Novell also provides the NetWare Access Server (NACS) for asynchronous communications. X.25 service is provided by a number of third-party vendors.

Novell's new improved relationship with IBM has led to better cooperation between the two companies in the area of network management. The NetView network loadable module (NLM) permits NetWare to generate and send Token Ring and Logical Link Control alerts to the NetView management console.

IBM and Novell recently agreed that NetWare would be integrated with LAN Server, OS/2's Communication Manager and Database Manager. The two companies have agreed on specifications that will permit NetWare servers to send information to Net-View for network management and have identified more than 125 alerts or commands that will permit control of a NetWare server from a NetView console. Novell has indicated that it will facilitate communications with IBM's DOS and OS/2 users by supporting NetBIOS and Server Message Block (SMB) protocols in a future release of NetWare.

Open Architecture and NetWare's Future Direction

Novell has stated that it is moving toward an open architecture. Figure 6-4 illustrates the structure of this architecture. Note that the architecture includes a low-level interface to device drivers (Open Data-Link Interface) and an interface between protocol stacks and NetWare services (NetWare Streams). What NetWare Streams offers is a common interface for transport protocols that need to deliver requests and data to NetWare services. Novell likes to refer to NetWare as a networking platform designed to run on virtually every current hardware configuration and operating system.

The OS/2 Operating System

In 1987, IBM announced Operating System/2 (OS/2) as the operating system for it
new family of PS/2 microcomputers. Requiring at least an Intel 80286 microprocessor
OS/2 represented a quantum leap in resource management over DOS. OS/2 wa
designed as a multitasking enviroment, one capable of addressing up to 16 Mb c
RAM. Developers are able to write to a standard interface, or "pipe," when they nee
to communicate with computer resources. OS/2 has taken two different directions
OS/2 (Standard Edition) has been Microsoft's primary responsibility, while IBM ha
been marketing OS/2 Extended Edition (OS/2 EE). Microsoft markets its LAN Man
ager network operating system in conjunction with OS/2, and IBM markets LAN
Server as its NOS. We'll examine these two products a bit later in this chapter
Although the two companies are taking different directions with their versions o
OS/2, IBM has indicated that the two products will remain compatible.

Applications running under OS/2 are divided into **processes.** A program and all the
memory areas required to support it can make up a process. The execution path within
a process is known as a **thread.** One key aspect of OS/2 is its scheduler component
which uses a preemptive time slicing scheme that can execute a thread for a period o
time and save the current results while it runs another scheduled thread.

Threads and processes communicate with each other under OS/2 through shared memory, semaphores, queues, and pipes. Under shared memory, a program places information in a certain memory location and then a second program accesses this
information. **Semaphores** are flags that are set so that two proceses do not try to
access the same network resource at the same time.

Queues also facilitate interprocess communications. Information can be placed in
queues, specific memory locations, as it is produced. Another process can then retrieve
this information as needed without having to take it in sequential order. The process
takes only the information it requires.

Pipes function as channels between two programs. The information flows in sequential order from one program to the other. OS/2 also offers **Named Pipes,** a very
sophisticated way of handling interprocess communications on a network. Named
pipes provide full duplex traffic within a computer and between two computers. They
create a virtual session between two computers with an unlimited number of such sessions on a network.

Finally, OS/2 supports **Named Mailslots** as a method for interprocess communications. This "quick and dirty" technique enables remote processes to send information
to each other by name—hence the name "mailslots."

OS/2 provides a **protected mode,** under which each program is granted its own protected area of memory and registers to hold information during processing. Under this
arrangement, the "crashing" of one program will not cause the other programs to fail.

Another OS/2 feature that distinguishes it from DOS is **virtual memory,** the ability to utilize hard disk space and RAM in such a way that large programs can be fooled into thinking the computer has more RAM than it really does. Portions of a program are moved from disk to RAM as needed.

BM's OS/2 Extended Edition

IBM released the first edition of OS/2 Extended Edition (OS/2 EE) in July 1988, and in November followed with LAN Server, a program enabling a workstation running OS/2 EE to function as a network server. OS/2 EE is fully compatible with IBM's Systems Application Architecture (SAA), a set of guidelines to enable programs running across IBM's entire computer family to communicate with each other and present a common user interface. Presentation Manager serves as OS/2 EE's graphical user interface, or "GUI." It presents a standard SAA display, utilizing windows and icons.

OS/2 Extended Edition contains a layered architecture. The top layer of its Communication Manager provides a number of application programming interfaces (APIs), including a NetBIOS interface and an IEEE 802.2 LAN interface to the LAN Requester. The LAN Requester serves the same basic function as the Requester under DOS; it intercepts application program calls for file and printer input and output onto the network and forwards these commands to the file server (LAN Server on an IBM system). The Communications Manager's upper layer also contains a number of emulators, including the Emulator High level Language Application Programming

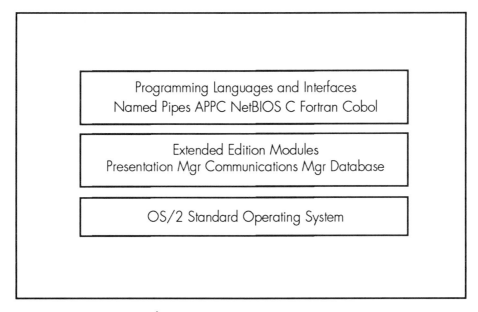

Figure 6-5. The structure of OS/2 EE.

Interface (EHLLAPI), 3270 terminal emulation and 5250 terminal emulation. Figure 6-5 illustrates the structure of IBM's OS/2 Extended Edition. The extended edition modules include the Communications Manager, the Database Manager, the LAN Requester, and the Presentation Manager.

The Database Manager includes a Query Manager, the component that provides the user interface as well as producing all reports. Users can opt for a command line interface if they prefer. Any database created is limited to a maximum size of 4,000 bytes or 255 columns, whichever comes first. The database, which can reside on a PC or on a mainframe, supports Structured Query Language (SQL). The database program also provides a number of utilities for file transfer and conversion. A Query Manager enables users to generate reports and perform queries.

The OS/2 EE Communications Manager also contains network management functions, including the ability to detect and log as well as forward this information to a mainframe running the IBM network management program NetView. This Communications Manager also keeps track of network statistics and logs this data to help with error diagnosis and problem resolution.

A Protocol layer provides support for such protocols as synchronous data link control (SDLC), X.25 and SNA's LU 6.2, PU Type 2.1. The Data Link Controls (DLC) layer of OS/2 EE roughly corresponds to the OSI model's Data Link layer. It it able to handle a number of protocols, including IBM's own IEEE 802.5 LAN, the synchronous data link control (SDLC) protocol that runs on IBM's larger computers, and 3270 coaxial links to IBM's mainframe world of systems network architecture (SNA).

The communications functions of OS/2 EE are its major strength. It is designed to be integrated into an enterprise network that includes IBM mainframes and token ring networks. Its SAA compatibility and Application program to program communications (APPC) interface means that the foundation is present to develop program-to-program communications in the future.

Why select IBM's OS/2 EE over Microsoft's version of this operating system? Network managers with heavy investments in IBM mainframe, minicomputer equipment, and token ring networks might very well select OS/2 EE for its Communication Manager's ability to facilitate LAN-to-mainframe communications. Also, since IBM apparently will continue to push SAA, this SAA-compatible operating system will appeal to some large companies that have decided to become SAA compliant.

A Microsoft 32-bit Version of OS/2

Microsoft has promised a new version 3.0 of OS/2 (OS/3 ?) that will require a 32-bit machine to run and will take full advantage of a 32-bit processor as well as incorporate its Windows product to serve as the graphics interface. The company has also promised such mainframe and minicomputer features as symmetrical multiprocessing, fault tolerance, and enhanced security.

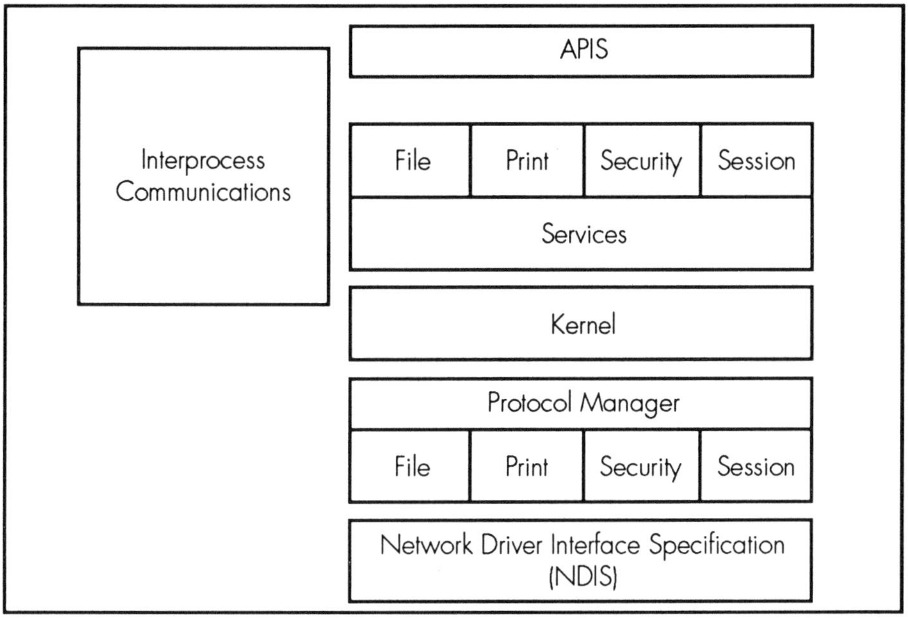

	APIS			
Interprocess Communications	File	Print	Security	Session
	Services			

Kernel

Protocol Manager			
File	Print	Security	Session

Network Driver Interface Specification (NDIS)

Figure 6-6. Microsoft's vision of OS/2 version 3.0.

OS/2 version 3.0 is expected to use dynamically loaded operating system application programming interfaces (APIs) on its common operating system foundation. This flexibility would enable different applications running under different APIs, such as Unix and Windows, to run concurrently. This approach is remarkably similar to the approach Novell has taken in NetWare 386 with its NLMs.

Microsoft's projected new OS/2 product will be built around the new kernel technology that Microsoft refers to as New Technology (NT). As Figure 6-6 illustrates, this approach will permit a true multiuser, fully distributed environment with the ability to support RISC-based Unix machines as well as Intel 80386 and 80486-based microcomputers. It is also expected to include symmetric multiprocessing, allowing multiple threads to be distributed from a single application to different processors.

IBM's OS/2 Direction

While IBM and Microsoft started as OS/2 partners, they have taken different directions. Microsoft has begun to push a Windows-supported version of OS/2, in recognition of the more than 2 million copies of Windows it has sold. IBM, on the other hand, has continually pushed for a version using Presention Manager for its graphical interface, but it will bow to the market pressure by making its version of OS/2 Windows-compatible.

IBM has also announced that it will unbundle its Database Manager and Communications Manager from the OS/2 EE package. These two programs will run as 16-bit applications on top of the 32-bit OS/2 2.0 Standard Edition and on systems made by hardware competitors. Also, IBM will move its OS/2 Requester program from OS/2

EE to its file server program, LAN Server. IBM will include a superset of the same function provided by Microsoft's LAN Manager 2.0 file server program with its own LAN Server so that the program can run across all vendors' equipment. IBM's OS/2 2.0 is expected to support both 16-bit and 32-bit machines. It is also expected to remain SAA-compliant while supporting Windows 3.0.

While making its future versions of OS/2 EE compatible with competitors' products, IBM has also moved to bridge the gap between its products and Novell's NetWare. In fact, it has begun to sell Novell's NetWare under its own label, and has announced plans to work with Novell to make NetWare more compatible with IBM's entire family of computer products.

Microsoft's LAN Manager

Microsoft's original intention was to market LAN Manager, its network operating system under OS/2, to other computer manufacturers such as 3Com, AT&T, Hewlett-Packard, and IBM, who would add value to the product and then market under their own names. Beginning with LAN Manager 2.0, Microsoft has standardized core NOS features including printing, file management, administrative functions, and security, which companies licensing the product cannot change. These licensees can add enhancements, however. A number of factors, including 3Com's failure to achieve a significant marketshare with its 3+ Open version of LAN Manager and NetWare's increasing marketshare, caused Microsoft to change its strategy. It now sells LAN Manager to the public under its own label and provides its own technical support. Let's examine some of the key features of this product.

LAN Manager senses whether it is running on an Intel 80386- or 80486-based file server. It will load the 80486 version of the High Performance File System (HPFS) when it identifies this microprocessor. HPFS optimizes disk usage as well as adding significant caching and storage addressing capabilities (48 gigabytes). HPFS matches Novell NetWare's **hot fix** feature. Using hot fix, HPFS will check a block before writing to it. If the block is bad, it will be placed in a hot fix table so that no data is written to it; data will then be written to a safe disk area.

Microsoft has also added a domain-based approach similar to that found with IBM's LAN Server to LAN Manager. Several servers can be grouped into a single entity to facilitate management and control. This approach enables network managers to modify user accounts only once rather than on each file server.

LAN Manager offers asymmetrical multiprocessing support. This means it can be used with the family of superservers that support this approach to handling heavy network traffic. One microprocessor can be dedicated to certain tasks while another microprocessor handles others.

LAN Manager runs on a file server under OS/2, but the client nodes can run DOS or OS/2. The structure of LAN Manager running on a file server is illustrated in Figure 6-7 The NOS consists of several modules, enabling Microsoft to add and modify modules without having to rewrite the entire product. The approximately 150 Application

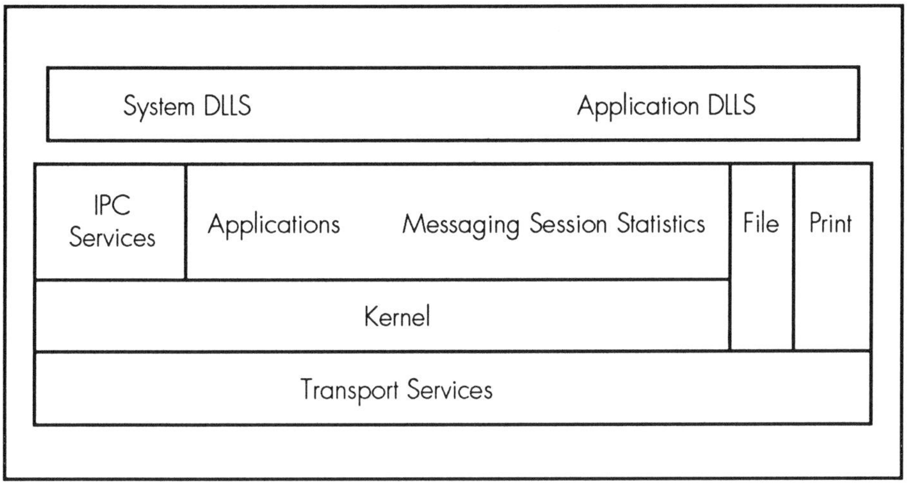

Figure 6-7 The structure of LAN Manager.

Program Interfaces (APIs) provide services for distributed applications in conjunction with **Dynamic Link Libraries (DLLs)**. The actual instructions for the APIs' functions are shipped by Microsoft as DLLs. The major advantage of this approach is that developers need only have their programs reference a DLL. The operating system links a program to the DLL when the program is run. Developers need not change their programs whenever Microsoft updates its NOS, since the DLL reference should remain the same. An advantage for network managers is that the data contained in a DLL need only be stored on one place; each program need not contain this additional code.

LAN Manager's services are handled by separate modules. One module concerns itself with security while another handles printing, memory management, and so on. These services in turn are controlled by the LAN Manager kernel. The interprocess communications discussed under OS/2 are an integral part of LAN Manager and provide communication between the programs that make up a distributed application. Named Pipes are particularly important in this context, because they permit developers to write to a standard interface when they want to control resources across the network.

The Protocol Manager includes NetBIOS Extended User Interface (Netbeui), a NetBIOS interprocess communication routine, and NetBIOS protocol, a Transport layer mechanism. Also included are support for Transmission Control Protocol/Internet Protocol (TCP/IP), AppleTalk Filing Protocol (AFP), and OSI protocols.

Network Driver Interface Specification (NDIS)

The **Network Driver Interface Specification (NDIS)** was developed by Microsoft and 3Com as a standardized interface for DOS and OS/2 platforms for access to the services provided by the Data Link layer. Software developers can write to the NDIS interface and NDIS-compliant drivers without having to write drivers for every NIC on the market. NDIS enables two protocols such as TCP/IP and Apple Filing Protocol to share the same MAC driver and adapter card. The LAN Manager Protocol Manager module gathers NDIS information during the system CONFIG.SYS initialization o the NIC drivers. It then parses this information into a Configuration Memory Imag that is accessible by other NDIS drivers. The Protocol Manager retains a complete lis of all active NDIS drivers, including their desired bindings. The actual binding doe not take place until a program initiates this process by issuing a call.

Several applications now support NDIS including Pacerlink (Pacer), LAN Works (DEC) and PC/TCP (FTP). 3Com, AT&T, Microsoft, and IBM all have versions of LAN Manager that support NDIS, and Banyan's VINES also supports this emerging standard.

LAN Manager's Packaging

Microsoft packages a five-user version of LAN Manager for $995 with an additional 10 users for $995. It also offers a 1,000-user version for $6,490. This approach is particularly appealing for small companies that have growth plans. The network can grow the network incrementally as needed.

LAN Server

IBM's LAN Server requires OS/2 EE as its operating system for its server while its client stations can run either DOS or OS/2. DOS client stations must run the IBM PC LAN Program. The server must also run the LAN Requester. This software package performs the same function under OS/2 that the Requester performed under DOS. It intercepts I/O calls and redirects them to network resources such as the file server or a network printer. In 1990 IBM and Microsoft announced that eventually everything found in LAN Manager will appear in LAN Server. Because the two companies seem to be taking different directions with their OS/2 products, LAN Server is probably a good choice for companies that have a large investment in IBM equipment. LAN Server running on OS/2 EE will no doubt continue to be SAA-compliant. This NOS is a good choice if communications with IBM mainframes or minicomputers is a major part of a company's business or if the company has several large IBM Token Ring networks. It should be pointed out, however, that the latest version of LAN Server does support 802.3 LANs.

At this time, IBM's LAN Server does a better job with its domain management than LAN Manager. IBM has integrated its OS/2 EE's Database Manager with the Domain Manager. A user can use one password and ID to access both the LAN Server and the Database Manager. IBM's pricing will vary by the time this book is published, but some figures will help you compare it with the other NOS products described in this chapter. LAN Server costs $1,040, which includes the DOS LAN Requester and LAN support program. Users are permitted to replicate up to 128 licenses for this network. In other words, IBM has a server-oriented rather than user-oriented pricing structure.

The Unix Operating System

For years some industry experts have predicted that Unix would become a major force in local area networking. After all, it is a true multiuser, multitasking operating system that was designed to support large networks and client servers without any degradation. Unix structure includes a kernel that is responsible for all resource allocation. Its shell provides a command language interpreter as well as interfaces to all other operating system services.

Unix is portable enough to run on virtually any hardware. Developed two decades ago by Bell Labs, Unix System V Release 4.0 has a number of built-in communications features. It offers an implementation of TCP/IP, including this protocol's E-Mail service (Simple Mail Transfer Protocol), its file transfer service (File Transfer Protocol), and its terminal emulator (Telnet). It supports Sun Systems' Network File System (NFS) and includes virtual file support (VFS) as well as memory management and network management functions. VFS enables different types of file systems to exist simultaneously on the network.

In this section we'll look at how AT&T runs its version of LAN Manager (StarGroup), while Banyan Systems runs its proprietary NOS software (VINES) under Unix.

VINES

Banyan Systems' Virtual Networking Systems (VINES) is a network operating system based on Unix System V that is designed specifically for very large multiserver networks. All VINES services, including its electronic mail, file management, and printing management, operate as processes under Unix.

With the release of VINES 4.10, this network operating system now supports client systems running OS/2 (both OS/2 and IBM's OS/2 EE) as well as those running Windows 3.0. Since VINES now supports Named Pipes and Mail Slots, Banyan is hoping that developers will consider writing programs for VINES concurrently with their work on OS/2 applications. One of the major stumbling blocks for VINES has been its lack of support from third-party vendors who have focused on the more lucrative NetWare market.

The two major strengths of VINES have been its naming service and its sophisticated wide area network and interconnectivity links. These two advantages are particularly important on very large enterprise-sized networks.

StreetTalk

VINES is best known because of its distributed database called **StreetTalk,** which provides a resource naming service. It really does not matter if there are hundreds of servers attached to a VINES network; a user can still access any of these network resources by name without having to know their network paths. When a new resource is added to a VINES network, the network is alerted and servers update their routing tables accordingly. When a user in New York wishes to retrieve information from the company's file server in San Francisco, only the correct name (let's say SF-FS1) is needed. VINES offers StreetTalk Directory Assistance (STDA) to help users look up StreetTalk names. That's far easier than the alternatives under NetWare, LAN Manager, or LAN Server.

StreetTalk enhances security, because this naming service informs all services across the network of the rights a user has when he or she logs on. Only one password is needed, since all servers share the same naming service information.

Enterprise Networking Features

VINES is particularly strong when it comes to linking LANs and forming wide area networks. A single VINES server can support up to four different LANs and integrate them into one coherent network. Banyan's Intelligent Communications Adapter card supports VINES's communications services and protocols, including support for asychronous host connections and server-to-server communication over dial-up connections. VINES also supports SDLC protocol for SNA/3270 mainframe connections, HDLC for server-to-server integration over leased lines, and X.25 protocol for server-to-server communications over public and private packet switched networks.

How VINES Is Packaged

VINES is packaged in a number of different ways. VINES 4.1 is sold as VINES Team (a ten-user version priced at $2,495). VINES Unlimited (a combination of earlier versions VINES 386 and Vines 486) sells at $7,495. Banyan also markets its symmetric multiprocessing version of VINES for $13,995.

AT&T's StarGroup LAN Manager and Unix

AT&T licensed Microsoft's LAN Manager and developed its own implementation running under Unix. StarGroup provides full support for DOS, OS/2, and Unix along with support for SQL servers. It supports virtually all LAN Manager APIs, including support for Named Pipes and Mailslots. In addition to server software, StarGroup networks require modules for the OS/2, DOS, and Unix client stations.

StarGroup and Enterprise Networking

StarGroup is particularly strong in the area of enterprise networking. It provides SNA gateways as well as asynchronous gateways, X.25 routers, TCP/IP support, and PMX/STARMail, AT&T's LAN-based electronic mail. AT&T offers the OSI Network Program, which provides protocol support for the first four layers of the OSI model, including the TCP/IP protocol. This program supports the Basic Networking Utilities, which provide a NetBIOS interface for the DOS world as well as tools for facilitating remote logins for Unix-based systems.

AT&T also offers a StarGroup Server for the Macintosh, which coresides with StarGroup LAN Manager. This software enables Macintosh users to share files and printers with DOS, OS/2 and Unix machines. AT&T currently prices StarGroup LAN Manager at $3,495 for an unlimited server configuration. StarGroup Server for the Macintosh is priced at $795 for eight users and $1,295 for an unlimited number of users.

AT&T's NOS provides extensive network management capablities. It gathers statistics from all OS/2, DOS, Macintosh, and Unix machines and is able to transmit this information over a wide area network to AT&T's own Unified Network Management Architecture (UNMA) or to IBM's NetView network management system.

Because the StarGroup server is running under Unix, it is able to support standard Unix System V APIs so that multiuser Unix applications can run simultaneously with the StarGroup network software. The file server is able to utilize all the sophisticated communications services offered by Unix while retaining its links to the DOS and OS/2 worlds. AT&T's products might be some of the best-kept secrets in the network world, since the company has never excelled at marketing its products. A company should give StarGroup server serious thought if wide area networks and communications with several different types of large computer systems are company concerns. This choice is particularly appealing for companies that can use the StarGroup server's ability to gather network statistics and pass them on to a sophisticated network management system such as NetView or Unified Network Management Architecture. We will examine these network management systems as well as others in Chapter 8.

■ CLIENT SERVERS

The major network operating system vendors are positioning themselves and their products for a new type of network architecture, one requiring a very powerful, multi-tasking operating system. Applications are beginning to appear that can utilize a client-server architecture. Let's spend a few moments examining what many industry experts believe will be a major trend for networking in the near future.

On a typical network, nodes request programs from the file server and receive the files along with associated data. This is not particularly efficient, since the node might need only a specific record or a few records, not several hundred records that have to be sorted through. The result of this approach is very heavy network traffic, much of it not really used. With client-server architecture, servers can be dedicated to specific tasks such as database servers. A client node requests specific information. This request is relayed from the file server to the application server, which processes the information and then transmits the specifically requested records to the client node.

Because the heavy processing is done on the application server, the client node might not need to be upgraded to the same level as the application server. The volume of traffic on the network is reduced considerably, since only needed information is transmitted.

The client node's "front-end" program provides it with a user interface for querying and making other requests. The "back-end" program runs on the application server and does the actual work. Because current applications do not communicate with each other using an agreed-upon syntax, there is a trend toward embracing IBM's Structured Query Language (SQL)—hence the term "SQL server."

Developers will incorporate SQL in their applications in a way that should be transparent to end users, who will probably have a much easier user interface. The applications will not be limited to databases, although this area seems to have the greatest impetus at the moment. Other applications that lend themselves to client servers could include E-Mail servers, CAD/CAE files, and accounting software.

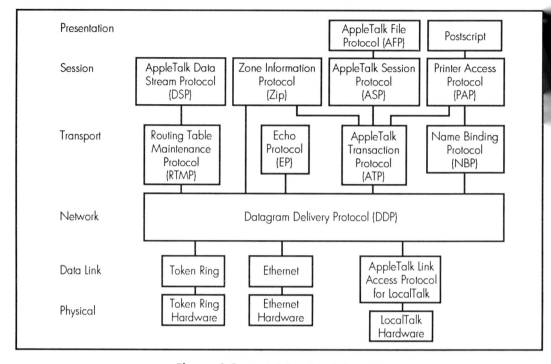

Figure 6-8. AppleTalk and the OSI model.

The flood of products has already started. Front-ends to Microsoft's SQL Server already announced include such products as dBASE IV, Paradox, Lotus, Revelation, Oracle, DataEase, and Focus. Front-ends already announced for NetWare's SQL Server include Revelation, Oracle, Paradox, WordTech, and DBXL.

■ APPLETALK AND MACINTOSH NETWORKS

Built into every Macintosh is a suite of layered network protocols whose functions can best be described by comparison with the OSI model. Figure 6-8 illustrates Apple-Talk's seven layers of protocols. Let's spend a few moments looking at the key components of AppleTalk.

At the Physical layer, AppleTalk provides specifications for Token Ring, Ethernet, and LocalTalk specific hardware; it also addresses what is required for twisted-pair, coax, and fiber optic cabling. The Data Link layer includes Apple's own AppleTalk Link Access Protocol (ALAP), designed for packaging data to travel over a LocalTalk interface. EtherTalk and TokenTalk drivers provide the Macintosh with specifications for packaging packets for Ethernet and Token Ring networks.

AppleTalk's Network layer consists of the Datagram Delivery Protocol (DDP). This protocol establishes the route a datagram will take from its source node address to its destination node address. It accesses routing tables to establish a network path for this datagram. While working out the specific details associated with a datagram's routing, the Network layer utilizes the Transport layer's Name Binding Protocol to translate a network server's name into an acceptable internet address.

It is AppleTalk's Transport layer that concerns itself with the specific details of services to be provided for the datagram's routing. The Routing Table Maintenance Protocol (RTMP) maintains the information needed by bridges and routers to link together AppleTalk networks. It determines how many "hops" a datagram must take before it reaches its ultimate destination. The Name Binding Service translates addresses into acceptable formats, while the AppleTalk Transaction Protocol provides an acceptable level of Transport layer delivery service.

AppleTalk Session layer is concerned with establishing and maintaining a network session. The Data Stream Protocol ensures that a communication session is established. The Zone Information Protocol maps networks into a series of zone names. The routing path AppleTalk establishes is based in large measure upon the ZIP. The Session Protocol is concerned with the correct sequencing of datagrams should they arrive out of order. Finally, the Printer Access Protocol provides a datastream for devices such as printers and streaming tape systems on the network.

The Presentation layer featuring the AppleTalk Filing Protocol (AFP) is absolutely critical to the ability of non-Macintosh networks to achieve some degree of interoperability with Macintosh networks. AFP is concerned with file service and file structure. AFP compatibility is a key issue for any non-Macintosh network that wants to exchange files with a Macintosh network. The PostScript Protocol provides an interface between network nodes and PostScript devices, including Apple's LaserWriter printer.

Apple's System 7.0 and Networking

For the past few years, industry experts have been awaiting Apple's long-delayed System 7.0 operating system. System 7.0 offers several features that will improve Macintosh networking. The Interapplication Communication Architecture (ICA) permits one application to send data or commands to another application located on the same machine or another network node.

The IAC includes Program-to-Program Communication (PPC), an editions manager, and AppleEvents. The Program-to-Program Communication (PPC) is that portion of System 7.0 that is responsible for routing, storing, and forwarding and other message-transport functions from one task to another.

The editions manager permits information changed in one application to be automatically updated in other applications. This feature has enormous potential for distributed databases that reside on several different machines in different cities. Finally, the AppleEvents feature provides a means for programs to send commands to other programs. In effect, IAC's features provide much the same intercommunication processes provided by OS/2 for the PC world.

Enterprise Networking with the Macintosh

Once virtually isolated from the world of PC networking, the Macintosh has become much easier to incorporate in an enterprise network. The easiest way to link the PC and Macintosh networking worlds is through Ethernet. An Ethernet NIC in a Macintosh and appropriate networking software makes it a viable part of a PC LAN. NetWare offers a Macintosh version that provides file translation and even truncates long Macintosh file names to conform to the eight-character limitation imposed by the DOS world. NetWare enables Macintosh users to enjoy the same network management and file resources enjoyed by PC users. VINES has also developed a Macintosh version, as has 3Com, with its version of LAN Manager.

AppleTalk provides drivers for Token Ring (TokenTalk) and there are even drivers currently available for Arcnet. Since TCP/IP protocols are now available for the Macintosh, it is possible to link Macintosh networks with the Unix world. There are also SNA gateways available to the IBM mainframe world and gateways to IBM's AS/400 minicomputer world.

7

REPEATERS, BRIDGES, ROUTERS, BROUTERS, AND GATEWAYS

Companies wishing to link all their computing resources into an enterprise network often find this a very complex task. Different types of networks have different degrees of interoperability. The solution to this problem is often the selection of the appropriate type of link.

In this chapter, we'll examine the ways networks can be linked together. Often, to gain efficiency, network designers subdivide large networks into smaller ones linked by bridges. Remote bridges can link networks to form a wide area network. Networks using different protocols can be linked via a router. Finally, networks that differ widely might require the services of a gateway. For example, gateways can link IBM's mainframe world with the PC world of LANs.

Other gateways enable network nodes on a LAN to access packet-switched networks. Asynchronous communications servers enable LAN nodes to access modems and communications software. This chapter will examine all these interoperability components.

■ REPEATERS

Before looking at the tools we have for connecting networks, it is worthwhile clarifying the role of a **repeater**. Functioning at the Physical layer of the OSI model, the repeater extends the distance a LAN can cover. On an Ethernet network, for example, the signal weakens after 500-meters. Two 500-meter segments can be linked together by use of a repeater, which regenerates the signal before transmitting it.

Repeaters can extend an Ethernet LAN to a maximum distance of 2,500 meters. There are limitations to a repeater, however, which explain the need for devices such as bridges and routers. Repeaters do not reduce the amount of traffic on a LAN, because they are not capable of filtering out packets. They do not look at the content of the packets they are transmitting. In other words, a repeater functions like a public address system added to a large meeting room in a convention center. It can transmit a message from one side of the room to the other, but it does not enable listeners speaking another language to understand the message, despite the fact that they can hear the sound.

■ BRIDGES

Bridges function at the Data Link layer of the OSI model. A bridge connects two separate LANs, permitting communications between nodes on each LAN. Bridges are capable of linking LANs with different hardware (Arcnet and Token Ring or Ethernet and LocalTalk, for example) as long as the network operating system (NetWare, VINES, LAN Manager, etc.) is the same on both LANs so that they share the same Network layer of the OSI model.

Bridges function as network traffic cops. They can read the destination address field on a packet and then forward that packet to the next network if that specific address is not found on the current LAN.

Perhaps an analogy will help explain how bridges work. Addresses in Tokyo are haphazard. People locate a particular office by stopping at a police box located in each neighborhood. The police officer checks the address and, if the office is not in his neighborhood, directs the person to the next neighborhood police box or, if it is located in his neighborhood, points out the specific building. Analogously, a bridge keeps a table that keeps track of all the nodes located on its LAN.

Bridges "age" entries in their routing tables. If a bridge does not see a node's source address for an extended period of time, it deletes this node's address from its table.

Advantages of a Bridge

A major design advantage of bridges is that they can be used to break up a single large network into smaller, more efficient networks, each of which carry a portion of the total traffic. When nodes need to communicate across the bridge, the process is transparent to end-users.

Another advantage to bridges is that they permit the use of mixed media. A factory area might require thick coaxial cabling while another area lends itself to 10BaseT. Still another area might contain Macintosh computers running Ethernet. Bridges can link these subnetworks smoothly.

Bridges can also isolate networks from the chaos caused by broadcast storms. These are massive amounts of packets generated by an errant broadcast that keeps replicating itself until the amount of traffic generated brings the network to its knees. A bridge set to restrict broadcast packets serves as a barrier protecting a network against such an invasion.

Today, most vendors offer "learning" bridges, bridges capable of learning the addresses of nodes that are added to their networks. These bridges automatically add the address of a new node to their address tables when the node is attached. Older bridges required the network manager to add new addresses manually every time the network configuration changed.

Bridges filter or forward packets, depending upon their destination address fields. If the packet's destination address appears in the bridge's table of addresses, the bridge filters it. If the packet's destination address is not in its address table, the bridge forwards it to the bridged network, where the process is repeated. An IEEE 802.3 bridge can forward approximately 15,000 packets per second and filter approximately 30,000 packets per second.

Bridges offer several advantages for the network manager. They are transparent to end users and able to respond automatically to node additions and deletions. While they are relatively inexpensive, they process frames at a much faster pace than alternative options such as routers.

Bridge Topologies

We've already noted that large networks are often subdivided into smaller nets that are bridged together. These bridges can be designed a number of different ways depending upon the overall needs of the network. **Cascaded bridges** are useful where network segments are relatively self-contained, having their own file servers, PC nodes, and communications servers. As Figure 7-1 illustrates, using a cascaded bridge topology it is possible to extend the length of a network without really increasing the network's overall traffic, since the heavy traffic is mostly confined within each segment. Cascaded bridge topology is useful when the number of segments is limited. If more than six segments need to be bridged, higher level protocols will respond to the length of time necessary to traverse these bridges by timing out and assuming that transmitted packets have been lost.

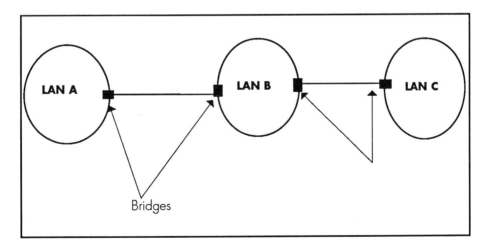

Figure 7-1. The cascaded bridge topology.

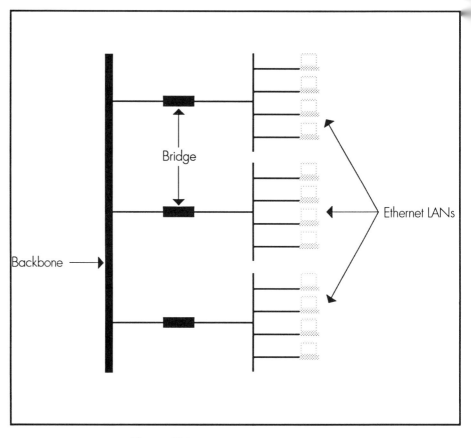

Figure 7-2. The backbone bridge topology.

A **backbone bridge topology** is useful when there are several different segments. As Figure 7-2 illustrates, this topology makes it possible for traffic to move quickly between networks without having to transverse several bridges. It is also useful for multifloor buildings that need to be networked.

A third type of bridge topology, the star, will be examined when remote bridges are discussed. The major advantage of a starlike topology is that a central location such as a corporate headquarters can be bridged directly to several different regional offices.

The Spanning Tree Algorithm (STA)

The **Spanning Tree Algorithm (STA)** was developed several years ago by Digital Equipment Corporation (DEC) and Vitalink. It has been adopted as a standard by the IEEE 802.1 committee. Each bridge under STA has a globally administered station address and a priority field.

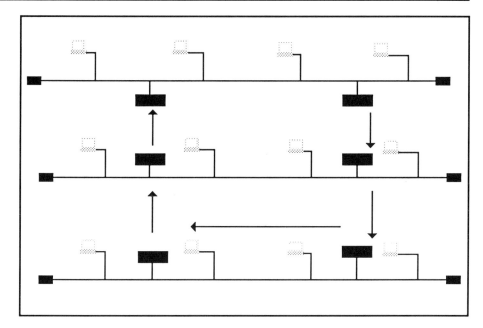

Figure 7-3. The effect of a Spanning Tree algorithm.

Bridges communicate with each other under STA and determine a root bridge on the basis of the station addresses of the various bridges' priority fields. Once a root bridge is selected, all bridges determine which of their ports points in the direction of the root bridge.

If multiple bridges exist on the same network, only one is included in the routing of a packet to the root bridge. The selection of this bridge is based on criteria determined by the network manager, such as the maximizing of line speed, the minimizing of network traffic, and the minimizing the number of "hops" or bridges that must be crossed from source node to destination node.

The Spanning Tree algorithm ensures that only one possible loop will exist for a packet's route from source node to destination node and then back again.

If a bridge becomes defective, it is no longer able to broadcast packets informing other bridges that it is active. The root bridge notifies all other bridges of this failure. A port that has been blocked off is activated, and it listens and "learns" by recording the information enclosed in bridge protocol data units (BPDUs), which are broadcast by bridges so that other bridges can update their routing tables. Figure 7-3 illustrates the effects of the Spanning Tree algorithm.

The IEEE 802-1D Standard

The IEEE 802-1D committee has selected the Spanning Tree algorithm as its standard for local bridges. This standard specifies a maximum period of one minute for rebuilding a new spanning tree after a network failure. While bridge failures are rare on local bridges, they can be more frequent on remote bridges depending upon phone line conditions. While some vendors are trying to extend the 802-1D standard to their remote bridges, the amount of time necessary to rebuild the spanning tree frequently could result in an unacceptable level of service on a remote bridge if 802-1D is used.

Source Routing

IBM's LAN bridges use an algorithm known as **Source Routing**. Source routing bridges function at the Network layer of the OSI model. Each bridged LAN ring is assigned a unique number. When a node attempts to transmit a packet to a node on a network that is bridged, the source node issues an all-routes broadcast frame to all rings attached. Bridges attach their unique numbers and the numbers of the two rings they bridge to the all-routes frame. When this frame returns to the source node, it is able to update its routing table and indicate the specific route its packet is to travel. It specifies precisely which bridges must be crossed and the order in which crossing must occur.

Because network nodes keep their own routing tables under source routing, source routing bridges do not maintain any routing tables. Bridges simply examine a packet's information to see if its bridge number and ring numbers of the rings on both sides are listed. If any of these addresses are missing or incorrect, the bridge will not forward the packet.

One negative feature of source routing is that, since each bridge copies each route determining packet it receives, the number of packets generated by an all-routes broadcast becomes exponential for each bridge that is traversed.

Linking STA (Ethernet) and Source Routing (Token Ring) Networks

The Ethernet and Token Ring packets differ in many ways, so linking these networks is problematical. Token Ring packets (around 5,000 bytes maximum) are approximately three times the size of an Ethernet packet (1,500 bytes maximum). Token Ring packets contain a number of fields (including the token itself) not found in an Ethernet packet. Currently, only special bridges can provide the conversion necessary to bridge Etherent and Token Ring networks.

The IBM 8209 LAN Bridge is an example of this highly specialized type of bridge. It will take a large Token Ring packet and segment it into smaller sized packets that an Ethernet network can handle. Conversely, to Token Ring nodes, the 8209 LAN Bridge looks like a source routing bridge. Ethernet nodes see all Token Ring nodes as Ethernet nodes on the same segment.

The major limitation of this type of bridge is that it is slow. The packet-format conversion takes time. As we'll see in the next section, IBM has proposed an alternative solution.

Source Routing Transparent Bridges

The new type of bridge IBM has proposed is known as a **source routing transparent bridge (SRT).** This bridge would examine the routing information indicator (RI) field to see if the packet uses source routing or transparent bridging. Source routing nodes would change the RI field to a 1 while transparent bridges would leave it unchanged at 0.

Bridging Ethernet LANs Via FDDI Backbones

As FDDI become more common, companies will want to bridge their existing Ethernet segments via FDDI backbones. The advantage of this approach is that traffic congestion can be eliminated at key points of a network by using the 100 Mbs speed FDDI offers. The problem with such an approach is that FDDI requires a format different from that of Ethernet.

One solution to this problem is a translation bridge, a bridge that translates the segment's Ethernet format into an FDDI format before transmitting it over an FDDI backbone. A bridge at the receiving end will translate the FDDI frame's format back into a standard Ethernet format.

A second solution the problem of bridging Ethernet segements via FDDI backbones is to use a bridge that encapsulates the Ethernet frame within an FDDI format. The vendors that offer this approach use proprietary protocols for performing this task. The limitation of this approach is that the company purchasing these bridges is locked into that particular vendor's products, since these bridges do not adhere to any international standard.

Remote Bridges

While information is transmitted over a LAN at speeds of millions of bits per second, remote bridges often become bottlenecks, since public telephone lines have been limited to a transmission speed of approximately 19.2 Kbs. Leased lines have upped the transmission speeds to 64 Kbs, but this is still not acceptable for heavy bridge traffic.

The Use of Load Balancing

Remote bridges often utilize **load balancing**, which is a uniform distribution of data over parallel links. Usually, these links can be similar or dissimiliar. One channel can have a transmission rate of 19.2 Kbs, for example, while the other channel might be transmitting at 56 Kbs. Similarly, one channel might utilize modems, while another channel utilizes microwave transmission.

Generally, the network manager will define the two links as a single logical link. The bridge has enough intelligence to build logical blocks in which a number of events take place.

Data packets are queued serially using a first in, first out approach. Each packet is assigned an identity number and then split into two or more links. The receiving block sorts the packets in order of transmission as well as the packet identity number. The logical block then transfers data packets to the bridge.

The bridge can ensure that packets will be sequenced correctly, but it cannot ensure that there will be no missing packets. Upper level protocols must be used to handle missing packets.

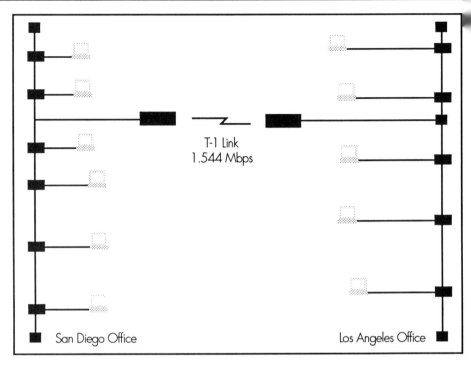

Figure 7-4. A remote bridge connects two lines via a T-1 line.

The T-1 Option

T-1 service offers a 1.544 Mb circuit that provides a quantum leap over 19.2 Kbs service. Where a remote bridge connects two LANs via a T-1 line, the bridge connects to a T-1 multiplexer that frames the data into the T-1 format. The multiplexer, in turn, is connected to a channel service unit (CSU), which handles long-distance carriers' electrical, testing, and alarm conditions. Figure 7-4 illustrates a typical remote bridge utilizing a T-1 connection.

Even T-1's 1.544 Mbs transmission rate is slow compared with the speeds frames travel on a LAN. A T-1 link could theoretically carry only 3,000 Ethernet packets per second, assuming that each packet contained only the minimum 64 bytes permitted.

Problems Associated with Remote Bridges

The major problem with remote bridges is that they are much more prone to fail because of line conditions than local bridges. For this reason, many companies will build a level of redundancy into their remote bridges. Figure 7-5 illustrates how the use of a spanning tree algorithm ensures redundancy. Should one link fail, the inactive second link would be activated and packets could still be transmitted.

Other algorithms besides spanning tree can be used with remote bridges. Several proprietary algorithms permit load sharing. Two T-1 lines could share ("load share") a remote bridge's traffic. Should one line fail, the traffic could be rerouted through the

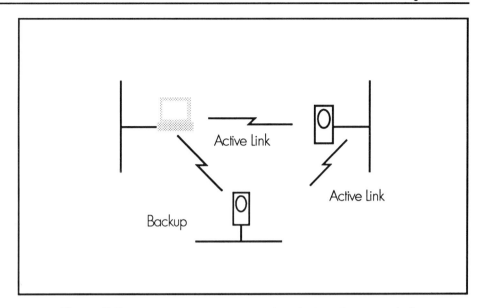

Figure 7-5. A spanning tree algorithm provides redundancy for a remote bridge.

remaining link. Companies can ensure even greater redundancy by requesting that the T-1 lines be on different circuits.

Because line noise can be such a problem with remote communications, one way of handling this problem is to use proprietary bridges that have automatic channel failure detection and fallback capabilities. Should its primary link fail, the bridge is then capable of falling back to an alternative link or dialup line.

While communications failure is the major problem associated with remote bridges, a second problem is the timing out of a packet because it has too many "hops" to travel on its trip from source node to destination node. One possible solution to this problem is to design a backbone structure so that packets need only cross certain bridges.

Selection Criteria

Here are some questions to ask when selecting a bridge:

1. What is the maximum number of packets that can be forwarded and filtered per second? A bridge must be fast enough not to result in massive network traffic congestion.

2. What type of network management software is offered with the bridge? Many of the newer bridges have network software that will monitor bridge traffic and provide statistics, the ability to program specific criteria to use for filtering, and the ability to diagnose specific problems.

3. What type of media does the bridge support? Some bridges have multiple ports enabling a network manager to select the type of media to be used.

4. Is the bridge capable of learning the addresses of new network nodes? Some bridges require the network manager to physically record any network changes.

5. Does the bridge offer load balancing? This feature enables multiple ports to carry information to the same destination, which provides a degree of redundancy that can keep a network bridge up even if one port fails. Unfortunately, this approach is often proprietary. Be sure that this type of bridge will work with your particular network.

6. If the bridge is to be linked to a wide area network, what is the maximum rate that the bridge's ports can support? Some ports can only support a 64 Kbs transmission rate while others are capable of supporting a 1.544 Mbs transmission rate.

7. How many ports does the bridge support? Some bridges support only two ports, while others support up to eight ports. Multiport bridges can connect LANs and WANs very effectively by connecting directly and avoiding multiple-hop delays.

■ ROUTERS

Routers are devices that function at the Network layer of the OSI model. More complicated and hence more expensive than bridges, routers are protocol-dependent devices that are sophisticated enough to be able to determine the most efficient route for a packet even when there are multiple paths. Some routers can handle multiple protocols such as TCP/IP, XNS, ISO, and X.25.

A major advantage of routers over bridges lies in flow control. On heavily congested networks, delays can cause a frame to be timed out before it reaches its destination and sends an acknowledgment back to the source node. Also, heavy traffic on a bridge can cause the bridge's buffers to overflow.

With routers, the data flow problem is handled by higher level protocols. These protocols send flow-control messages to reduce congestion and queueing delays. While buffer overflow is still possible, this extra level of control makes it far less likely with routers than with bridges. But nothing is free in the world of data communications. The price of this greater data flow control on routers is added overhead. These high-level protocols require control information that must be transmitted on a regular basis.

Routers have another major advantage over bridges. They provide a "fire wall" that shelters a network from broadcast storms that might be transmitted by another network. Network managers can divide a large network into several smaller subnetworks. Segmenting the network protects it against broadcast storms and improves overall efficiency, since each subnetwork can filter frames based on the limitations imposed by the network manager.

Internet Protocol (IP)

One of the most common protocols used by routers on large networks is **internet protocol (IP)**, the routing protocol associated with TCP/IP (Transmission Control Protocol/Internet Protocol). Internet protocol provides a connectionless service and does not guarantee such niceties as flow control, guaranteed delivery, or acknowledgment

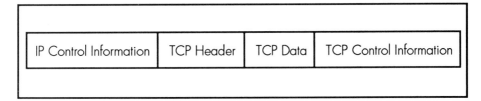

| IP Control Information | TCP Header | TCP Data | TCP Control Information |

Figure 7-6. IP control information is added to the front of a TCP packet to form an IP datagram.

of delivery. Looking at the information carried by IP will help you understand how routers use such information to route packets successfully across large networks.

Figure 7-6 illustrates an internet protocol control header that is added to the front of the TCP packet to form an IP datagram. A Version field indicates the version number of the protocol being used to ensure that both sending and receiving routers are using the same version.

The Internet Protocol Header Length indicates the number of 32-bit words in the IP header. The Type of Service field indicates the level of service and type of priority the datagram requires. The Total Length field contains a number (in bytes) representing the total length of the IP header and accompanying data. The Identification number uniquely identifies the datagram even if it is later divided into segments.

A Flags field contains various information, including whether or not to fragment the datagram and whether or not this particular datagram is the final segment if a datagram has been fragmented. The Fragment Offset field reveals how this particular fragment should be segmented so that the original datagram can be reassembled. The Time to Live field indicates how much time remains for the packet to live before it times out. This field has a maximum value of 255 seconds. It is decremented as it travels and then discarded when this field reaches zero.

The Protocol field indicates what protocol is found after the IP header. In most cases, this is likely to be TCP/IP. The Header Checksum field is used to determine if there has been an error in transmitting this IP datagram header. The Source and Destination addresses are 32-bit fields that indicate the network number and host address for source and destination nodes.

Finally, there is an Options field. This field is not required and can be padded with zeroes. It can be used for a number of functions, though—for example, carrying error information and providing debugging functions.

The Internet Control Message Protocol

Internet Protocol is accompanied by the Internet Control Message Protocol (ICMP), which is used to provide IP with information on routing problems. Internet Protocol receives ICMP messages describing trouble conditions such as the failure of a datagram to reach its destination. IP takes this ICMP message and encapsulates it with the IP header before transmitting it to the destination node.

The ICMP messages can take a number of forms that help explain how routers and router protocols work. These messages indicate whether a datagram's time has been exceeded and, if a parameter is in error, which particular field is incorrect. A Source Quench message indicates that the source node should reduce its transmission rate. A Redirect message indicates that a shorter, better route is indicated for the datagram.

Routing Information Protocol (RIP)

Many routers use **routing information protocol (RIP)**. The RIP approach uses the Bellman-Ford protocol, which means that it keeps track of the route between source and destination address in terms of "hop count," or the number of routers a packet must cross. This protocol imposes a limit of 15 hops for any route.

Another limitation with RIP is that it requires routers to transmit their entire routing tables frequently over the network to update other routers. This approach is time consuming and an ineffective use of bandwidth.

Open Shortest Path First (OSPF) Protocol

The internet community has been developing an improved routing algorithm known as the **Open Shortest Path First (OSPF)**. Rather than requiring routers to broadcast their entire routing tables, OSPF requires them simply to broadcast descriptions of their local links; this takes far less time and consumes less bandwidth.

OSPF does not have the 15-hop limitation found under RIP. Also, it offers eight different classes of service, which means that network managers can specify how different types of information should be routed. Critical information could be given highest priority and travel via expensive phone links while time-insensitive information might be routed via satellite with several hours delay.

Point-to-Point Protocol (PPP)

A working group of the Internet Engineering Task Force (IETF) developed the first specifications for **Point-to-Point Protocol (PPP)**. PPP was developed to provide serial point-to-point communications links so that interoperability could be improved among different vendors' equipment.

PPP is designed to improve upon the way some routers now communicate. Vendors now support transmitting IP over a serial link such as a dial modem, a protocol known as the Serial Line Internet Protocol (SLIP).

PPP will provide a standard way of encapsulating IP datagrams. It can be used to design high-speed direct serial connections between TCP/IP routers.

Figure 7-7 illustrates the PPP encapsulation format. The High Level Data Link Control (HDLC) header is followed by a PPP Protocol ID field, which is used for demultiplexing the packets. PPP ID values have been specified for TCP/IP, OSI, DECNET Phase IV, XNS, Appletalk, and IPX protocols, among others, so that different protocols can run over serial PPP links.

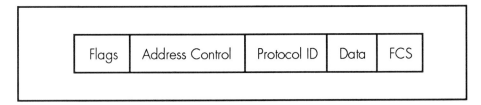

Figure 7-7. The PPP encapsulation format.

The PPP Protocol ID field is followed by a variable data field. A Frame Check Sequence (FCS) field provides error checking. PPP is intelligent enough to be able to negotiate use of 16-bit or 32-bit FCS algorithms.

Limitations to Routers

Routers are far more expensive than bridges. A major limitation to routers is that since they are protocol-dependent, they must be updated whenever an evolving protocol is modified. Also, they are not capable of routing low-level protocols (those residing below the Network layer of the OSI model). This means that routers cannot route such protocols as DEC's Local Area Transport (LAT) protocol or IBM's LU 6.2 application-to-application protocol.

Criteria for Router Selection

Here is a list of questions to ask when selecting a router:

1. What protocols are routed? This is the key question to ask. Does the router support XNS? IP? ISO? DECnet? What protocols does your network currently have and what protocols might be added in the near future?

2. Is the router capable of routing multiple protocols simultaneously? On networks with heavy traffic and several protocols running, this feature might be a major advantage.

3. What is the forward rate (packets per second) of the router? This number can vary widely. Some simple arithmetic based on current network statistics can show whether or not the router can handle the current and project workload.

4. Is the router static or dynamic? A dynamic router is capable of adjusting its routing tables when a node is added or deleted or a device fails. Static routers require a network manager to update all routing tables when a change is made.

5. What type of processor is used? Some routers use a Motorola 68000 while others now use Motorola 68020s; the processing speed varies considerably.

6. What routing algorithm is used? While RIP is still the most common, some vendors do offer OSPF. Proprietary algorithms are restrictive, particularly if the network needs to communicate with networks that do not use this protocol.

7. Some routers support network management protocols. We will be discussing such network management protocols as Simple Network Management Protocol (SNMP) in Chapter 8. It is worthwhile determining whether or not the router

supports a network management protocol standard such as SNMP or a proprietary network management protocol. Standard protocols are preferable, because they do not lock customers into a particular product line.

■ BROUTERS

The **brouter,** a relatively new development in network interoperability, is a device that incorporates some of the best features of the bridge and the router. Brouters combine the multiprotocol hardware capabilities of bridges with the flexibility of software-controlled routers. They can be programmed to act like bridges for some protocols while handling data using a different protocol as a router.

While a brouter can pass or filter packets at the MAC layer level like a bridge, it has the ability to route packets over closed loops in which all links are used. Unlike the spanning tree algorithm, brouters are intelligent enough to route packets through the best and second-best path on the network.

The brouter automatically learns the names of all node addresses on its own network and constructs a LAN table to hold this information. Nodes not active for a certain time period are deleted.

Brouters send broadcast messages to all other existing brouters. These messages contain both a HELLO message and an UPDATE message. The UPDATE message contains information on all new nodes that have joined its netwrok as well as information on nodes that have been deleted or changed addresses.

In a separate table, the brouter keeps track of all other nodes on the network. A separate routing table contains directions for sending packets through the best path and second-best path to each bridge or brouter on the network.

The brouter assumes responsibility for routing packets through the optimal path available. They also prevent packets from circling endlessly in loops. They discard packets that have traveled more than the maximum number of hops permitted. Finally, they control broadcast messages so that they are transmitted only once on each link.

■ GATEWAYS

Network gateways link the LAN world of PCs with networks that utilize different types of computers and operating systems.

The Role of Gateways

Gateways support functions performed by the upper layers (Transport through Application layers) of the OSI model. Gateways are capable of performing protocol translation so that networks with different protocols, such as SNA and NetBIOS, can communicate. In fact, gateways are used any time it is necessary to connect networks such as DECnet and SNA that do not share a routing protocol.

Gateways are mainly used to link LANs to minicomputer and mainframe networks, networks to packet-switched (X.25) networks, and different E-Mail systems. Gateways generally require two different circuit cards in the node serving as a gateway—

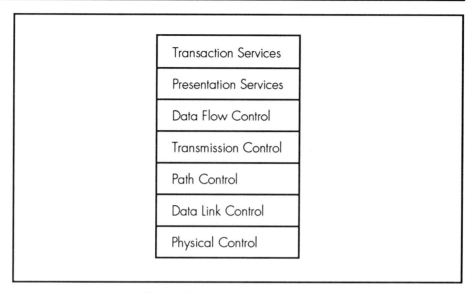

Figure 7-8. SNA's layered architecture.

one for the node's current network connection and a second to perform the protocol conversion and other functions required to convert packets into a form the second network can understand. This card is also responsible for translating incoming packets into its own network format.

In this chapter we will examine two major gateways—SNA and X.25.

Systems Network Architecture (SNA)

Since the overwhelming majority of mainframe computers are IBM hosts, it is necessary to examine the proprietary protocols associated with IBM's network architecture so you can understand the functions gateways must perform to communicate with these mainframes. IBM introduced **Systems Network Architecture (SNA)** in 1974. Since that time, the company has continually modified this network architecture, though it has not changed its focus on the mainframe computer. We'll see that SNA's focus on the mainframe as the hub of a network has created serious problems, particularly now that customers are demanding a way for their microcomputer programs running on LANs to communicate as transparently as possible with programs running on the mainframe.

SNA's Layered Architecture

Figure 7-8 illustrates SNA's layered architecture. The Physical layer concerns itself with specifications for connecting nodes physically and electrically. The Data Link layer is concerned with the reliable transmission of data among nodes. The IBM protocols supported by this layer include Binary Synchronous Control (BSC) and Synchronous Data Link Control (SDLC).

BSC is a character-oriented protocol that continues to live despite IBM's efforts to phase it out long ago. Control information takes the form of characters (ACK, for example). This approach is more limited and not as efficient as IBM's newer SDLC which is bit oriented. Control information is identified in SDLC's fields by bit patterns rather than by characters. Eight-bit control fields can generate 2^8 different codes.

The Path Control field handles network routing. It also concerns itself with traffic control and congestion reduction. The Transmission Control field handles data flow by packing data exchange to match end-point processing capacity. It also handles the encryption of data for security purposes. The Data Flow Control field is responsible for synchronizing the flow of data between end points. This layer handles full-duplex transmission as well as several different varieties of half-duplex transmission.

The Presentation Services layer formats data for different presentation media and coordinates resource sharing. Finally, the Transaction Services layer provides such services as distributed database access and document interchange.

SNA's Network Addressable Units (NAUs)

SNA provides addresses for all its network components that can either send or receive data. These **network addressable units (NAUs)** include physical units (PUs), logical units (LUs), and system service control points (SSCPs).

Physical Units (PUs)

Physical units (PUs) perform control functions for the devices in which they are located as well as for any attached devices. An IBM 3274 control unit is an example of a PU. It can support 16 or 32 devices and is used for local as well as remote locations.

Logical Units (LUs)

The **logical unit (LU)** is a point of access to an SNA network for an SNA user. Because it is a logical unit, it is not a physical connection. LU types 2,3, and 4 support communications between application programs and different types of workstations. LU types 1, 4, and 6.2 support communication between two programs. LU 6.2 will become increasingly important for LAN gateways in the future, so we will return to this topic later in the chapter.

System Service Control Points (SSCPs)

The third type of network addressable unit, the **system service control point (SSCP)**, provides the services necessary to manage a network or a portion of an SNA network.

An SNA Network in Operation

Figure 7-9 illustrates an SNA network in operation. The host computer runs the SSCP software. The SSCP software establishes a session with the network control program (NCP), which usually resides on a communications controller. The SSCP then establishes ownership of all resources that wish to communicate with the host. Application programs running on the host establish an SSCP-LU session. When a terminal wishes to communicate with a host, an SSCP-PU session is first established with a cluster controller. Then, an SSCP-LU session is established between the SSCP and the terminal.

PCs that need to communicate with IBM host computers must do so by emulating (imitating) an IBM 3278/9 terminal. The gateway runs software that enables it to emulate an IBM cluster controller. In the IBM mainframe world, the host computer communicates only with IBM equipment. All non-IBM devices (such as a PC or an asynchronous terminal) must emulate an IBM device in order to communicate with a host.

Types of SNA Gateways

LAN SNA gateways can take the form of local DFT coaxial gateways, token ring interface coupler (TIC) gateways, and remote gateways. In any event, the gateways perform the same basic function. The major function is to distribute mainframe sessions to PC users in the form of LU sessions. LU sessions are allocated to users, including printers and terminals, on a first come, first served basis.

Most gateways permit users to have multiple simultaneous sessions on the host. Gateway software maps the PC keyboard to emulate a 3270 terminal. Often, gateways permit a hot key that enables users to jump back and forth between DOS and a mainframe session.

Local DFT Coaxial Gateways

Distributed Function Terminal (DFT) coaxial gateways are designed so that the gateway PC functions as an IBM cluster controller. The PCs run software that enables them to emulate a DFT terminal such as an IBM 3278. The PC's terminal software accesses the gateway via the LAN's transport protocol. The number of concurrent sessions available on this type of gateway depends upon the software vendor.

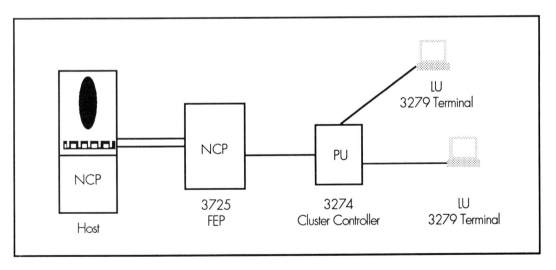

Figure 7-9. An SNA network in operation.

The gateway is attached directly to the host computer's communications controller by coaxial cabling. As far as the communications controller is concerned, it is communicating directly with a cluster controller that is processing the input of several 3278 terminals.

The Token Ring Interface Coupler (TIC) Gateway

The token ring interface coupler (TIC) gateway is a way for a token ring network to link directly to a host's front-end processor. The advantage of this approach is speed; the TIC can provide 4 Mbs or 16 Mbs transmission speed, depending upon the model installed. It is possible to link an Ethernet LAN to a front-end processor via a TIC gateway, but the transmission speed (2.35 Mbs) is not as attractive.

The host computer is viewed by the host as a cluster controller. It is polled for input on a regularly scheduled basis by the mainframe.

Remote SNA Gateways

LANs located at remote sites can communicate with SNA networks via remote gateways. The LAN gateway PC runs remote gateway software that enables it to emulate a cluster controller. It communicates with a front-end processor via synchronous modems at both sites using IBM's Synchronous Data Link Control (SDLC) protocol.

Synchronous modems can achieve speeds of up to 64 Kbs. Because this transmission speed is very slow compared to internal network transmission speeds, remote gateways can become traffic bottlenecks. One possible solution is to have multiple gateways. Another possible solution is to use T-1 links when available.

LAN-to-SNA Communications in the Near Future

IBM has developed **Advanced Program-to-Program Communications (APPC)** for the IBM PC to complement the versions of this program already available on its minicomputers. APPC includes the SNA protocols PU 2.1 and LU 6.2. PU 2.1 permits intelligent remote nodes to communicate on a peer-to-peer basis.

The LU 6.2 protocol enables two application progams on micro, mini, or mainframe computers to have a peer-to-peer conversation. These programs can exchange information without users even being aware that the exchange was taking place. As developers begin to write programs containing the "hooks" necessary to take advantage of the PU 2.1 and LU 6.2 protocols, there should be an increase in APPC-compliant programs and increased levels of communication between programs running on different platforms.

Criteria for Selecting an SNA Gateway

Here is a list of questions to ask when selecting an SNA gateway:

1. How many sessions are supported by the gateway? Since gateways range from 16 to 254 sessions, it is important that companies estimate the amount of their projected growth. They should also ask whether limited-session software can be upgraded should users' needs change.

2. What kind of file transfers capabilities are needed? Some gateway vendors offer

proprietary file transfer software that can speed up this time-consuming process significantly, particularly if file transfers are to be a major function on the gateway.

3. What type of gateway management features are available? Some gateways allow the network manager to enable and disable devices and to compile statistics.

4. Does your company plan to do its own programming? If the answer is yes, then does the gateway support programming interfaces and IBM's APPC?

5. If the gateway is remote, what kinds of transmission speeds are supported? As modem transmission speeds increase, will the gateway keep pace with the new technology?

6. What kinds of terminals are supported? If graphics are important for specific applications, does the gateway support emulation of a graphics terminal?

7. What kind of printer support is offered? Does the software support a printer attached to the host? Does the PC node software support a printer attached to it?

8. Does the gateway offer dedicated and/or pooled LUs? Dedicated LUs ensure that a critical user will always have a session available, but they result in poor overall utilization of LUs. Some gateways permit both dedicated and pooled LUs simultaneously.

Asynchronous Communications Servers

Network users are often astonished to discover that their network has a dialout service. LANs with asynchronous communications servers do not require users to have their own modems or communications software, because they can share the LAN's modem(s) and software. Users are able to dial out to an information service, perhaps access an X.25 packet-switching network, or communicate with the company's minicomputers or mainframe computers.

Modem Pooling

On networks where several modems exist, the asynchronous communications server software can be run at each modem station so that a pool of modems exists. This means that network users can access any of the pool modems that happen to be free. But there is a down side to having individual network users share their own modems by running ACS software at their local node. When they turn off their workstations, the modem is no longer available.

One solution to this limitation is to have a group of nodes functioning as dedicated communications servers. A second solution is to purchase a special ACS box to connect directly to the network without the need for a separate PC acting as a server.

Novell's NetWare Access Server

Novell's NetWare Access Server (NAS) illustrates the services asynchronous communication servers provide. NAS provides up to 16 PCs or Macintosh computers to dial in and simultaneously access NetWare resources. The NAS supports LAN-to-LAN communications. A NetWare Loadable Module runs on a NetWare 3.11 server translating AppleTalk protocols into NetWare native IPX protocols, so a Macintosh user running NetWare for the Macintosh 3.0 can locally or remotely log in to the NetWare server and initiate a DOS session on the NAS.

There are several ways in which asynchronous communications servers save money. Companies can purchase a few high-speed V.32/V.42bis modems rather than buying several lower speed 2,400 bps modems. And they can license software for the modem for concurrent use instead of buying copies for each network node. Finally, if LAN users are accessing a minicomputer or mainframe, the use of the asynchronous communications server can save ports, since network users share a common port. Saving ports often means putting off the need to replace or upgrade a minicomputer or even a mainframe.

Criteria for Selecting an Asynchronous Communications Server

Here's a list of questions to ask:

1. What network interfaces does the asynchronous communications server support? Does it support your network's interface (NetBIOS,IPX/SPX, TCP/IP, LU6.2, etc.)?

2. Is password security provided?

3. Can the software run in the background?

4. What transfer protocols are supported? Most programs support Kermit, but some add such useful protocols as Xmodem, Ymodem, Zmodem, and CompuServe B.

5. Is a script language provided? Some powerful script languages support as many as 300 commands and have scripts for common information services such as CompuServe, Dow Jones, MCI Mail, AT&T Mail, etc.

6. What kind of terminal emulation is provided? Obviously, a company connecting to a DEC would like to have VT 220 emulation.

7. What kind of hardware is available? Some ACS boards contain their own RAM and microprocessors so that they are able to buffer large amounts of information. The advantage of a microprocessor is that it speeds up operations.

X.25 Gateways

Since 1976, packet-switched networks have been used to transmit data to form a wide area network. Companies such as Telenet that offer packet-switched networks take data transmitted by their customers and package it in the form of packets. Customers are usually charged on the basis of the number of blocks or packets transmitted. These packets are of limited size and are transmitted via a connection-oriented connection. Connections are established, data is transferred, and then the connection is terminated.

Public packet-switched network vendors offer a number of services that are particularly appealing to network users. The network can either use its own packet assembler/disassembler (PAD) to frame its packets or use a modem and transmit data in conventional form to the vendor, who will convert the information into packets in turn. Vendors offer protocol conversion so that network users can take data utilizing ASCII, for example, and transmit it to the vendor, where it will be converted to EBCDIC before being forward to an IBM mainframe.

Unlike T-1 remote bridges that utilize a point-to-point link, X.25 wide area networks utilize a mesh architecture. As Figure 7-10 illustrates, each LAN has an X.25 gateway.

A major advantage of X.25 networks is that they are not distance sensitive. Users are charged for the amount of data they transmit and not how far the data is traveling. The major limitation of X.25 links is their lack of speed. Most users access them with 9,600 bps or 10.2 bps modems. The X.25 network can transmit up to 64 Kbs.

The X.25 Standard

Packet-switched network gateways are based on the CCITT X.25 standard for an "interface between Data Terminal Equipment (DTE) and Data Circuit Terminating Equipment (DCE) for terminals operating in the packet mode on public data networks." The major significance of this standard is that it defines how nonpacket equipment (DTE) can communicate with the packet-switching world through a packet-switched node (the DCE).

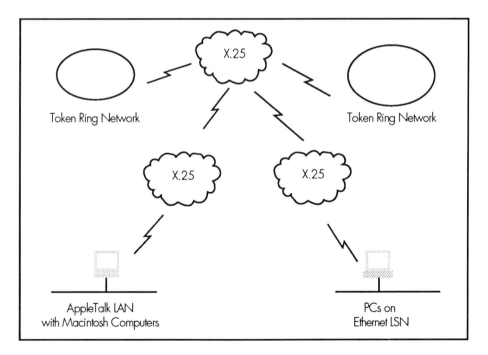

Figure 7-10. An X.25 WAN connects several LANs.

The CCITT X.25 standard defines a Physical level corresponding to the OSI model' Physical layer. The actual physical hardware and electrical connections used by X.2 are defined in CCITT Recommendation X.21. The X.21 specification defines a code string of characters for each interface function; the advantage of this approach ove simply defining each pin in an interface is that there is no limit to the number of func tions the interface can have. The X.21 specification also includes built-in dialing capa bilities so that trouble with a connection can be reported quickly and easily.

The X.21 specification refers to four different operating phases: a Quiescent phase, ε Call Control phrase, a Data Transfer phase, and a Clearing phase. The role of the DCE and DTE in each phase is spelled out in the X.21 specifications.

During the Quiescent phase, either the DCE or DTE can initiate calls to each other. I both stations are in a ready state, communication can take place. The Call Control phase includes both the call request and the connection and ready-for-data state. Packets flow between DCE and the DTE during the Data Transfer phase in a full-duplex mode.

Finally, the Clearing phase describes the termination of the data transfer. It can be initiated by either the DCE or DTE by the issuing of a Clear signal. This signal is responded to with a Clear Confirmation and then a Ready signal.

While X.21 is the defined Physical level interface for X.25, it has not received much support in the United States. The CCITT does permit an alternative interface known as X.21 bis which is equivalent to the CCITT standard V.24; this, in turn, is compatible with RS-232C. This equivalence permits the numerous RS-232C devices in the field to connect to packet networks without modification of existing interfaces.

The X.25 standard also defines a Link or Frame level that corresponds to the OSI model's Data Link layer. Software programs are run on the DCE and DTE to maintain control of transmission, conduct error checking, and add and later strip off control information before a packet is delivered in layer 3. High-level Data Link Control (HDLC) protocol implements two procedures to accomplish these tasks: Link Access Procedure Balanced (LAPB) and Multiplink Procedure (MLP).

The LAPB procedure enables any network node to initiate or terminate transmission activity; these nodes share the management and error-recovery responsibilities associated with data transmission. The MLP procedure permits more than one concurrent data transmission.

The Packet Level is the third layer of the X.25 Recommendation. It defines procedures for packet handling between the DCE and the DTE. Packet-handling responsibilities include call initiation, data transfer, and packet-level error handling. The DTE begins the process by transmitting a Call Request packet, which asks that a logical channel be established.

This Call Request packet both identifies the logical channel to be used and lists the source and destination addresses for this packet. When the packet reaches its destination, the receiving DTE responds with a Call Accepted packet. The DCE associated with the calling DTE sends it a Call Connected packet. The channel is now in the Data Transfer state and ready for data to be transmitted over it.

Control packets also travel over a packet-switched network. When serious errors occur, a Clear packet is generated. This packet results in the clearing of the entire communications session and then its re-establishment.

The Packet level of the X.25 Recommendation is responsible for routing the packet. This layer corresponds to the Network layer of the OSI model.

The X.75 Recommendation

The X.75 Recommendation was adopted by the CCITT to establish standards for communications between packet-switched networks. It enables packet-switched networks in different countries to communicate with each other.

Criteria for Selecting an X.25 Packet Switch

Here is a list of questions to ask:

1. What kinds of protocols are supported? Does the switch support X.75 as well as X.25?

2. The hottest new development in packet switching is known as frame relay. Does the switch support this new technology? Is it upgradable to frame relay?

3. How many ports are available? What speeds do these ports support?

4. How many packets/second throughput does the switch support? Models can vary from 300 to 4,000, depending on the system and configuration.

5. What physical interfaces are supported? Most switches include an RS-232 interface, but what about V.35 or RS-449?

8

NETWORK
MANAGEMENT

One major concern of network managers is how to monitor and control their networks. While various network devices such as bridges, routers, and multiplexers might be capable of generating alarms and alerts, is there a central network manager program capable of understanding these signals that might be using proprietary protocols?

In this chapter, we'll examine some emerging network management protocols such as the Simple Network Management Protocol (SNMP) and the Common Management Information Protocol (CMIP). We'll also look at some major network management tools such as protocol analyzers and network monitoring programs. Finally, we'll examine some enterprise-wide network management programs that are still emerging, including IBM's NetView, AT&T's Unified Network Management Architecture (UNMA), DEC's Enterprise Management Architecture (EMA), and Hewlett-Packard's OpenView.

◄ WHAT IS A NETWORK MANAGEMENT SYSTEM?

A **network management system (NMS)** is a group of integrated programs that monitor and control a network's functions, including its performance, security, accounting, resource and configuration management, and the alarms and alerts from various network components. Let's examine some of the major functions performed by a NMS.

Performance Management

Network management systems monitor a network's overall performance, especially its response time, quality of service, and availability. How many packets are transmitted in a given time period? How many collisions are taking place? How many defective packets ("runts") are being transmitted? Where are the bottlenecks on the network? Performance management usually includes graphic presentations of network activity—for example, graphs revealing peak-activity periods. Some systems will use a color code to show levels of response time, with green for normal operation, yellow for degrading response time, and red for unacceptably high response time.

Fault Management

Fault management includes notification as to when an alarm occurs. Some sophisticated network management systems make an attempt to identify the type of error and, in some cases, take appropriate action. This action can take the form of deactivating node or other network device. The NMS might be able to test to see if a condition no longer exists and then reactivate the network device.

Accounting Management

Accounting management is concerned with allocating network expenses. The accounting features associated with Novell's NetWare illustrate this accounting function. NetWare's accounting enables the network manager to charge users for such network resources as disk space occupied, file server processing, and network printing. Furthermore, it permits differential pricing based on day and time of the week. Users who decide to print after 4 pm might be charged considerably less than users who insist or printing long reports at 10 am.

Configuration Management

Configuration management can mean many different things, depending upon the network management system. An NMS might be able to read user workstation information—such as DOS version, hardware configuration, and network login—and then place this information into a database. Such systems can then check on users during their subsequent logins and identify any hardware or software changes on the specific workstation. McGee's Network HQ is an example of a program that performs these tasks.

Configuration management can also include tracking network cabling in a database, initiating user moves and changes, and planning where bridges should be placed. It can also mean altering the port settings for a network's communications server. With wide area networks, configuration management can include automatically switching from one link to another because noise has compromised data reliability. Similarly, with dynamic routing, a network management system can reconfigure routing tables and reroute traffic when a link is down, or a key network router is removed.

Security Management

Network management systems must address security. An NMS might restrict users by day and hour, utilize a callback modem to frustrate hackers, or limit users' rights at the directory and even the file level. An NMS might maintain detailed audit trails so that a network manager can retrace every directory and file accessed by a particular user.

Resource Management

Some network management systems provide the ability to administer all network resources via a specific database. This means that the database keeps detailed records of such information as purchase dates, warranty information, and serial numbers for network components—for example, network interface cards, monitors, and printers. This database often generates "trouble tickets" for a trouble desk.

Staff at the trouble desk can record information on various user network problems and then allocate resources to solve these problems. Computer Associates' CA-NET-MAN/PC, for instance, is a product designed specifically for administering network resources. Among its many functions are the abilities to track inventory, track network equipment purchasing and receiving, provide an on-line training library for network users, and provide management analysis reports. These reports provide information on such topics as comparative expenditures based on department, product category, vendor, manufacturer, and cost center.

Network Management Protocols for an NMS

A network management system must receive alarms and alerts in a format it can understand. Similarly, it must be able to issue commands that can be understood by network devices, including bridges, routers, and multiplexers. Two of the major network management protocols we will examine are SNMP and CMIP.

Simple Network Management Protocol (SMNP)

Simple Network Management Protocol (SNMP) has become very popular, because it has been associated with the Transmission Control Protocol/Internet Protocol (TCP/IP) that is the basis of this nation's internet. SNMP was designed as a way to manage network devices designed by different vendors. Each device functions as an **agent** capable of reporting alarm information to and receiving orders from a manager known as the **Network Management Station (NMS)**. Devices that do not understand the SNMP protocol must be connected as proxy agents to devices that do understand SNMP and act as translators.

The SNMP NMS uses a trap-initiated polling system. It receives requests from various agents and then polls these agents about their current status. The NMS issues orders to agents using a connectionless User Datagram Protocol (UDP). This connectionless protocol requires very little overhead and no acknowledgment. The manager's orders and the agent's responses take the form of Protocol Data Units (PDUs) that have been defined as part of the SNMP standard.

Each SNMP agent is defined as an object in a network database known as the **Management Information Base (MIB)**. Each object's definition includes such information as its name, the syntax used to communicate with it, and various variables associated with it. Vendors can add their own devices as objects to the MIB by issuing Private Enterprise MIB extensions.

Novell's LANtern Services manager can be used to monitor SNMP alarms on a NetWare LAN. The alarms are displayed under Microsoft Windows. Both Hewlett-Packard's OpenView and Sun's SunNet Manager are examples of network management systems that utilize SNMP. Both systems can monitor and display the activities of all network devices functioning as SNMP agents. SNMP is built on several specifications

known as Requests for Comments (RFCs). RFC 1157 defines SNMP, while RFC 115(
(MIB-1) and 1158 (MIB-2) define the Management Information Base (MIB). RFC 115
defines the structure of management information (SMI) itself. The structure of manage
ment information includes rules for defining and accessing through NMS network vari
ables or objects. While SNMP is not an international standard, it has become a de fact
standard in the United States. It is governed by the Internet Activities Board.

Common Management Information Protocol (CMIP)

Network managers contemplating a network management system must consider the
long-term implications of the battle taking place today between advocates of SNMP
and the **Common Management Information Protocol (CMIP)**. CMIP has bee
developed by the International Standards Organization (ISO) as part of its OSI model
CMIP offers a far more sophisticated, comprehensive approach than SNMP, but so fa
its popularity has lagged far behind its competitor.

CMIP makes a clear distinction between objects in its MIB and the attributes of those
objects. New objects can be defined easily by incorporating attributes already defined.
CMIP's event-forwarding discriminators enable the protocol to filter alarms and
events and display only the more serious alarms; this prevents the clutter that can
occur when thousands of devices are reporting even the smallest deviations.

CMIP's greater functionality than SNMP comes at the price of a considerable amount
of additional overhead (more than 300 KB on a workstation). Its connection-oriented
nature means that it is more reliable than SNMP but also slower. Its ability to provide
all the information on a specific object is criticized by SNMP supporters, who point
out that sometimes only a specific piece of information is needed.

Virtually all industry experts predict that CMIP eventually will become the major network management protocol; after all, the Government OSI Profile (GOSIP) will
require it and the prospect of government contracts will spur vendors. Also, although
SNMP is very popular in the United States, Europe and the other countries of the
world have tended to gravitate toward international data communications standards
such as those incorporated in the OSI model.

CMIP Over the Transmission Control Protocol (CMOT)

One possible solution for the short-term for companies trying to decide between
SNMP and CMIP is **CMIP Over the Transmission Control Protocol (CMOT)**. This
compromise consists of running both protocols as a dual-protocol stack. While this
approach is inefficient, it provides companies with some flexibility as they look
toward their eventual migration to CMIP.

CMIP Over Logical Link Control (CMOL)

Another version of the CMIP network management protocol is **CMIP Over Logical
Link Control (CMOL)**. CMOL offers a smaller version of CMIP that requires less
overhead (only about 20 KB) and an agent about the same size as a SNMP agent.
Developed specfically for managing a local area network, CMOL lacks an Internet

Protocol header, so its messages cannot travel through routers. CMOL incorporates part of the Heterogeneous LAN Management (HLM) architecture developed by IBM and 3Com. CMOL incorporates the IEEE 802.2 Logical Link Control protocol, which corresponds to a portion of the Data Link layer of the OSI model. CMOL's implementation of HLM is compliant with the Microsoft and 3Com Network Driver Interface Specification (NDIS) standard for interfaces between network operating systems and network interface cards.

The Element Management System (EMS)

Many manufacturers of network devices or elements offer **element management systems (EMSs)**. The EMS is a proprietary software system designed to support multiple network devices from a single manufacturer. The EMS filters alarms and alerts coming from network components and then forwards this information to a network command center. At the network command center, a console operator can issue commands to the various network components.

The Racal-Milgo Communications Management System (CMS 8800) illustrates a typical EMS. It is designed to handle up to 255 multiplexers. The CMS color codes alarms and also indicates them audibly. It provides a network topology map illustrating all network nodes.

What characterizes an EMS is its proprietary limitations. It monitors and controls one small part of a network. A network manager with several EMSs would need several different consoles to monitor different aspects of a network. The solution to this problem is the enterprise-wide network management system.

Enterprise Network Management Systems and Their Links to LANs

Element management systems can provide only a portion of the network management function, because they usually only communicate with a portion of the network's devices, those using certain proprietary protocols. In this section we'll examine some enterprise-wide network management systems that are still developing. Someday these NMSs will be able to monitor and control networks composed of multivendor products located at several different sites.

NetView

IBM's network management is built around its NetView program running on a mainframe computer. The management protocol utilized by this network management system is known as the **Network Management Vector Transport (NMVT)**. IBM has also indicated that it will support CMIP. The host computer is known as a **focal point** and serves as a network manager. System Network Architecture (SNA) devices are linked to these focal points via entry points, which are agents embedded in a management resource. Non-SNA devices connect to focal points via service points, an example of which is a PC running the NetView/PC program.

Theoretically, non-IBM devices such as LANs could link directly to focal points without going through NetView/PC if they utilized the IBM SNA protocol known as

Logical Unit 6.2 (LU 6.2). This link would require extensive programming on the par
of the company wishing to use this approach. Figure 8-1 illustrates IBM's networl
management approach and how LANs would link to NetView.

IBM has announced that CMIP transported over the OSI transport protocols as well a:
CMOT. It will incorporate CMIP in its System Network Architecture (SNA). It wil
also support SNMP transmitted over TCP/IP.

IBM also offers LAN Network Manager programs that can manage Token Ring LAN:
independently or in conjunction with NetView. The IBM LAN Manager Program (no
to be confused with Microsoft's LAN Manager) can send LAN alarms and bridge

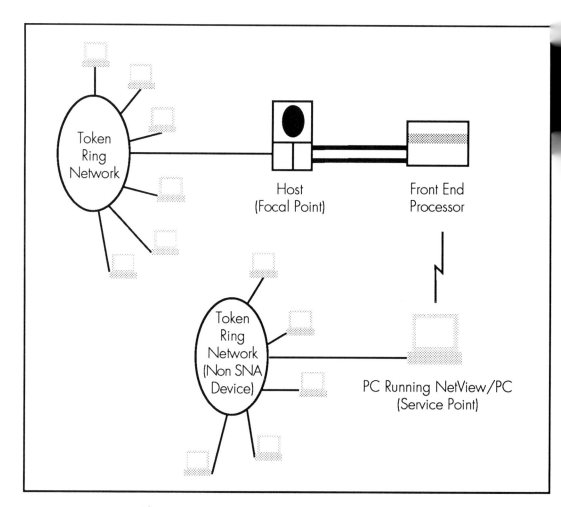

Figure 8-1. LANs and IBM's network management approach.

alarms to NetView and also receive commands from NetView. This program provides a graphic view of a LAN, uses CMIP, and uses IBM's own OS/2 EE Database Manager to store and retrieve network management information. Of great significance to LAN managers is IBM's working agreement with Novell. IBM has agreed to provide a set of NetView network management variables (NMVs) that can be used to manage alerts from a NetWare LAN. These NMVs are expected to be available in NetWare version 3.2.

The focus of LAN network management from IBM's perspective is mainframe-oriented, which should come as no surprise. IBM perceives network management as a centralized function performed by a manager who must control mainframes, minicomputers, and LANs as part of an enterprise-wide perspective.

Unified Network Management Architecture (UNMA)

AT&T's **Unified Network Management Architecture (UNMA)** has devices (or elements) reporting to Element Management Systems (EMSs). Each EMS manages day-to-day operations for its elements. When an EMS receives significant alerts or alarms, it forwards them to the network management system using AT&T's Network Manage-

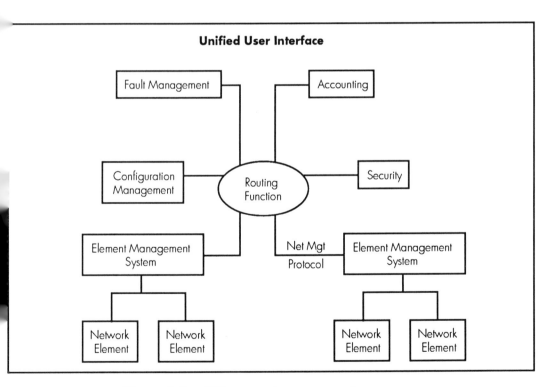

Figure 8-2. AT&T's concept of enterprise network management.

ment Protocol. As Figure 8-2 illustrates, the information is then routed to a softwa
module that handles that particular task. A network management station known as a
Accumaster Integrator views the entire network, including LANs, wide area ne
works, PBXs, and mainframe computers.

AT&T's network management system software runs on an AT&T minicomputer und
the UNIX operating system. The network management console is a Sun workstatio
which means that the software can take advantage of the Sun's ability to display info
mation graphically with windows and icons. AT&T intends to run CMIP as its netwo
management protocol, but it has "frozen" CMIP at one stage of its development so tha
software developers can begin writing applications for UNMA. While AT&T has put
lished its network management protocols, it must depend on third-party vendors to wri
links so their devices will communicate as UNMA elements.

AT&T's Accumaster Integrator already has the links to its StarGroup Network Mana
ger and StarGroup Computer Manager. This means that Accumaster Integrator ca
already manage StarLAN LANs. AT&T has worked with Network Computing Inc. t
utilize that company's LANAlert management system for NetWare LANs as a collec
tion point for SNMP alerts.

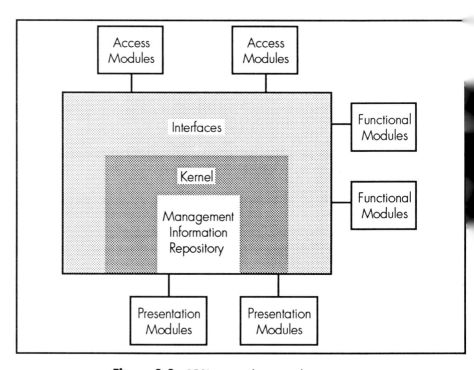

Figure 8-3. DEC's approach to network management.

DEC's Enterprise Management Architecture (EMA)

DEC's **Enterprise Management Architecture (EMA)** is designed specifically for a distributed, multivendor Enterprise network. Running on DEC's own VMS operating system, the EMA product known as **DECmcc** is built on a network manager known as the Director kernel. Functional modules provide such services as control, performance analsysis, and configuration management, while Access modules are designed to provide interfaces to DECnet, bridges, and third-party devices. A Management Information Repository serves as a database to hold all network management information. Figure 8-3 illustrates DEC's approach to network management.

In addition to support for CMIP and DEC's own proprietary protocols, the company has announced that it will develop access modules for TCP/IP, Ethernet, bridges, terminal servers, and FDDI products. Managers with token ring networks might just have to wait a while for DEC support.

OpenView

Hewlett-Packard's **OpenView** is a network management system designed to manage LANs and WANs. Running on an HP 3000 minicomputer, the software can monitor local and remote HP minicomputers as well as LAN MAC-level bridges. Under OpenView, network elements are known as objects. Object managers serve as translators that send OpenView messages to elements in a format they can understand and forward element alarm information to OpenView in a form it can understand. Hewlett-Packard offers OpenView DOS-based and Unix-based managers supporting both CMIP and SNMP.

OpenView is designed to focus on seven functional areas: fault management, accounting management, security management, configuration management, performance management, inventory management, and system management. The last item refers to the ability to manage a large network from a single point.

OpenView's Network Node Manager is used for network monitoring, data collecting, and applications building. A Single View Management component enables network managers to manage a network from a single screen. Third-party applications can be integrated into OpenView's graphical interface using this component. The Dynamic Data Collection and User-Defined Threshold component monitors alerts and permits managers to set parameters for variables. Finally, the Application Builder component enables developers to write their own SNMP applications for OpenView.

OpenView still lacks an integrated database management system for integrating information on all network elements. While it is able to handle TCP/IP networks as well as HP proprietary networks, it is not yet able to handle alarms and alerts from LANs.

LAN Network Management

While enterprise networks will require enterprise network management systems such as those offered by IBM, AT&T, DEC, and Hewlett-Packard, the network manager responsible for a local area network needs tools today to help monitor and control the

LAN. Network management tools for LANs include a number of software and hardware products that are examined below.

LAN Management Hardware Tools

LAN Management hardware tools include devices to check cabling as well as very sophisticated protocol analyzers for diagnosing network problems.

Breakout Boxes (BOB)

The network manager utilizes a breakout box to determine if two devices are connected correctly. This device is particularly handy when a cable is being built to connect a printer via an asynchronous (RS-232C) connection. Printer manufacturers often use the same pin for different functions, so the breakout box becomes a handy tool for ensuring that both ends of a cable have been configured correctly.

Most BOBs are handheld devices that display interface signals via LEDs. They also provide switches so that leads can be reconfigured and a new configuration tested.

Bit Error Rate Testers (BERTs)

A bit error rate tester is used to measure bit-error rates. It compares the received test pattern with the pattern transmitted to detect bit errors.

Cable Testers

One of the most common network problems is a defective cable. Comline's Wireman is an example of a group of cable testers that can solve most cabling problems. This unit can test token ring cabling by plugging the remote Wireman unit directly into a wiring block while the main Wireman unit is attached to the token ring. The Wireman indicates which cables are defective.

For twisted-pair cabling, the Wireman uses its Toner and Tracker features. The remote unit generates an audible tone to indicate a good connection.

Time-Domain Reflectometers (TDRs)

The Time-Domain Reflectometer is used to check cables. It can identify breaks, shorts, and opens. TDRs are particularly valuable on coaxial cable topologies such Ethernet and Arcnet, where specific impedances are needed and cable ends must be terminated. A TDR can detect an open cable end and determine the distance to its location. In fact, TDRs can also determine the lengths of entire Ethernet segments.

A network manager will make sure that the network is entirely quiet and then inject signals onto the network. The reflections of these signals comes back to the TDR, and the amount of time they take to return reveals how far down the cable the problem lies. A look at the signal's waveform reveals whether the problem is an open, a short, a bad connector, or an improper termination.

LAN Probes

LAN probes are diagnostic devices that are commonly used with Ethernet networks. They enable network managers to continuously monitor traffic, track errors, set alert thresholds, and log critical network events. Hewlett-Packard's LANProbe is an example of how this type of device works.

ProbeView software runs on a PC or compatible and serves as a network monitoring station. LANProbe devices attached to Ethernet segments are linked to the monitoring station via an Ethernet connection or an RS-232 link. They also can be linked via modem for remote network management.

The LANProbe provides maps of the entire network as well as segment maps identifying Ethernet addresses and NIC vendor names. It also identifies cable breaks, shorts, and faulty termination. It can monitor LAN packets and then provide reports on trends as well as packet-size distribution. A log keeps track of all critical events on each segment. The network manager can set threshold values so that alerts are sent only when activity exceeds these thresholds.

Protocol Analyzers

Protocol analyzers are the network manager's most powerful tool for diagnosing network problems. They can be programmed to look for specific conditions, which could take the form of errors or packets from specific workstations. They can also be programmed to look for packets with certain designations such as "secret." On a network in which several different protocols are transmitted, the protocol analyzer can be programmed to look for packets with a specific protocol and ignore packets with other protocols.

While protocol analyzers can perform real-time filtering for managers who need to know just how many packets are being transmitted at that very moment, it is not very practical given the limited amount of buffer space on most of these units. A more practical approach is to direct the filtered packets to a disk file and then examine the results. Many protocol analyzers have export functions that enable the files to be exported into spreadsheet or database files.

Protocol analyzers perform the following major functions:

- network monitoring;
- specific condition testing;
- filtering based on specific criteria;
- data collection and analysis.

Let's examine each of these functions.

Network Monitoring

The protocol analyzer is often used to monitor network performance by providing a graphic display of the network's current state of health. Color-coded graphs can display the network's traffic, the number of collisions, the number of bad frames, and so on.

Some protocol analyzers, such as Novell's LANanalyzer, have a station monit screen that enables a network manager to check network activity at the workstatic level. Using this screen, it is easy to see if a particular station is generating unusu amounts of traffic, particularly during peak traffic hours. A user might be trying print large graphic files at 10:00 am and causing a traffic jam. The protocol analyz will reveal the culprit.

Monitoring a token ring network enables a network manager to pinpoint defective st tions quickly. By running an error monitor program on a protocol analyzer, it is possib to identify which stations are sending BurstErr messages, indicating that a proble exists between the station sending the message and a station upstream from it.

The protocol analyzer can then run a map application to generate a list of users on th token ring in sequential order. This list reveals which stations are upstream from th station sending the error message and can quickly narrow down the "suspects" to few stations. Sometimes all that is needed at this point to restore network health is th tightening of a loose connection.

Network managers can customize a protocol analyzer's monitoring function so that i displays alarms for a number of conditions—for example, a user-defined load leve has been exceeded, a user-defined error level has been exceeded, a station doesn' transmit any traffic during certain times, and a new station has started transmitting o receiving on the network.

Specific Condition Testing

Some protocol analyzers can transmit frames on a network to simulate certain condi tions. This feature is useful for benchmarking the network as well as capacity plan ning. Using this technique, a network manager can send certain types of frames and check the operation of specific bridges and routers.

Filtering Based on Specific Conditions

If a network manager suspects that a defective NIC is transmitting broadcast messages that are causing congestion on the network, the protocol analyzer can be programmed to filter frames and look at their source and destination addresses.

Another example of the protocol analyzer's usefulness is using it to check for frames that have timed out, or taken too long to reach their destination. By examining these frames, it is possible to discover whether the time-out has been set too low or whether the traffic congestion on the network simply makes it impossible for frames to reach their destination in the maximum time alloted. The network manager might use the results of this analysis to justify segmenting the network by adding bridges to reduce traffic congestion.

A protocol analyzer is an ideal tool for detecting broadcast storms. A network manager can filter based on broadcast packets. A quick look will reveal that a specific station is initiating these broadcast packets. After turning off this station, the manager can have the protocol analyzer display the percent of network utilization to determine whether the traffic congestion problem has been solved.

Data Collection and Analysis

Protocol analyzers most often are used for data collection and analysis. The data is usually time stamped as it is collected. The "burst rate," or maximum rate at which the device can collect data without losing any information, is an important feature of protocol analyzers. Network General's The Sniffer has a traffic generator feature that permits traffic to be collected to a file and then replayed using a playback feature. The data is replayed as if it were occurring in real time.

LAN Management Software Tools

A number of programs are available for monitoring and controlling LANs. These programs vary in complexity and cost and can prove invaluable for enhancing printing functions as well as providing audit trails and monitoring network traffic.

Network Monitoring

A number of programs perform some of the same network monitoring functions handled by a protocol analyzer. Invisible Software's Netdiag illustrates some typical network monitoring functions. It provides a real-time display of network activity, including displays of all stations on the network and traffic and error statistics for each station. It also has a stress-test function that tests the network and provides a real-time display of each station's response to heavy traffic.

A network manager can run Netdiag at the end of a day and see cumulative figures on traffic and error conditions for each station. This information is valuable for determining which stations need hardware upgrades.

Frye Computer Systems' NetWare Early Warning System (NEWS) goes even further than Netdiag when it comes to monitoring a network. NEWS can be instructed to notify the network manager by written message, voice, fax, MHS, or paging once it observes that network thresholds have been exceeded. NEWS can also be instructed to run another program, should a threshold be exceeded.

One network manager might instruct NEWS to run a program that tells users not to print graphic files when it observes that a traffic congestion level has been exceeded. Similarly, when NEWS notes that free disk space has fallen below a threshold, it could run a backup program that archives files and then deletes them from the file server.

Menu Management

Many network operating systems provide rudimentary menuing tools such as NetWare's MENU utility. But third-party vendors offer menuing programs that often include versions for Windows workstations. The Saber Menu System illustrates just how sophisticated these programs have become and just how useful they can be for a network manager.

The Saber Menu System enables a network manager to create customized menus for all network groups; individual users have the option of customizing and controlling the physical appearance of their own menus. Programs can be metered through Saber so that single-user programs can be placed on the network without violating single-user licensing agreements.

The network manager can program function keys so users can access particular programs, exit to DOS temporarily, or log off the network. By requiring users to log on through a menuing system such as Saber, the network manager can automatically map network drives and prevent the user from learning the precise location of files that have to be protected.

One company has used the Saber menuing system to create several different menu picks based on different groups' access rights to a database. Some users see only the option to "read-only" from the database, while others see a menu option to "enter information in limited fields." Only a select few users see the menu option to "add or delete database information." Each of these menu options results in a different command to the Advanced Revelation database, and each user enters the database with the appropriate set of rights.

Printing Management

Printing management has not been the strong point with most network operating systems. A number of print management utilities can make the network manager's job easier. A program such as LANSYSTEMS' LANSpool, for example, converts any MS-DOS workstation into a print server supporting multiple network printers. Printer utility programs enhance such weak NetWare features as form printing and print-queue management. Brighwork Development's QueueIT provides a pop-up printer-selection menu, the ability to resequence print jobs, sophisticated form-handling ability, and user notification of required form changes.

Security Management

One common concern of network managers is whether or not users are violating software licensing agreements. A program such as Sitelock can control users' access to programs that have specific license limitations. It also can provide full reports of software usage. These reports are particularly useful for justifying additional copies of a program or for "bumping" disks to bring up the number of legally authorized users.

Audit Trails

Audit trails are particularly valuable on large networks with a wide range of users who have different rights and access privileges. The LT Auditor program, for example, shows log-in and log-out times for each audited user. It also shows which users have accessed which files as well as when and where they have done so.

Performance Analysis

Dozens of available programs analyze network performance. Cheyenne Software's Monitrix, for example, examines NetWare servers, bridges, and workstations and provides alarms that can be set for certain conditions. Assuming a network manager has used the program to establish benchmarks when the network was running smoothly, these results can be compared to current Monitrix values.

Resource Management

It is useful for LAN managers to keep track of network users' hardware and software. A program such as Magee's Network H.Q. can silently interrogate workstations, retrieve information on their hardware configurations and the version of DOS they are using, and place this information in a database. Such information can benefit a network trouble desk, purchasing, and warranty and service work.

Generally such programs load Terminate and Stay Resident (TSR) agents into network workstations and then gather information from these sources. Network H.Q., for example, uses its TSR agents to gather information on the workstation's microprocessor, its coprocessor, its network interface card, its network address, disk drives, RAM still available on the workstation, and the network user's login.

9

NETWORK SECURITY AND RELIABILITY

A network's security and reliability are critical. Network managers must take measures to prevent unauthorized users from accessing the network. They must also protect the network from such unwelcome intruders as Trojan horses, viruses, and worms. Even if the network is relatively secure from intruders, network managers must also concern themselves with increasing the network's reliability by building in levels of system fault tolerance.

Will the network fail if there is power blackout? What happens if the file server's hard disk drive fails? These are some of the issues that network managers must consider when designing their network's level of system fault tolerance. In this chapter, we will examine a number of steps a manager can take to keep a network secure and reliable.

■ PREVENTING UNAUTHORIZED NETWORK ACCESS

Historically, mainframe environments have been protected from intruders by badges, magnetic cards, and so on, but the LAN environment is more difficult to protect because its resources are distributed over a large area. Some resources such as file servers and communications servers can be isolated and secured behind closed doors. Often, network managers will physically remove the keyboards from file servers to prevent direct access. However, there are more sophisicated ways to keep unauthorized users from accessing network resources. One option is a retina-scanning device that matches a person's retina pattern with patterns in its memory. A second option is a palm-recognition system. People attempting to gain admittance must type a private seven-digit number into the machine and then place a hand on an illuminated screen. A machine such as Mitsubishi's Palm Recognition System can store up to 200 different palm prints for matching with users.

Password Protection

While most networks require passwords, network operating systems such as NetWare can enhance password protection. Users can be required to use passwords of a certain minimal length or change their passwords at designated intervals. One division of Litton Industries, for example, requires passwords to be changed every six weeks.

NetWare can prevent users from ever using the same password again. This feature prevents users from continuing to use the names of spouses, pets, and children. NetWare also enables network managers to restrict the times during which users can log onto the network. A network manager might routinely limit most users to 8 am to 5 pm Mondays through Fridays and then accept requests from users who require weekend or evening access.

One of the limitations of password protection is that users often write out their passwords and then tape them near their computers in case they forget them. One network manager makes it a point to walk through the plant and physically remove all such password references. She then changes the offending people's passwords and requires them to come to her to get a new password (along with a lecture on the need for security).

Another related security issue is the tendency of many network users to log onto the network and then leave their computers for extended periods of time. Anyone can walk up to these computers and instantly be on the network with all rights of the person who logged in. One solution is to use a network utility program that will automatically log off any network workstation that has not had any keyboard activity for at least one hour.

Call-Back Modems

Call-back modems can ensure that only users calling from authorized sites can log onto the network. Users log in from a remote site and type in a password and then hang up. The modem dials back the user at a number it has listed in a table. The user might be required to enter a second password at this point to verify identity.

Many call-back modems offer additional features, including the ability to enter a temporary phone number if the user is at a different site. These modems often provide detailed audit trails of caller attempts and even bill cost centers for remote user logins.

Individual network workstations also need protection from unauthorized access. Vacant workstations are inviting targets for people wandering around unsecured areas. Authentication systems can provide security far beyond that offered by passwords alone. Users attempting to log onto a network can be required to enter a personal identification number as well as a random code number from a hand-held authentication device. Since this number changes each time, it does an intruder absolutely no good to memorize the number used previously. Each device can be coded for a particular user and workstation so that users cannot "borrow" each other's authentication devices.

oftware Threats to a Network

A network is a ripe target for today's hacker. The movie *War Games* alerted the public about the threat to computer systems from hackers. More recently the book *The Cuckoo's Egg* revealed how even very knowledgeable network managers at major defense installations overlook "back doors" and other ways of breaking into computers. Often, hackers will make themselves "superusers" with all network rights, browse through computer files, and then remove any evidence that they had broken the computer's security. While some hackers argue that they never do any real damage, others break into computers and then leave destructive programs—Trojan horses, viruses, or worms—that can cripple all operations.

Trojan Horses

Trojan horses are programs that appear to be harmless applications or files until they are loaded. Once inside an operating system, they can do enormous damage. On many occasions, the Trojan horse has taken the form of a time bomb, a program "set" to begin on a certain date. April 1 and Halloween are commonly used dates, but sometimes, as in the case of the famous Jonas virus, the date is the program creator's birthday. These programs can also be triggered by a hard disk reaching a certain percentage of capacity.

Viruses

The term **virus** refers to any program that is capable of attaching itself to other programs and infecting them. These programs are designed to be self-replicating, so they spread throughout an entire hard disk or even an entire network.

Worms

Worms are programs that are designed to enter a system, burrow into a secluded area, and then perform a task. This task could be as benign as issuing a message or as sinister as slowing down or even crashing the file server.

Antiviral Utilities

Network managers have fought viruses by purchasing and installing antiviral utility programs that can search, find, and then destroy most of the more common viruses. Among the more popular programs in this field are the McAfee Associates Viruscan series of shareware programs. The number of additional features these programs offer grows with each new release.

Virus Scanning and Removal

Some programs will scan network software for viruses and then identify them (usually by matching common hexadecimal code sequences) by name whenever possible. They will also destroy the viruses they identify. Sometimes virus destruction is accomplished by overwriting the infected file several times and then erasing it. If the boot sector of a hard disk is infected, the program might perform a low-level format.

Some programs create signatures of files and boot sectors and then use these signa
tures to identify any significant changes or discrepencies. These change could indicat
a virus infection.

Controlling Floppies

Some programs lock out floppy drives when a workstation boots up. This feature ca
eliminate one of the most common ways of spreading a virus across a network.

Virus Protection

Protecting files from becoming infected is an important function of many programs
These programs check each executable file before permitting the program to execut
its instructions.

Virus Protection Updates

New viruses are constantly being created. Some programs offer regular updates and
even BBS services for downloading new antivirus remedies.

Terminate and Stay Resident Versions

Rather than increasing network traffic, some programs load a Terminate and Stay
Resident (TSR) portion that resides on the network workstation and checks executable
code before running it.

On-Line Sources of Virus Information

The Computer Virus Industry Association maintains a Virus Information Bulletin
Board (408/988-4004) that provides downloadable shareware and public domain
virus-scanning software as well as virus-fighting software. This bulletin board also
provides the latest upgrades to a number of antivirus software programs.

The National Institute of Standards and Technology Computer Security Bulletin Board
(301/948-5717) provides lists of government-sponsored security conferences as well
as downloadable files containing information on risk assessment and encryption.

The National Computer Security Association Bulletin Board (202/364-1305) focuses
on LAN security. It contains a number of downloadable shareware and public domain
virus-scanning software and virus-fighting software. Particularly valuable for network
managers new to the field of network security, the bulletin board contains a number of
tutorials on this subject.

Additional Security Measures for PC LANs

Even if the network is protected from hackers and viruses, there is always the danger
that someone will tap into the network and read sensitive files. In this section, we'll
look at some ways to encrypt data so it will be meaningless even if stolen.

Encryption

One of the major network security dangers on a network is that packets travelling
around a network will be easy prey to anyone who can tap into the network. On

Ethernet networks, for example, knowledgeable computer users have been known to alter their network interface cards so that they copy packets with other stations' destination addresses. One solution to this particular problem is encryption. When data is encrypted, it is meaningless to anyone capturing it unless they possess the key to deciphering it.

One encryption method utilizes a public key. This means that both the sender and the recipient must have the same key to decrypt a file. One part of this key is made public and published in a directory. The other part is private. No one who does not have the private portion of the key can decrypt the message.

A second encryption method utilizing a private key. Both sender and recipient use this private key to encrypt and then to decrypt the same message. Private keys are faster than public keys, but require a more sophisticated distribution system. This includes a distribution center for distributing private keys to individuals and companies needing to exchange encrypted information.

The DES Standard

The Defense Department Encryption Standard (DES) was developed by IBM in conjunction with the National Bureau of Standards (now known as NIST). While it has been available since 1977, more sophisticated encryption methods have only recently become popular.

The RSA Encryption System

The Rivest-Shamir-Adelman (RSA) encryption system is a very popular encryption alternative to the DES standard. It uses two separate keys to encrypt messages, and is thus considered by many industry experts more secure than DES.

The ANSI X9.17 Encryption Standard

The ANSI X9.17 has a larger key size (112 bits versus 56 bits) than the DES. It also offers some additional safeguards against the reusing or compromising of keys. Unencrypted key variables are stored within the encryption chip itself.

Message Authentication Code (MAC) Protection

Some companies use the message authentication code (MAC) for protecting information. Data is transmitted as clear text, but a MAC field is added to the message. The MAC is used for a cyclical redundancy check (error check) and is composed of the message itself as well as a private key. It is possible to make a message even more secure by combining encryption with message authentication code.

LAN Security Programs

Network managers can turn to a number of network security programs that augment the security offered by network operating systems such as NetWare. Programs such as Watchdog, Security Guardian, OnGuard, and Access II can restrict access to files, directories, floppy disk drives, and external ports and can provide extensive audit trails.

Many security programs offer both DES encryption and their own proprietary encryption schemes. Some of these programs offer audit trails that both track users' particular program usage and keep track of the time these users are on the network. Among the key questions network managers should ask when considering these programs are the following:

1. Does the program offer compatibility with the latest version of Windows?

2. How many users will the program support? Is there a site license available? PC Watchman, for example, offers a site license for approximately $195.

3. How much RAM does the program require if it includes a Terminate and Stay Resident portion?

Protecting the Network From Physical Danger

Assuming that a network is protected from unauthorized access, there is still the danger that the data itself might be damaged by a physical network failure, such as a defective file server, a break in cabling, or a fire. How rapidly a company recovers from such a disaster depends upon how carefully it has planned for such emergencies and how much attention it has paid to the subject of system fault tolerance. This section will examine these critical topics.

Uninterruptible Power Supplies (UPSs)

While most large networks have uniterruptible power supplies (UPSs), there is some debate about what type of UPS is really needed. Does the network require an on-line model, or can it get by with a standby unit?

The Standby UPS

The **standby** UPS is like the understudy in a play. It stands ready to take over should an emergency occur, but it takes no active part in the drama taking place on stage. A Standby UPS contains a battery pack and an electronic inverter to convert its batteries' DC output to the AC power required by computer equipment.

The standby UPS is inexpensive insurance. There is a brief time while it takes over as a power source. Standby UPSs do not usually provide line conditioning while they are waiting "in the wings".

The On-line UPS

An **on-line** UPS is connected directly to the computer. It serves as a line conditioner and filters AC electricity through a rectifier circuit where it is converted to DC power. This DC power charges its batteries and then passes through an inverter and on to the computer system.

A UPS can generally supply up to ten minutes of emergency power, enough for the file server to close files and shut down properly. Many of the major network operating systems such as NetWare and LAN Manager provide interfaces to UPS units so that network managers can control this shutdown procedure more efficiently.

On-line units are far more expensive than standby units, but they might be needed in areas where power is particularly "dirty." The on-line units will both provide line conditioning and stand ready to take over should an emergency occur.

A UPS for Workstations

Some companies have opted to install lower cost UPS models for each network workstation. Voltage fluctuations can cause a workstation's hard disk to write data incorrectly. If this data is then uploaded to the file server, the data remains corrupted and unreadable. These UPS models for workstations can be purchased as plug-in half-cards that provide approximately four minutes of backup power plus the ability to restore the workstation to its exact state just prior to the power interruption.

A UPS for Bridges, Hubs, and Routers

While the file server is an obvious target for a UPS and workstations are increasingly being protected this way, bridges, hubs, and routers also require protection. Power failure to these vital network links can result in destruction of routing tables and significant delays while the devices reconfigure themselves.

Backup Technology

All networks should be backed up so that files can be retrieved and restored should a disaster occur. The range of media options for backup continues to expand. Should the network manager use tape cartridges, the newer digital audio tape approach, or optical disks?

Cartridge Tape Backups

Quarter-inch tape cartridges remain the most common LAN backup medium today. They are inexpensive and reliable, but many brands are limited to a 150-Mb capacity. Colorado Memory Systems has a quarter-inch tape product that achieves a 500-Mb capacity by use of data compression and longer tape. Other manufacturers, such as Mountain Computer, achieve a 600-Mb capacity by combining four 150-Mb tape drives with one controller.

4mm and 8mm Cartridge Drives and Tape

Both 4mm and 8mm cartridge drives use helical scan recording technology. Rather than using a stationary head to write data linearly across a rapidly moving quarter-inch tape, these newer drives use a rotating head to write data diagonally across slowly moving tapes.

The 8mm drives support up to 2.2 Gb of storage, far more than the 4mm models can support, although both use the helical scan recording technology. The new digital audio tape drives that are growing in popularity support 4mm tape.

Optical Disks

While still very expensive, optical disks are growing in popularity as a backup medium. Write-Once Read-Many (WORM) drives use lasers to record data permanently. Double-sided disks can hold up to 1 Gb of backup information. Newer magneto-optical

optical drives have the ability to write over data. A base unit can cost several thousand dollars, so this option might be a future consideration for most networks.

Regardless of the type of optical drive selected, the technology ensures that an optical disk has a shelf-life of up to 50 years, which makes it an ideal medium for archival purposes. Unlike tape, optical disks do not deteriorate over time, nor do they stretch. Optical drives provide much quicker transfer of information from optical disk to file server than is possible from a tape drive to the file server. Erasable optical drives cost between $4,000 and $6,000 and have access times ranging from 30 to 80 milliseconds.

Backups Systems

A number of backup systems are available for LANs, but their features vary considerably. Among the features network managers often request are file encryption, attended and continuous backups, and archive tape/library management functions. While most large networks use data encryption for transmission, some network managers back up files to tape without recognizing the potential security danger.

Attended backups are sometimes necessary, but often not desirable because they require the network manager to be present during the entire backup process; on a large network with several file servers this process could take all night. A continuous backup feature backs up each transaction so the network can be restored to a previous condition quickly and accurately.

Archive tape library management features enable managers to archive and retrieve specified files, keep track of numerous checkpoints for files, and maintain detailed histories. On Palindrome's Network Archivist, for example, the software keeps track of when files have changed and thus when they need to be backed up. The program enables network managers to select the specific checkpoint (date) they want retrieved when a user needs to replace a garbled file. The Network Archivist even tells network managers which tapes need to loaded for the current backup and which tapes will be needed for the next backup. Network managers can schedule when they want the backup process to begin unattended.

System Fault Tolerance

System fault tolerance refers to the measures that can be taken to keep a system from failing even if one or more of its key components fail. While local area networks have not achieved the degree of system fault tolerance found in mainframe systems, the level of sophistication is growing. We'll use NetWare as an example of the type of system fault tolerance possible on a LAN.

Multiple File Allocation Tables (FATs)

One Achilles Heel for most file servers is the file allocation table (FAT). This key table maintains the addresses on the hard disk where files are located. Should the section of the hard disk containing the FAT become damaged, this information would be unavailable to the file server; consequently, the file server would not know where to look to retrieve files and all file server functions would fail.

NetWare's system fault tolerant solution to this problem is to write multiple file allocation tables to different parts of the hard disk. If one FAT becomes unavailable, the file server's hard disk drive controller would automatically look to the other FATs for the key information it needs to access files.

The Hot Fix

One way data can become unusable on a file server is if the disk drive controller writes a block to a sector that has become bad. A hard disk sector that has gone bad after the disk drive has been formatted will not have its address in the bad block table.

NetWare's system fault tolerant solution to this problem is the **hot fix**. A NetWare hard disk controller will check a sector before attempting to write data to it. If the sector is bad, the controller will add the sector's address to the bad block table. It will then write the data to a good section of the hard disk known as the hot fix area. This area is reserved for just such situations. Figure 9-1 illustrates this process.

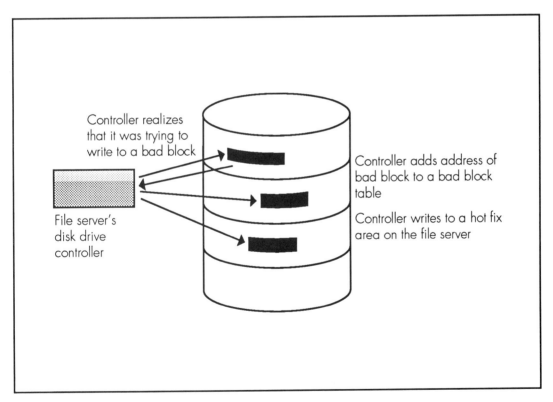

Figure 9-1. The hot fix.

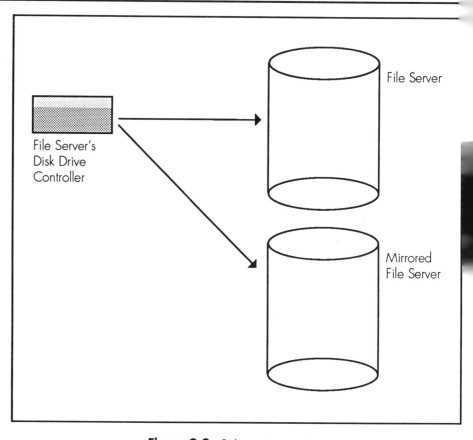

Figure 9-2. Disk mirroring in action.

Disk Mirroring

Another potentially fatal file server failure is the failure of the file server's hard disk drive. NetWare's system fault tolerant solution is to have two disk drives mirrored and connected to the same hard disk drive controller card inside the file server. The file server writes identical information to both hard disk drives. If one drive fails, the file server switches automatically to the second drive without any disruption in service. Figure 9-2 illustrates how **disk mirroring** works.

Disk Duplexing

One danger to disk mirroring is that the hard disk drive controller linked to both drives could fail and bring down the entire network. NetWare's system fault tolerant solution is **disk duplexing**. The file server is equipped with two identical hard disk drive controllers, each of which is connected via a separate cable to its own hard disk drive. Should one disk drive controller card fail, the file server automatically switches to the second circuit card and continues its operations.

A second benefit of disk duplexing is that both controller cards can be used to access file requests. The result is that file server performance is improved by 50 percent. Figure 9-3 illustrates disk duplexing in action.

Transaction Tracking

Another key NetWare system fault tolerant feature is **transaction tracking**. All file operations identified with a "transaction" are performed without any partial "writes" to the file server's hard disk. Only when the transaction has been completed are the files associated with it updated.

The advantage of transaction tracking is that should a transaction such as an accounting entry be interrupted before it is completed, the integrity of the files associated with this transaction will not be breeched.

When the physical network problem such as a power failure is corrected, the file server can "roll back" to the point just before the transaction and the transaction can be re-entered without the network manager worrying about incomplete or inaccurate data files.

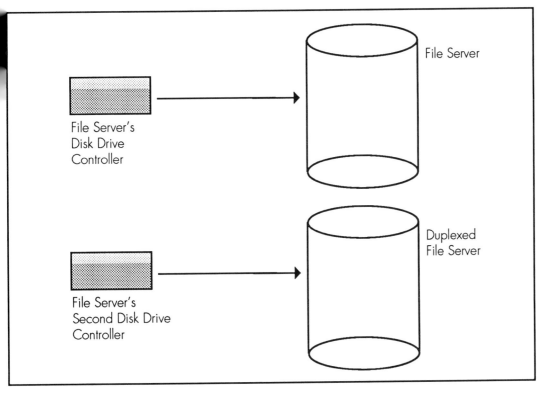

Figure 9-3. Disk duplexing in action.

Additional Network System Fault Tolerance

Some networks—such as those associated with hospitals, police departments, or fir departments—cannot afford to be down even for short periods of time. One solutio adopted by many such organizations is to increase system fault tolerance by addin redundant cabling and even an additional file server. Should one file server fail, th network can switch automatically to the second. Should a cable break, the second s can be used to continue network operations.

Finally, network managers increase the system fault tolerance of their networks b maintaining inventories of key network components such as network interface card: If workstations have the same network configurations, it is relatively easy to replac defective cards quickly.

Criteria for Security and Reliability

Here's a checklist for ensuring network security and reliability:

1. Have a regular backup schedule and store copies of these backups off-site.

2. Require users to change passwords at regular intervals. If users have to change passwords every 60 days, they soon will exhaust the names of their spouses, children, and pets.

3. Make sure there is a procedure for ensuring that logins for guests and former employees are eliminated immediately after these people leave.

4. Keep all system files off-limits except for the network manager. As a rule, restrict users to Read, Open, and Search rights in all but their own user directories.

5. Do not permit users to upload executable files to the network; this is a job for the network manager. All new programs should be loaded and tested first on a stand-alone PC to ensure that they do not have a virus.

6. Restrict users by day and time and keep a detailed audit trail of when people log in and what files they attempt to access.

7. Control remote login carefully. Consider call-back modems as a way of ensuring that hackers do not break into the network.

8. Use a network menuing system so users never know precisely where directories and files are located.

9. Delete all extra COMMAND.COM files from network file servers. Make all executable program files write-protect status.

10. Place write-protect tabs on all program disks and do not use them to store data files.

11. Physically protect a network by using a UPS.

12. Use a file server backup system that is powerful enough to maintain archiving information and permit easy retrieval and restoration of files.

13. Make sure this backup system encrypts files.

14. Provide as much system fault tolerance as is necessary for the network.

10

E-MAIL AND FAX SERVERS ON THE NETWORK

E-Mail is one of the most popular applications on local area networks. Unfortunately, companies with several different networks often have a number of incompatible E-Mail programs running that make it difficult for intracompany communications to take place. In this chapter we will examine some of the major issues associated with E-Mail on LANs, including the CCITT's X.400 Recommendations, which establish an international standard. We will also examine the CCITT X.500 standard for a global directory, which will make it possible to address and send E-Mail across the country or around the world.

Before looking at E-Mail on LANs, however, we will examine a new type of product that could become as popular as E-Mail: fax servers. The abilities to monitor and control fax transmissions and use powerful E-Mail functions in conjunction with them have made this new type of product very appealing to network managers.

Group	Signal	Speed	Communications Network
1	Analog	6 minutes	Public telephone network
2	Analog	3 minutes	Public telephone network
3	Analog	<1 minute	Public telephone network
4	Digital	< 10 seconds	Dataphone or ISDN

Figure 10-1. The CCITT facsimile machine groups.

■ CCITT FAX STANDARDS

The International Consultative Committee on Telephony and Telegraphy (CCITT) ha established several standards for fax machines. Figure 10-1 describes the four majo fax groups defined by the CCITT and defines them by their type of signal, their spee (per page), and what type of communications lines are required.

Groups 1 and 2 consist of machines that are obsolete, although large companies migh still have models operating at remote sites. The vast majority of fax machines operat ing in the United States fall into Group 3 and utilize the CCITT V.29 half-duplex 9,600 bps transmission speed. Group 3 machines compress the white space on a page by using the Modified Huffman compression scheme. Modified Huffman will com press the approximately 2 million bits onto a single page to about 200,000 bits, a 10:1 ratio. That is still a lot of transmitted data that could be garbled by a poor telephone connection. The CCITT also defined an error correction mode that breaks data into frames, which are transmitted to a fax machine that then analyzes them for errors by calculating a cyclic redundancy check (CRC). Frames with errors are then retransmit ted. Some vendors also offer their own proprietary methods for error checking.

By definition, Group 3 machines are capable of 200 dpi resolution in normal resolu tion (98 lines per inch). Graphics can be transmitted using a fine mode, which pro duces 196 lines per inch and doubles the transmission time. Group 3 machines can "fall back" to a speed slower than 9,600 bps if they need to transmit to older Group 2 machines or to Group 3 machines when line conditions are poor.

The CCITT has also modified its existing V.33 communications standard, designed for leased lines, and created a V.17 standard for public telephone lines. This standard enables Group 3 machines to increase their transmission speed from 9,600 bps to 14,400 bps while retaining compatiblity with current fax equipment. V.17 uses an error correction technique known as trellis encoding to eliminate the poor quality and data errors associated with high transmission speeds.

Group 4 machines transmit a page in approximately 10 seconds by doing so digitally. These machines transmit at 56 Kbs or 64 Kbs over Integrated Services Digital Net work (ISDN) lines or leased lines. Group 4 machines are not compatible with Group 3 machines unless a second modem is added for transmitting over an analog line. Currently, the major disadvantage of Group 4 machines, besides their incompability with Group 3 machines, is their cost—still over $10,000.

Selecting the Right Type of Network Fax Server

There are two different types of network fax servers. One type uses a network operat ing system's print capture capability and takes advantage of services offered by a net work's file server. A user transmits a fax message in ASCII format to the network file server using a terminate-and-stay-resident (TSR) program or going through a window if Windows is being run.

The file server routes the message to a fax queue, which resembles a print queue. The fax server receives this message when it polls the file server. It then extracts the document along with the control information it needs, such as the telephone number it must call. The fax server then transmits this document at 9,600 bps after first converting it from its ASCII format to a Group 3 format.

This approach utilizes the strengths of a file server. A NetWare server, for example, offers system fault tolerance, including disk mirroring or disk duplexing to prevent the loss of data. Also, users must know the appropriate password even to log onto the file server.

A second approach taken by some fax server vendors is to "piggy-back" onto popular electronic mail (E-Mail) programs and create an E-Mail gateway to their fax servers. A fax gateway program resides on the E-Mail server and provides the necessary communications between the two services.

E-Mail users specify that a document is to be transmitted via fax. Appropriate E-Mail addresses as well as fax phone numbers must be entered for this process to work correctly. The E-Mail server routes the document to the appropriate fax queue for transmission. The fax server receives this document, strips off E-Mail-specific control information, converts the document to Group 3 format, and then transmits it.

An advantage of this approach to network fax transmission is that the fax server can utilize some of the powerful features offered by E-Mail programs. VINES's Street-Talk, for example, is a very powerful network directory and provides directory information for all users regardless of their location. A fax server attached to VINES mail service could use StreetTalk's "yellow pages" feature to look up the network address of a network user at a different site and then transmit a fax.

Unfortunately, though, E-Mail is based on the concept of "store-and-forward," which means that documents are stored and then forwarded later, at designated times. But fax transmissions usually have some kind of urgency associated with them, and a network user who decides to fax a message via an E-Mail gateway will not have the measure of control over the document's transmission that is possible with the fax server functioning via a print capture approach.

Just as a user can use NetWare's PCONSOLE program to cancel a job that is currently printing, a network user of a fax server using print capture rather than an E-Mail fax server can cancel a fax job that has begun transmission.

Routing Faxes to Network Users

Most fax servers receive a fax and print it out using a laser printer, so the network user must still travel to the printer to pick up the fax. While not usually a problem in small companies, the distances involved in larger companies can make this pickup process very inefficient and costly. Some vendors have solved this problem by using Direct Inward Dialing (DID) trunk lines from the phone company. Assuming a company's phone system permits each user to have a separate telephone extension, outside calls (such as a fax transmission) could be routed to a specific extension number. Some fax servers have their own internal telephone directories and can perform this routing function. Network users can receive faxes at their network workstations, view them, and then print them.

The DID approach is very expensive, since it requires separate lines for each user. much more cost-effective approach is taken by All The Facts Inc.'s FaxPac gatew. network server.

FaxPac uses a technology known as universal autoroute. Users send a fax to remo PCs by adding a personal identification number to the end of the fax phone numbe The fax server at the receiving end uses FaxPac software to route the message direct to the appropriate network workstation.

Security For Network Fax Servers

Until recently, fax machines simply printed every document they received. The onl security possible was to call the recipient and announce that a confidential docume was being faxed. The recipient would run to the fax machine if it were in a commo area and wait for the transmission.

Today some fax machines have storage areas that serve as confidential mailboxes t hold sensitive documents until a personal identification number (PIN) is entere Another solution offered by vendors is to have a sensitive document held in the mem ory of the originating fax until the receiver calls and enters a password by pressin selected numbers that produce a coded group of dial tones.

Criteria for Selecting a Fax Server

Here is a checklist of points to consider:

1. Is the server capable of printing out fax activity logs and then transmitting copies of these reports to another designated fax machine? Network managers with several fax machines could collect such reports at one site and then run a program to consolidate the information.

2. Does the machine follow CCITT international standards or does it offer proprietary algorithms for transmission, compression, and so on? While some proprietary features might be very attractive, selecting such a machine means that all future purchases of fax machines that need to communicate with this machine will probably be limited to models from this same vendor. Do you want to lock yourself into a single-vendor solution? Some vendors do offer machines that are compatible with international standards while still providing proprietary features. Such machines can be an attractive solution.

3. Does your company transmit a lot of graphics? If so, does the fax support such common file formats as AutoCAD, HPGL, and PCX? Can it handle PostScript files?

4. How much flexibility does the fax server offer the network manager? How many fax boards can be placed in a single fax server? Can the individual lines be configured as in-going or out-going depending upon the traffic?

5. A corporate network file server might need several different distribution lists. How many lists can the server handle? Can it distribute the same message to multiple recipients around the world? Can it be programmed to prioritize messages and then send them at specified times?

6. Do network users run Windows? Some fax servers are Windows-compatible and offer a TSR (terminate and stay resident) program that the network user runs. The fax menu appears in a window enabling the user to perform other network activity while the fax is being transmitted. A related issue is selecting a product, such as FacSys, that will work on both DOS and Windows workstations.

7. Does the product provide a fax confirmation feature? This feature can save money, since it permits users to find out if the fax arrived safely without having to call.

8. Are users notified when a fax arrives? Some products freeze the user's keyboard to announce the arrival of a fax. Other products work in background mode and simply beep to announce a fax.

◀ ELECTRONIC MAIL ON LOCAL AREA NETWORKS

Electronic mail evolved on local area networks as proprietary software. Developed mostly by small companies, this software was written without any regard for international or even national standards. This meant that a program designed to work on one LAN would not communicate with E-Mail packages on other LANs. Nor would it communicate with the E-Mail software running on a company's larger computers, such as IBM's DIOSS and PROFS or Digital Equipment Corporation's All-In-1. With today's push toward enterprise networks, companies are becoming very concerned about linking their various E-Mail packages. In this section, we will take a look at some emerging E-Mail standards and the advantages they will offer for enterprise networks.

The MHS De Facto Standard

Action Technologies developed a Message Handling System (MHS) a few years ago that is now part of Novell's product line. Renamed the Mail Handling System, the MHS has become a de facto standard for many LAN E-Mail systems. It serves as a message transfer agent (MTA), the E-Mail entity that delivers messages from one user to another or from one application to another. Although the two terms are identical, the Action Technology/Novell MHS is different and not compatible with the CCITT X.400 Recommendations for a standard MHS. We will discuss this emerging standard in the next section.

MHS is based on the store-and-forward approach to mail service. This means that a message transmitted by a user can be placed in a storage area where it will be accessed at a later time and then forwarded to its recipient. If the recipient is located on a different computer network, the message will have to go through a gateway. MHS gateways are currently available to IBM's mainframe E-Mail system (DIOSS) and to popular E-Mail systems such as cc:Mail. The MHS Connectivity Manager is a program that usually runs

on a dedicated E-Mail server. This program periodically monitors an E-Mail director
looking for files that need to be transmitted.

The Connectivity Manager will transmit a message over a gateway to an E-Mail system
a fax, or even a telex machine. An E-Mail system will store the message until a use
agent notices it and transmits it to the user's workstation. As mentioned earlier, the limi
tation of E-Mail gateways to fax machines is that the service is not as fast as transmittin
a fax directly because of the store-and-forward approach that E-Mail systems take.

Two different types of messages are possible under MHS. Message Control Block
(MCBs) is the older and by far simpler type. An MCB file consists of a text file i
which the first 18 lines provide control information such as the sender, recipient, sub
ject, and so on. An accompanying text message can be up to 8 Kb in length.

The MHS Seal program prepares the MCB for transmission. At the receiving end, the
MHS Unseal program is run to prepare the message for reading.

X.400   Overview of the Message Handling System Model (MHS)

X.402   Description of MHS architecture

X.403   Methods of testing E-Mail systems to ensure they are compliant with the
         1984 set of X.400 Recommendations

X.407   A description of an information processing system model

X.408   Description of rules for converting one type of information into another type

X.411   Description of a Message Transfer System

X.413   Description of a Message Store

X.419   Description of protocols used by the different components of a Message
         Transfer System

X.420   Description of types of information that can be included in a message

Figure 10-2. The CCITT X.400 Recommendations.

MHS also offers a Standard Message Format (SMF). Programs written by developers to use SMF perform the functions normally performed by the Seal and Unseal programs used by MCB. SMF provides many more features than MCB (such as distribution lists), but it requires a developer to write the program to utilize its power.

ome Background on CCITT X.400 E-Mail

In 1984 the CCITT issued its first set of **X.400 Recomendations**. It followed these in 1988 with a second set of Recommendations that rounded out a very robust Message Handling System compatible with the Open Systems Interconnect (OSI) model standards. The purpose of the X.400 Recommendations was to make it possible for users regardless of their computers' hardware configuration to transmit mail to each other using a store-and-forward approach.

X.400 applications are found at the Application layer of the OSI model. They utilize the services of the Presentation layer to define the data structures that will be transmitted during a session. Figure 10-2 describes the set of CCITT X.400 Recommendations.

Figure 10-3 illustrates a typical X.400 MHS. **User Agents (UAs)** are programs that reside on a stand-alone PC or on an E-Mail server. They format documents for transmission and also receive incoming messages, retrieve them when requested, and then display them.

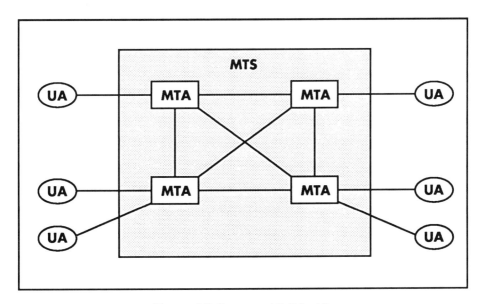

Figure 10-3. A typical X.400 MHS.

The **Message Transfer Agent (MTA)** displayed in Fig. 10-3 functions like a p
office. It handles the actual transmission and routing of messages and provides t
"mailboxes" where incoming messages can be placed. The **Message Store (MS)** w
added as part of the 1988 set of X.400 Recommendations. It serves as a continuous
available storage system to take delivery of messages addressed to a specific us
While the MS is not required, a UA that subscribes to an MS communicates only wi
that MS and not with an MTA. The user agent submits a message to the MS, which
turn submits it to the MTA.

The messages transmitted via X.400 Recommendations consist of an envelope and t
content. The envelope contains control information regarding the sender and recipie
The content can consist of a message from sender to recipient, a report containi
information about the delivery or nondelivery of messages, or a probe that carries
information itself but determines whether or not it is possible to deliver a message to
specified recipient. The X.400 Recommendations also defined the protocols, or rule
followed by the elements composing the MHS. MTAs communicate with each oth
using the P1 protocol. The P1 protocol describes the contents of a message's envelop
which specifies how two computers that will be routing messages communicate wit
each other. User agents communicate with each other using the P2 protocol, whic

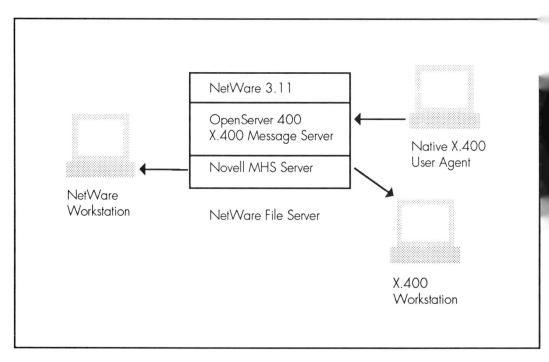

Figure 10-4. A Novell MHS Gateway to an X.400 MHS.

describes the way messages must be structured for transmission and retrieval. The P3 protocol provides specifications for remote user agents to MTA communications. This protocol has been revised and enhanced into the P7 protocol, which provides more remote services.

Some Major X.400 Features

The CCITT X.400 standards define a full-featured E-Mail system. Basic functions include a submission time stamp indication (When was the document submitted?), an indication of the document's content, and an indication of when the document was delivered or that it failed to be delivered.

Senders of X.400 documents can request multidestination delivery as well as specific grades of delivery service. They can also request notification of when a "receipt" arrives. More important, senders can specify a document's level of importance and sensitivity and can request that the contents be encrypted to prevent unauthorized people from attempting to read it.

A NetWare X.400 Gateway

Since Novell's NetWare enjoys close to 70 percent of the LAN market, many corporate LAN managers need to know how they will be able to link their NetWare LANs using Mail Handling System E-Mail systems with networks using X.400 E-Mail systems. The solution is a gateway linking the Novell MHS world with the X.400 MHS. Figure 10-4 illustrates the Retix OpenServer 400, which is implemented on a NetWare 3.11 server as a network loadable module, or NLM. Applications that use the X.400 application programming interfaces are able to directly access the X.400 service. This means that X.400 and Novell NHS applications can coexist.

Public and Private E-Mail X.400 Gateways

Some companies who foresee limited communication between their existing proprietary E-Mail system and networks running X.400 E-Mail can use public E-Mail X.400 gateways. Vendors such as AT&T Mail and MCI Mail can provide the conversion to X.400 format and then transmit messages to X.400-compliant E-Mail systems.

For larger companies that want to link incompatible E-Mail systems and also utilize the X.400 format, the answer might be an X.400 gateway to several different E-Mail protocols. WorldTalk/400 made by Touch Communications is an example of this new class of gateway. This gateway is divided into two components: a gateway engine that resides on a Unix-based workstation and LAN-specific gateway modules that reside on LAN servers or on dedicated E-Mail servers.

The gateway engine establishes links with private as well as public X.400 backbones, while the LAN gateway modules perform both address mapping and conversion from the LAN's proprietary addressing scheme to the X.400 specifications.

What makes the WorldTalk/400 gateway interesting is the large numbers of LAN-specific modules available or announced. Gateways include Action Technologies /Novell's MHS, Microsoft's Microsoft Mail, cc:Mail Inc.'s cc:Mail, TOPS' INBox Plus, CE

Software's QuickMail, and Unix systems using SMTP or UCCP. It also suppor
IBM's PROFS and DEC's All-in-One.

E-Mail Cross-Platform Gateways

Some companies have found that they must grapple with as many as ten different E
Mail systems that are unable to communicate directly with each other. End-users ar
accustomed to using these programs and unwilling to learn a common mail program
The expense of replacing these existing systems with a new mail program, even a
X.400 mail system, might not be justifiable.

One solution for such companies is to use a mail system such as IBM's PROFS as :
platform. Since PROFS has such a large share of the mainframe E-Mail market, mos
E-Mail programs have some kind of gateway to PROFS. While Higgins and cc:Mai
users cannot communicate directly with each other using their own E-Mail systems
they can send messages back and forth if they are both listed in the PROFS directory a
PROFS users. A message sent from the Higgins mail system to a cc:Mail mail system
user (listed as a PROFS user) will be forwarded from PROFS to the LAN running
cc:Mail.

Companies with many different hardware/user-interface platforms—say PCs running
DOS, PCs running Windows or OS/2 , Unix workstations, and Macintosh computers—
need to consider offering gateways to link the E-Mail on these various machines. Unix
machines are likely to require a gateway to Simple Mail Transfer Program (SMTP) or
UUCP. cc:Mail is particularly strong in the area of cross-platform gateways, offering
gateways for PROFS, Telemail, Easylink, MCI, Telex, Unix (UUCP), and fax. Third-
party vendors add gateways to cc:Mail for DISSOS, All-in-One, GEISCO, HP Desk,
and Unix running SMTP. There is also an X.400 gateway from Retix.

Transmitting Electronic Data Interchange (EDI) Over X.400

The CCITT has developed an X.435 Recommendation for users of electronic data
interchange (EDI) who wish to exchange documents over X.400 E-Mail systems. EDI
has grown in importance in paper-intensive industries such as banking, because it
enables users to create electronic forms such as purchase orders and then transmit data
electronically directly into these forms. General Motors, for example, requires its vendors to use EDI if they want to do business with it.

Many aerospace companies such as Boeing have expressed interest in X.435, because
the federal government is putting pressure on its major contractors to transmit data to
it electronically.

Network Directory Services and the CCITT X.500 Standard

Network directory services are a convenience for users of large networks and a
necessity for users of enterprise-wide networks. For E-Mail to function on an enterprise-wide network, a user in Los Angeles, for example, must know the network
address of the intended recipient in New York. A user in Chicago might need a file
located on a file server in Philadelphia. How does he or she learn the name of this

device? Printers are another area where directory services can make network life much easier. Users can print out documents on remote printers by looking up the printers' names in the directory.

The **CCITT X.500** standard will establish a form of digital directory assistance for E-Mail users nationally and internationally, but a number of issues remain to be resolved. Different E-Mail systems use different addressing schemes. How will these systems be able to understand each other? What format will the X.500 directory information follow? Do companies really want outsiders to be able to gather names of its employees and send them unsolicited messages?

The current CCITT X.500 directory service uses a hierarchical directory structure. A user accesses the directory through a **directory user agent (DUA)**. The DUA communicates with the directory by using the **directory access protocol (DAP)**.

Several **directory system agents (DSAs)** each have their own associated databases, which hold portions of the global directory database. The database as a whole is known as the **directory information tree (DIT)**. Each entry in the DIT is an object made up of attributes and distinguished by a unique name. The DIT's associated DSAs communicate with each other using their own protocol, known as directory system protocol (DSP).

Users of X.500 directory services will be able to use LIST commands to browse through the directory tree. By combining the LIST command with a READ command, users can view the equivalent of directory white pages to locate a particular person or organization. Since directory entries can be listed by attributes, it is possible to create and view directory yellow pages so that a user can search through, for example, accounting firms or publishing companies specifically.

VINES' StreetTalk and Network Directory Services

Banyan's Virtual Networking System (VINES) is a network operating system that incorporates a network directory naming service called StreetTalk. This is by far the most sophisticated naming service available today.

StreetTalk is a distributed naming service database. Names are divided into three parts: Object/Group/Organization. Any user on a VINES network can ask for StreeTalk Directory Assistance and see a list of the names of all users and resources on the network. StreetTalk permits the use of nicknames, so that a user might be identified simply as "Red" or "CarolynT." Similarly, users with the necessary network rights can request a file without knowing the directory, subdirectory, or even file server on which this file resides. StreetTalk would use its directory to locate the file. At the current time, neither StreetTalk nor the NetWare and LAN Manager products we will discuss shortly are compatible with the X.500 standard, but all three companies have indicated that they will eventually offer X.500 compatible products.

NetWare's Naming Service

NetWare has its own naming service, known as the NetWare Name Service (NN While not as sophisticated as StreetTalk and not a directory service, NNS does make easier for users to log into a network without having to log onto several differe servers. Under NNS, users and resources such as file servers and printers are group together into **domains,** where they can be managed as a single object. The NETCC utility program is designed to enable managers to manage domains under NNS. group that performs similar functions can be described in a profile. Users meeting th profile would be logged into the appropriate domain.

A single domain might contain several file servers and several profiles. The Accou ting profile, for example, might have access to the file server containing accounti programs and data as weil as a wide carriage dot matrix printer for printing ledge and a laser printer for printing reports.

When a network manager changes something on one server through NETCON, the changes are automatically made on all other servers in the same domain when the pr gram is exited. A network manager can create a print configuration job on one fi server, and all other servers in the same domain will be able to use this job.

LAN Manager's Name Service

Microsoft's LAN Manager also has a name service, which establishes networ domains so that a set of servers can be administered from a single server. LA Manager has a related replication service permitting files and even directories to b duplicated across an entire domain. At the present time, LAN Manager's domains ca recognize the names of users and the names of groups. This means that a user ca access information on a group such as WORDPERF from any server in a domai where this group resides on a server. LAN Manager and NetWare both lack the direc tory services found in StreetTalk, but both companies have announced that they wi offer these services in the future and that these services will be compatible with th emerging CCITT X.500 standard.

Criteria for Selecting E-Mail Software

Here is a checklist of questions to ask:

1. If network management is a corporate edict, what plans does the prospective E-Mail vendor have for supporting the Common Management Information Protocol (CMIP)? Does the vendor have a scheduled delivery date for this product?

2. The ability of an E-Mail system to use X.500 directories will become increasingly important, especially for large companies with multiple branches. What plans does the E-Mail vendor have for providing X.500 compatibility?

3. Can the E-Mail gateway be reconfigured to T-1, X.25, or other possible configurations? Heavy E-Mail traffic can cause a real bottleneck at the gateway, and it only grows worse. What is adequate today might be inadequate a year from now.

4. Does the E-Mail system have a notify function? Can network users examine mail without having to leave their current network application? Some E-Mail packages use Terminate and Stay Resident (TSR) programs that can be opened from within any application.

5. Is a network-wide scheduling capability important for your company? Some E-Mail programs such as The Coordinator have this module. A secretary can write a memo to a distribution list announcing a committee meeting and use the E-Mail's scheduling capability to look at committee members' calendars to select a date and time when they are available.

6. Does the vendor offer versions of the E-Mail product for all the hardware/software platforms your company uses? E-Mail loses its power if the entire company cannot use it.

7. Can remote users be accommodated via remote post offices? How difficult and/or expensive is it to link these remote users?

8. Are there certain features your company needs very badly? For example, would the ability to produce custom forms be valuable? For heavy mail users, can mail be searched and prioritized? Can a user look at a mail log? Can the messages be filed under certain topics and then retrieved?

9. Are special printing capabilities important? For example, does your company want to print E-Mail messages from a PC E-Mail system to a PostScript printer?

11

CHECKLISTS FOR NETWORK EVALUATION AND SELECTION

The purpose of this chapter is to make you aware of the types of questions one must ask when evaluating an existing network or selecting a new one. While this list is not exhaustive, it should help you understand the process a consultant goes through when planning a company's network.

THE NEEDS ANALYSIS

When planning a corporate network, one of the very first things to do is to conduct a needs analysis. One must ask several questions at this stage in order to design the optimum network. An experienced network consultant will probe to discover not only how the company currently conducts its business but also how it plans to do business in the future.

The Firm's Mission and Structure

To automate a company, the consultant must start with the company's business mission and its organizational structure. If the company's goal is to establish a national sales network with regional distribution centers, then designing high-speed remote communications links to the corporate LAN will have a high priority. If the company's mission is to establish itself as a leading stock brokerage firm that will offer fast service and reliability, then the consultant must build in these design priorities.

A company with several autonomous divisions or with a lot of in-fighting among its department managers might require a network that can be easily segmented to give each department or division control over its own network traffic and ensure that information on a particular segment is secure.

A company that has a strong MIS department and centralized mainframe computer operations faces a number of difficult issues when it downsizes to a local area network.

How will the network be segmented? Who will be responsible for managing and controlling the network? Is MIS supportive of this movement toward LANs, or is the department fighting the decision?

Following the Current Paper Trail

A consultant might begin by looking at how the company currently handles its paper work. What is the typical customer business transaction? How many separate pieces of paper are involved? A retail store might currently be using a cash register at its point of sale and handwritten invoices written by salespeople. Company purchase orders might currently be handwritten as well. The consultant needs to ask several questions to determine if there is an integrated point in the sales system at which data could flow from an electronically created invoice directly into an accounting program that can generate a corporate balance sheet. Similarly, purchase orders could be created electronically, and the information supplied could flow into the company's accounts payable accounting module. In one company salespeople might be required to call in to check current inventory levels and then handwrite their orders. These salespeople might hand in these orders the next morning so that this information can be typed into a computer. How much more efficient would it be if these salespeople could use laptop computers with modems to dial into the corporate network to place their orders?

If a company generates hundreds of memos and then requires secretaries to duplicate copies for everyone on a distribution list, how much time could be saved by using electronic mail and sending a memo to all network users on a distribution list? If hundreds of documents are faxed daily, would a network fax server prove more efficient especially if it were linked to the company's electronic mail system?

Analyzing the Necessary Software Needed

It is an old computer industry truism that a company should find its software first and then buy the hardware required to run these programs. A consultant must look at the specific software features different departments require. Marketing might require a customer database that can be used for telemarketing new products as well as servicing regular customers. The engineering division might want to link the customer database with specific trouble reports so it can track engineering problems that need to be solved. Finally, the maintenance division might want to use the same database to track the maintenance it sells. Does a customer have a 24-hour on-site maintenance contract? The maintenance division needs to know this information.

A consultant will ask the questions necessary to discover which software features are absolutely required and which features are desirable but not required. Some companies might absolutely require the ability to include pictures with a database record, while other companies might be more concerned with the ability to produce complicated reports.

A look at accounting distribution software will show why consultants must ask very specific questions about a company's software needs. Does the company provide multiple discounts to different types of customers? Are some customers taxable while others are tax exempt? Does this same company want to offer different types of discounts on different product classifications? An irrigation supply company, for example, might provide different discounts to landscape architects, resellers, and the general public. It might also offer different levels of discounts on sprinkler heads than it offers on pipes. What about a nut and bolt company that requires the ability to price items at less than a cent? Can the software handle such complications?

Current Hardware and Software

If a company is currently computerized but not networked, how much of the current software is networkable? If network versions are not available, can the programs be metered so that one user at a time can use them without damaging files? What kinds of computers are currently being used? If the company has original IBM PCs running the Intel 8088 microcprocessor, the consultant might feel that it would be more economical to buy new Intel 80386SX- based machines than to try to update the old machines to this performance level.

Does the company have a mixture of Macintosh and IBM PCs and compatibles? Can these machines be incorporated into a network that will run the software the consultant has selected?

Plans for Future Growth

The company's plans for future growth will help the consultant design the appropriate type of network. A company with no plans to grow beyond 50 workstations might be ideal for an Arcnet LAN, while a company starting with 250 users with plans to expand to more than 1,000 users might require a network with greater bandwidth and the flexibility to add optic fiber cabling and FDDI in the future.

The Physical Environment

A company's physical environment will help determine the type of network to be installed. Are the buildings spread over a campus environment encompassing several miles or is the company situated in a single high-rise building? Are a couple of offices located on the other side of a freeway?

A manufacturing company with heavy equipment that generates electromagnetic interference will require a network that provides protection against these signals. A company located in Houston with several buildings spread over a campus setting could present cabling problems, because conduits and cabling must be able to handle the very heavy rainfall and flooding found there.

The Overall Network Design

The network consultant must make sure that corporate management agrees on design priorities for a LAN before designing the network. Each company will use its own performance-to-cost ratio as a guideline. A company that is thinking of going public and wants to show the most positive bottom line might tell the consultant to keep equipment costs down to a minimum while a company whose customers expect performance and responsiveness might tell the consultant that performance and reliability are the two most important criteria. The key point, though, is that the consultant must raise thi question and receive an answer that reflects total agreement within the company.

Data Traffic

How much data traffic will be on the network? Are some users going to send larg graphics files? Are several users going to access accounting programs? Will a data base be accessed frequently? Printing long reports on the network can also generate enough traffic to slow down the entire network.

A consultant might try to determine if users will generally send short bursts of packet: rather than large numbers of packets, since this information can help determine the type of network topology (contention or noncontention) to be used. If users will be transmitting short bursts of data, a contention network such as Ethernet might be ideal since it was specifically designed for this type of traffic.

The consultant might also determine that certain departments will be transmitting so much traffic that they should be segmented to prevent their traffic from slowing down the entire network. Similarly, such departments would be better served by their own network printers on their segment to generate their reports.

Performance

Closely related to the amount of network traffic is the level of performance required. If the network is to be used to respond to inquiries, then response time is a major consideration. To keep response time short even when data traffic is heavy requires a high-performance network such as the 16 Mbs IBM Token Ring network or perhaps even a proprietary very-high-speed network such as those offered by Proteon. Companies requiring high performance under heavy data traffic conditions might even need the 100 Mbs transmission speed offered by FDDI.

Interoperability

One of the major network design considerations is how well the proposed network will be able to communicate with other corporate networks. If a company has IBM mainframes that have Systems Network Architecture (SNA), DEC minicomputers utilizing DEC Network Architecture (DNA), and IBM and Apple microcomputers, it has major interoperability problems. None of these machines was originally designed to communicate with the others, but it is possible to link them using a combination of hardware and software.

Bridges

Networks that utilize the same low-level protocols even though they differ in their high-level protocols can be linked by bridges. A company might already have some Macintosh computers linked in an AppleTalk network and a group of PCs linked in an Ethernet network. Since both 802.3 networks utilize the same low-level protocols defined in the IEEE 802.2 specifications, the two networks can be bridged.

Routers

Does a company have Unix computers running the TCP/IP protocol and a local area network running the NetWare IPX protocol? A consultant might recommend Novell's LAN Workplace for DOS so that the LAN workstations can access the Unix network.

If a company's computers are utilizing several different protocols, a consultant might consider a multiprotocol router. This router could act as a switching station to connect the various networks.

Gateways

Because IBM mainframe computers talk only to IBM devices or devices that emulate them, LANs require the appropriate gateway hardware and software to link them with a mainframe. Consultants must closely question companies with mainframe equipment contemplating LANs in order to discover what level of connectivity these companies need. If a company is using a specific mainframe database application and want to transmit data from this program into LAN workstations, the consultant might look for a PC version of the same program or another program that has a mainframe environmental bond. As an example of this situation, a company that has its customer data on its mainframe in DB2 format could run Advanced Revelation on its LAN and use the product's DB2 environmental bond to move data transparently into the LAN and then back to the mainframe.

Open Versus Proprietary Network Architecture

Does a company plan to link its computers to other companies' computers? Does it intend to bid on government contracts that require Government Open Systems Interconnect Profile (GOSIP) compatibility? A company that intends to remain a 100 percent "IBM shop" has no need to abandon IBM's proprietary closed architecture, since this software is optimized for its computer hardware.

If a company does need to link its computers to companies using different computers, there might be a need for an open architecture. The International Standards Organization's Open Systems Interconnect Model (OSI Model) provides an open architecture that enables diverse computers running this protocol stack to communicate with each other.

Network Topology

A company's present cabling might lend itself to a bus topology or perhaps a star topology. Does the company have distance requirements that go beyond the limitations of Ethernet even with its maximum number of repeaters? A consultant might look at IBM's Token Ring Network under such circumstances. A company's concern about its network's robustness might lead a consultant toward a clustered star topology that enables the network to remain functional even if one star's hub is disabled.

Many consultants are leaning toward the 10BaseT star topology, because it offers excellent diagnostics as well as the ability to remain functional even if a MAU goes down.

Security

Security might be a major corporate priority. The consultant then would design a net work that incorporated as many internal and external security measures as possible. A centralized file server approach such as that found under NetWare or LAN Manager provides a clear audit trail, effective login password protection, and the ability to limit users' rights to key directories.

A consultant planning to design a secure network must begin by examining what rights different types of users really need and not what rights they want. Who should be able to view personnel records? Who should have the rights permitting the deletion or modification of these records?

The security of data transmitted over the network is also a major concern. Optic fiber cabling provides considerably more protection than coax or twisted pair. Does data travel in encrypted format? What about data that is backed up to tape?

A consultant might consider diskless workstations in public areas so that data cannot be downloaded. Users might also be restricted to using the network 8 am to 5 pm on weekdays.

Reliability and System Fault Tolerance

Some organizations cannot afford to have their networks go down. A consultant designing such a network must examine each of the potential points of failure and make them as fault tolerant as possible. The network might include disk duplexing as well as a duplicate set of cabling and NIC cards so that if one network fails, users can continue their work on the second network.

A company must weigh the cost in loss of business when its network is down versus the expense of building in enough redundancy to make a system fault tolerant network.

Maintenance

How much maintenance does the company intend to do internally? Will it have its own factory-trained technicians to maintain the network or will it rely on service contracts? If the company wants to maintain its own network equipment, then the consultant will look at network components, such as MAUs, that contain their own diagnostics. The network budget must also include a significant number of spare parts so that NIC cards can be swapped quickly.

Cost Effectiveness and Company Priorities

While a mainframe-oriented company that has opted to build a LAN will find the cost of network components reasonable by mainframe standards, a company that has decided to build its first network might have no idea how expensive it will be. The consultant needs to meet with top corporate officials and reach consensus on what the company is willing to spend.

If the company's budget is limited, the consultant must sacrifice performance and look to such alternatives as Arcnet or even AppleTalk if the company already has Macintosh computers. Rather than selecting LAN Manager or NetWare, the consultant might look at a network operating system such as Lantastic that can economically handle up to around 100 workstations in a peer-to-peer arrangement.

The consultant must also examine whether the company can afford the top tier of microcomputers (such as Compaq, IBM, or Dell) or whether it must go with lower cost clones whose MTBF numbers might not be as good.

SELECTING NETWORK COMPONENTS

Once the consultant has established a company's priorities for its overall network design, it is time to look at specific network components. Knowing the level of data traffic, the type of work that will be done on the network, and the plans for future growth helps determine such specifics as the type of network interface card or file server.

Cabling

Network cabling used to be a nonissue, because options were limited. Today the cost of optic fiber has dropped to the point where it is competitive with coax even though its components (connectors, NICs, and the like) are still expensive. A company that already has a very heavy investment in cabling designed for 3,270 terminals might be a candidate for Arcnet, which could utilize the existing cabling.

A company might have a large telephone system comprising several unused twisted-pairs as well as designed wiring closets. The consultant would have to consider whether or not to use this medium, since the major expense associated with twisted pair is the installation.

The major advantage of twisted-pair and 10BaseT topology is that moves and changes can be made easily. A user who moves his or her computer from one office to another can be hooked up in minutes. Cabling is much easier to manage with wiring closets, and this approach seems to be growing in popularity.

A consultant must ask enough questions to learn whether or not there are potential sources of electromagnetic interference that might require using coax or even optic fiber as the network medium. One company discovered after installation that its cabling was running adjacent to fluorescent lighting, resulting in a major network disruption.

The File Server Platform

What kind of performance does the network need from its file server? Very heavy traffic demands might require one of the "superservers" now available from companies such as Netframe or Compaq. Does the file server require an Intel 80486 microprocessor? Can the network operating system support this chip?

Has the company resolved the EISA-versus-microchannel architecture question? A company that thinks of itself as an "IBM shop" might prefer microchannel architecture, because it offers a one-vendor solution. What type of architecture does the company want and how does this selection make sense in terms of the company's long-term plans?

Network Users' Workstations

Does the company prefer going with a major microcomputer manufacturer or does want to save money and go with clones? What potential compatibility problems could result from going with clones? Do certain departments require higher performance workstations owing to the nature of their work (for example, computer assisted drawing, programming, and so on)?

Can the company buy complete off-the-shelf workstations with the appropriate size hard drives, video cards, monitors, and other peripherals? Are the power supplies adequate for future expansion?

Ergometric Design

The consultant must probe corporate officials to learn what the company really wants to do to promote employee safety and health. Some companies will opt for more expensive terminals and keyboards because their electronic emissions have been reduced and they limit hand strain. These same companies might also want adjustable monitors that prevent neck strain. Other companies, however, will insist on the least expensive equipment available.

Network Interface Cards

Are 32-bit cards (and appropriate drivers) available for the file server? Are NICs software configurable so that switches do not have to be changed manually? What kind of memory management does the NIC use? Is it fast and reliable? 3Com cards are rated so reliable that the company now offers a lifetime warranty. Do network workstations need 16-bit NICs or can they use fast 8-bit NICs?

Network Operating Systems

NetWare dominates the network operating system market, but it is not appropriate for every situation. LAN Manager and LAN Server offer advantages to companies that have substantial mainframe operations and want to establish close LAN-to-mainframe links. VINES might be ideal for companies that plan large wide area networks (WANs) because of the software's StreetTalk naming service. It might also be preferable in an Unix environment, since the software itself is Unix-based. Other companies might be perfectly happy with the peer-to-peer services provided by Lantastic.

One major question presents itself: What does the network operating system have to do for this particular company? A company that has Sun workstations using the NFS protocol and wants to link these workstations to a LAN might look at a network operating system, such as NetWare 3.11, that has an NFS network loadable module (NLM) to establish this link.

Backup Systems

What kind of backup system will the network have? How fast can the network be restored if necessary? What scheme will be used for backups? A backup system such as the Network Archivist will establish a backup schedule and then prompt the network supervisor when to back up the network and which tape to load.

The UPS

What kind of uninterruptible power supply (UPS) is required? Can the network use a standby unit or must it go with an on-line system? Is the UPS capable of handling the load imposed by multiple file servers if they are situated in the same room? What kind of software comes with the UPS?

NETWORK SOFTWARE

A network is a way to share software, so the software should drive the network. Here are some basic network-related questions one needs to ask to select network software.

E-Mail

What E-Mail services do network users need? Do users need to link a fax server to its E-Mail? What gateways are required to link LAN E-Mail with other mail systems, such as PROFS or All-in-One? What kind of licensing is available? Is it by file server or by site?

One overlooked network issue is the ability of the E-Mail package to notify users that they have mail. Does this feature require a Terminate and Stay Resident program? If so, how much memory does this TSR require?

If the company expects to link its network mail with mail systems located overseas, the consultant might want to find an E-Mail program that has X.400 gateways. Another useful feature, particularly on a network, is E-Mail packages that can be linked to scheduling packages. This combination enables managers or their administrative assistants to schedule meetings by having the program locate dates and times when everyone on a distribution list is available.

Network Database Management Software

A consultant needs to match a company's needs with the various databases available. How many fields will be required in a database? Are links required to other databases such as DB2? If customized programming is required, does the database program offer a powerful enough language to accomplish this task?

How complex are the reports that users will need? How difficult will it be to train network users? Are training materials available for this program? One major database issue that will become increasingly important in the near future is the ability of the database program to run on an SQL server. Database programs pump out an enormous amount of traffic, while SQL versions send only the records that are requested. If the network requires high performance, then SQL compatibility might be very important.

Network Word Processing Software

Most of the top rated word processing programs offer complete network versions, but they do differ in subtle ways. How easily can printers be configured for the word processing program? How easily can individual workstations be configured for the program? Since word processing will probably be the most common function on a network, how easily can users be trained? Are tutorials available?

Network Application Software

Network application software should not require users to change everything about the way they normally conduct business. A customer entry program, for example, should not make it difficult for salespeople to enter orders nor should a point of sale program increase the lines at a checkout counter. Ideally, a consultant should be able to set up demonstrations of leading software candidates for a particular task and then let users try each program.

A consultant must consider the strength of the companies offering the application software. If the company's business will depend on a particular program, what would happen if the software vendor goes bankrupt? Is source code available for an additional price? If the network workstations will be using a special environment, such as Microsoft's Windows, does the application provide a Windows version? If not, are such versions scheduled for future release?

Maintenance Contracts

What kind of maintenance contracts are available for network components? Can the company contract for 24-hour on-site service? How much more is weekend service than eight-five weekday service? Does the vendor promise a one-hour response time? Will the vendor supply loaners if it does not have a part required to make a machine operational? Can the vendor fix software problems remotely via modem? Is one vendor willing to take responsibility for coordinating repair in a mixed-vendor environment?

On-Site Spares

As mentioned earlier when we looked at a company's budget for a LAN, is the company committed to maintaining an on-site collection of spare parts to keep the network up and running? Is there a place to store these parts?

Network Management Tools

Network management tools are expensive. Is the vendor willing to spend $15,000 to $20,000 for a protocol analyzer and an additional couple of thousand dollars to train personnel to use these machines? A consultant must determine what kinds of tools are necessary. Will the company's own personnel be maintaining both the network software and hardware? If so, then the company will require special cable-testing equipment such as TDRs to test for cable breaks.

How useful are the reports generated by the network diagnostic tools? Are these tools programmable and capable of being customized to meet the special needs of this network?

Network Management and Control

What specific management and control functions are required for this network? Will a network manager be able to manage the entire network from a single workstation?

Will network components such as bridges and routers be able to send alarms to a network monitor? Does the company require the management services offered by Simple Network Management Protocol (SNMP)? Must it wait until the ISO's CMIP protocol is available in commercial products?

Network User Training

What type of network training will users require? Is the vendor prepared to do on-site training and continuing training as users' needs change? Does the company want a network menuing system such as Saber's in order to reduce the need for users' network training?

■ THE NETWORK PROCUREMENT PROCESS

The network procurement process is complex, because so many of the building blocks must come from different vendors. It is imperative that a single vendor take responsibility for systems integration, installation, training, and maintenance. After a company has a clear picture of what it needs, the next step is often a request for proposal (RFP).

The company issuing an RFP must have a very clear set of priorities for its network. Ideally, it will set a certain amount of points to be awarded for vendors' proposals in each of several categories (file server, workstation, network operating system, training, and so on). The company should weight the number of points awarded in each of these categories to reflect its own priorities. If network security is the absolutely highest priority, for example, then the single greatest number of points should be awarded in this category. If the clarity of network documentation is less important than the file server's performance or the bandwidth available, then the documentation should be awarded less weight.

Some points will probably be awarded for such nonproduct-related categories as the vendor's financial stability, the quality of its customer recommendations, and its staff's level of expertise as reflected in resumes.

Some points might be awarded for vendors who formally agree to assume responsibility for service calls regardless of whether it is their product that is malfunctioning.

Ideally, the vendors with the highest point totals can provide demo models for a kind of computer "bakeoff." Staff members who will be the end users for this equipment can try out each system and record their reactions and evaluations.

One final word of advice to network consultants: draft the network contract so that vendors receive portions of their funds as they complete different phases of the job. The installation of a network is not an overnight process. It might require several weeks before all software is installed and operational, particularly if accounting charts of accounts must be built or manufacturing inventory entered.

A detailed checklist should include such items as a benchmark test under simulated heavy data traffic, a file server backup and restore, and interoperability tests if different protocol stacks are being used. Only after all these tests have been passed successfully and all training has been successfully completed should a vendor receive all its funds.

Remember, a customer who still has some funds held back usually has phone calls returned more promptly than one who has paid everything before the network is completely operational.

BIBLIOGRAPHY

Breidenbach, Susan. "Bus Masters Prolong Life of PC AT Servers,"
Network World. March 26, 1990: 13–14.

Cole, Gerald. *Computer Networking for Systems Programmers*.
John Wiley, 1990

Connor, Deni. "ISA, MCA, EISA, and the Winner Is . . . ,"
LAN Times. September 1990: 59–63.

Madron, Thomas. *Local Area Networks: The Next Generation*. 2nd edition.
New York: John Wiley, 1990.

Schatt, Stan. *Understanding Local Area Networks*. 2nd edition.
Howard W. Sams, 1990.

———. *Linking LANs*. Tab, 1991.

Sidhu, Gursharan S., Richard F. Andrews, Alan B. Oppenheimer, and Apple
Computer Inc. *Inside AppleTalk*. 2nd edition. New York: Addison-
Wesley, 1990.

Tanenbaum, Andrew S. *Computer Networks*. 2nd edition. New York:
Prentice-Hall, 1988.

Stallings, William. *Local Networks*. 3rd edition. New York: Macmillan,
1990.

GLOSSARY

Accumaster Integrator: A network management station under AT&T's UNMA.

Advanced Program-to-Program Communications (APPC): IBM's programming tools to enable developers to write programs that can communicate directly with each other.

Agent: A device under SNMP that is capable of reporting alarm information to a manager.

American Standard Code for Information Interchange (ASCII): A data encoding scheme commonly used with PCs. While there are different versions of ASCII, a popular version uses seven bits to represent a character and an eighth bit (the parity bit) for error checking.

Amplitude Modulation: Modulation based on varying the power of the signal's transmission.

AppleTalk: Apple Computer's suite of network protocols.

Backbone Bridge Topology: A backbone is directly connected to several bridges. This topology is particularly useful in multifloor buildings.

Bridge: A device functioning at the Medium Access Control level of the OSI model that permits two LANs to communicate with each other. It is insensitive to higher level protocols and basically filters or forwards based on destination address.

Brouter: A device that combines features offered by a router and a bridge. They can act as bridges for some protocols while routing packets with other protocols.

Cache Memory: High-speed RAM used to hold information in the expectation that it will be requested again.

Carrierband: A baseband network that includes some modulation to reduce noise.

Carrier Sense Multiple Access with Collision Detection (CSMA/CD): Network nodes listen to the network medium to identify any network traffic before transmitting.

Cascaded Bridges: Bridges that are linked together to connect several different networks or network segments.

CMIP Over Logical Link Control (CMOL): A smaller version of CMIP designed specifically to be used with LANs.

CMIP over the Transmission Control Protocol (CMOT): A dual-protocol approach to running both SNMP and CMIP.

Common Management Information Protocol (CMIP): A network management protocol developed by the ISO as part of the OSI model.

Connection-Oriented Service: IEEE 802.2 service that incorporates flow control, error recovery, and acknowledgments into the LLC and MAC layers.

Contention Networks: Networks in which nodes contend or compete for network access.

Data Communications Equipment (DCE): A data communications term often used to describe a modem.

Data Terminal Equipment (DTE): A data communications term often used to describe a computer or terminal.

DECmcc: DEC's enterprise management architecture product.

Directory Access Protocol (DAP): The protocol used by the directory user agent to access an X.500 directory.

Directory Hashing: A technique used by Novell NetWare in which the file server maps all directory files and keeps this information in RAM as a kind of super index.

Directory Information Tree (DIT): The entire X.5OO directory database.

Directory System Agents (DSAs): Different databases that comprise an X.500 directory.

Directory User Agent (DUA): The component of an X.500 system that is used to access an X.500 directory.

Disk Caching: A technique used by Novell NetWare file servers in which they anticipate file requests based on a frequency chart and keep those files in RAM.

Disk Duplexing: A NetWare system fault tolerant measure in which a file server's hard disk drive and its hard disk drive controller are duplicated.

Disk Mirroring: A NetWare system fault tolerant measure in which a file server's hard disk drive is duplicated and connected to the same disk drive controller.

Distributed Processing: Processing is spread or distributed across a network so that network nodes can do their own processing rather than having all processing done by a central computer.

Domains: The term used for grouping resources under a network management system so they can be managed as a single object.

Dynamic Load Libraries (DLL): Libraries under OS/2 that contain the actual instructions for APIs' functions. Programs link to the DLL when they run so that data contained in a DLL need only be loaded once.

Element Management Systems (EMSs): A proprietary software system designed to support multiple network devices from a single manufacturer.

Elevator Seeking: A technique in which a file server retrieves files physically located in the same area of the hard disk rather than blindly retrieving files in the strict sequential order in which they were queued.

Enterprise Management Architecture (EMA): DEC's network management architecture.

Enterprise Network: A network that links together all computing resources within a company; this network can encompass LANs, minicomputers, and mainframes.

Ethernet: A bus network utilizing the CSMA/CD technique for network access. Ethernet LAN specifications were developed by DEC, Intel, and Xerox.

Extended Binary Coded Decimal Interchange Code: An eight-bit data encoding scheme used by IBM mainframe computers and some minicomputers.

Extended Industry Standard Architecture (EISA): 32-bit microcomputer bus architecture that is backward-compatible with 16-bit ISA machines.

Fan Out: A device that acts as a transceiver multiplexer under Ethernet.

Fiber Distributed Data Interface (FDDI): An ANSI standard for a counter rotating ring cable of transmitting data at 100 Mbs over fiber optic cabling for distances up to 200 km.

File Caching: A technique in which the file server keeps frequently requested files cached in RAM so that it does not have to go to disk to retrieve them when they are requested.

File Server: A computer with a large hard disk that serves as a network's central repository for application programs and data files.

File Transfer Access and Management (FTAM): An OSI Application layer protocol for exchanging files between different networks.

Focal Point: The host computer on an IBM's network.

Frequency Modulation: Modulation based on changing the number of cycles per second (the frequency) of a sine wave.

Go-Back-N ARQ: A techinque that utilizes the data unit sequence numbers provided by the LLC. The receiving node indicates a specific number of data units that need to be retransmitted.

Guardbands: Safety bands that separate assigned frequency bandwidths so that they do not interfere with each other.

Hot Fix: NetWare's system fault tolerance measure, in which the hard disk controller checks a sector before attempting to write data to it. If the sector is bad, the controller will write data to a good area.

IEEE 802.3: IEEE specifications for a bus network utilizing CSMA/CD.

IEEE 802.4: IEEE specifications for a token bus network.

IEEE 802.5: IEEE specifications for a token ring network.

IEEE 802.6: IEEE specifications for a metropolitan area network.

Industry Standard Architecture (ISA): Microcomputer 16-bit-architecture resembling the IBM AT's bus.

Interleaved Memory: Memory divided into two or four portions that process information alternatively.

Internet Protocol (IP): The routing protocol associated with TEP/IP. IP provides a connectionless service.

Load Balancing: The uniform distribution of data over available transmission lines.

LocalTalk: Apple's network specification for its shielded twisted-pair cabling system.

Logical Link Control Layer (LLC): The IEEE 802.2 layer concerned with establishing, maintaining, and terminating a communications path between two network nodes.

Logical Unit (LU): A point of access to an SNA network for an SNA user.

Management Information Base (MIB): A database under SNMP that contains definitions for each SNMP agent.

Manchester Encoded Binary: A network encoding scheme that provides a signal transition for every bit.

Manufacturing Automation Protocol (MAP): A protocol based on IEEE 802.4 developed specifically for manufacturing networks.

Media Access Control Layer (MAC): The IEEE 802.2 layer responsible for taking the LLC layer's data units, adding the necessary control information for accessing the specific type of LAN hardware involved, and successfully transmitting frames over a network.

Message Store: Under X.400, a storage system to take delivery of messages addressed to a specific user.

Message Transfer Agent (MTA): The X.400 component responsible for the actual transmission and routing of messages.

Micro Channel Architecture: IBM's proprietary 32-bit bus-mastering architecture for its PS/2 family of microcomputers.

Modem: A device that modulates (converts) a digital signal to an analog signal, changing to reflect the information it is conveying. A second modem demodulates this signal back into digital form for the receiving computer.

Multistation Access Unit (MAU): A wiring hub.

Named Mailslots: A "quick and dirty" method under OS/2 for remote processes to send information to each other by name.

Named Pipes: Channels that can provide full duplex traffic between different processes within a computer or on different computers by creating a virtual session.

NetWare Loadable Module (NLM): Software modules developed for NetWare 3.1 and later versions that link dynamically to the operating system and enable server-based applications to be added while the server is running.

Network Addressable Units (NAUs): Under SNA, NAUs include physical units, logical units, and system service control points. All these elements can be addressed on the network.

Network Driver Interface Specification (NDIS): A specification developed by Microsoft and 3Com as a standard interface for DOS and OS/2 platforms to access services provided by the Data Link layer.

Network Interface Card (NIC): A circuit card placed inside a network node that provides it with the ability to transmit data over a network.

Network Management Station (NMS): A manager that receives alarm information under SNMP.

Network Management System: A group of integrated programs that monitor and control a network's functions, including its performance, security, accounting, resource and configuration management, and alarms and alerts from various network components.

Network Management Vector Transport (NMVT): The management protocol utilized by IBM's network management system.

Non Return to Zero Inverted (NRZI): A network encoding scheme that provides a signal transition only on every binary zero.

Noncontention Network: A network in which nodes are assigned periods to access the network so that there is no contention for network access.

1Base5: An IEEE 802.3 network capable of transmitting at 1 Mbps for 500 meters over baseband cabling. This specification is sometimes referred to as "Starlan."

Open Data-Link Interface (ODI): A standard for device drivers developed by Novell and Apple that enable NIC manufacturers to write one device driver for as many protocol stacks as they want to address.

Open Shortest Path First (OSPF): A routing algorithm that enables routers to broadcast descriptions of their local links rather than entire routing tables.

OpenView: Hewlett-Packard's network management system.

Phase Modulation: Modulation that shifts the entire sine wave a certain number of degrees.

Physical Units (PUs): An SNA NAU that performs control functions for the devices in which they are located as well as for any attached devices. An example is an IBM 3274 control unit.

Pipes: Channels between two programs. Information flows in sequential order from one program to the other.

Point-to-Point Protocol (PPP): A protocol developed to provide serial point-to-point communications links so that interoperability among different vendors' equipment can be improved.

Processes: A program and all the memory areas required to support it under OS/2.

Protected Mode: A mode under OS/2 in which a program is granted its own protected area of memory and registers to hold information during processing.

Repeater: A device that rebroadcasts a network signal.

Routing Information Protocol (RIP): A routing protocol that utilizes the Bellman-Ford algorithm to keep track of the route between source and destination nodes by "hop" count.

Semaphores: Flags set so that two processes do not try to access the same network resource at the same time.

Service Access Point (SSP): The specific element in a node involved in a data exchange according to the IEEE 802 committee's specifications.

Simple Network Management Protocol (SNMP): A network protocol originally designed to be used on the internet to manage network devices designed by different vendors.

Source Routing: A routing scheme utilized by IBM networks in which bridges function at the Network layer of the OSI model. Source nodes broadcast requests for routing information and then determine the path for a packet and attach this "roadmap" to the packet when it is transmitted.

Source Routing Transparent Bridge: A bridge that combines the best features of the Spanning Tree Algorithm and Source Routing. A routing information indicator field (RI) is set for Source Routing nodes and unset for Spanning Tree nodes.

Spanning Tree Algorithm: Bridges communicate with each other and determine a root bridge. Other bridges determine their paths to this bridge so that there is only one complete loop. This standard has been adopted by the IEEE 802.1 committee.

Spread Spectrum Technology: Technology that spreads a data signal across a wide range of radio frequencies.

Standby UPS: An uninterruptible power supply that stands by in case of power failure. It contains an electronic inverter to convert its batteries' DC output to the AC power required by computer equipment.

Static Column Page-Mode RAM: A chip's address is broken into two parts—the column and row address. Since both parts of this address are not always needed, read/writes can be done more quickly.

Stop-and-Wait ARQ: A node waits for an acknowledgment that a data unit was received correctly before beginning to transmit again.

StreetTalk: A distributed database under VINES that provides a very sophisticated resource naming service.

System Fault Tolerance: Measures that can be taken to build redundancy into a system to keep it from failing even if one or more of its key components fail.

System Network Architecture (SNA): IBM's network architecture for its large computers. This is a host-oriented layered architecture.

System Service Control Point (SSCP): Under SNA, an NAU that provides the services necessary to manage a network or a portion of a network.

10Base2: An IEEE 802.3 network capable of transmitting data at 10 Mbs for 200 meters. This specification is sometimes referred to as "Cheapernet," because it utilizes cheaper thin coaxial cabling.

10BaseT: An IEEE 802.3 network capable of transmitting data at 10 Mbs over twisted-pair wiring.

10Broad36: An IEEE 802.3 broadband network that uses 75 ohm coaxial cabling to transmit 10 Mbs for a distance of up to 3,600 meters.

Thread: The execution path within a process.

Unacknowledged Connectionless Service: LLC and MAC layers do not provide any acknowledgment (ACK) that data has been received or offer flow control or error recovery services.

Unified Network Managment Architecture (UNNA): IBM's network management architecture.

User Agents (UAs): Programs under X.400 that reside on stand-alone PCs or E-Mail servers.

Value Added Processes (VAPs): Programs written for NetWare 2.2 and later versions that permit the server to host additional applications. These programs function as interfaces to third-party developers' products.

Virtual Memory: The ability under an operating system to utilize a hard disk's memory and RAM in such a way that large programs can be fooled into thinking the computer has more RAM that it really does.

Wait State: The period of time a PC must wait for the RAM to be cleared before it can write to it.

X.400 Recommendations: CCITT recommendations for an international standard for electronic mail.

X.500 Recommendations: The CCITT standard for creating a global E-Mail directory.

A GUIDE TO
NETWORK VENDORS

This list is not intended to be exhaustive, but it is intended to be a handy place to look when you can't remember a vendor's phone number or address. If you are planning a LAN or expansion of an existing LAN, this guide might be a useful place to begin gathering information. By calling several vendors for a product such as Ethernet cards and requesting sales literature, you can do some quick research before talking to a local distributor.

Bridges and Routers

3Com
3165 Kifer Road
Santa Clara, California 95052
408-562-6400

Advanced Computer Communications (ACS)
720 Santa Barbara Street
Santa Barbra, California 93101
800-444-7854

BICC Data Networks
1800 West Park Drive
Westborough, Massachusetts 01581
800-4-ISOLAN

Cisco Systems
1525 O'Brien Drive
Menlo Park, California 94025
800-553-NETS

CrossCo Corporation
133 East Main Street
P.O. Box 699
Marlboro, Massachusetts 01752
800-388-1200

Develcom Electronics, Inc.
856 51st Street
Saskatoon, Sask. X7K 5C7
306-933-3300

Gateway Communications
2941 Alton Avenue
Irvine, California 92714
800-367-6555

Racal Interlan
155 Swanson Road
Boxborough, Massachusetts 01719
800-LAN-TALK

Retix
2644 30th Street
Santa Monica, California 90405
213-399-2200

E-Mail Software Manufacturers

Accton Technology
2109 O'Toole Avenue, Suite S
San Jose, California 95131
408-432-3042

cc: Mail
2141 Landings Drive
Mountain View, California 94043

Da Vinci Systems
4200 Six Forks Road, Suite 200
Raleigh, North Carolina 27609
800-328-4624

Enable/Higgins Group
1150 Marina Village Parkway, Suite 101
Alameda, California 94501
415-521-9779

Microsoft Corporation
16011 NE 36th Way
Redmond, Washington 98052
206-882-8080

Retix
2644 30th Street
Santa Monica, California 90405
213-399-2200

Ethernet Network Interface Cards

3Com
3165 Kifer Road
Santa Clara, California 95052
800-638-3266

David Systems
701 East Evelyn Avenue
Sunnyvale, California 94086
408-720-6867

Digital Equipment Corporation
146 Main Street
Maynard, Massachusetts 01754
508-493-5111

Racal Interlan
155 Swanson Road
Boxborough, Massachusetts 01719
800-LAN-TALK

Standard Microsystems Corporation (SMC)
35 Marcus Blvd.
Hauppauge, New York 11788
800-762-4968

Thomas Conrad
1908-R Kramer Lane
Austin, Texas 78758
800-332-8683

Tiara Computer Systems
1091 Shoreline
Mountain View, California 94043
800-NETIARA

Network Management Tools

Network General
4200 Bohannon Park
Menlo Park, California 94043
415-688-2700

Novell Lanzlyzer Products
2180 Fortune Drive
San Jose, California 95131
800-243-8526

Spider Systems
12 New England Executive Park
Burlington, Massachusetts 01803
817-270-3510

Network Operating Systems

Artisoft
575 East River Road
Tucson, Arizona 85704
602-293-8965

AT&T Computer Systems
1 Speedwell Avenue
Morristown, New Jersey 07960
800-247-1212

Banyan Systems
120 Flanders Road
Westboro, Massachusetts 01581
800-2-BANYAN

Hewlett-Packard
3000 Hanover Street
Palo Alto, California 94304
415-857-1501

Novell
122 East 1700 South
Provo, Utah 84606
800-453-1267

Microsoft Corporation
16011 NE 36th Way
Redmond, Washington 98052
206-882-8080

Superservers

Compaq Computer Corporation
P.O. Box 17220
houston, Texas 77269
713-370-0670

Dell Computer
9505 Arboretum Blvd.
Austin, Texas 78759
800-426-5150

Netframe Systems
960 Hamlin Court
Sunnyvale, California 94089
408-745-1520

Token Ring Network Interface Cards

Andrew Corporation
2771 Plaza del Amo
Torrance, California 90503
800-541-5021

Cisco Systems
1350 Willow Road
Menlo Park, California 94025
800-553-NETS

Gateway Communications, Inc.
2941 Alton Avenue
Irvine, California 92714
800-367-6555

IBM
1133 Westchester Avenue
White Plains, New York 10604
800-IBM-2468

Madge Networks
534 Salem Avenue, S.W.
Roanoke, Virginia 24016
800-TR-MADGE

Proteon, Inc.
2 Technology Drive
Westboro, Massachusetts 01581
800-545-RING

INDEX

Access Control field, 73

Access II, file access restricted, 145

accounting management, NetWare, 126

Accumaster Integrator, 132

Acknowledged Connectionless Service (Type 3), 54

Acknowledgment frame, Arcnet, 75

AC (*see* Access Control field)

Active Hubs, Arcnet, 76

Addendum (AD), 9

Advanced Program-to-Program Communications, 118

Advanced Revelation database, 138

AFP (*see* Apple Filing Protocol)

ALAP (*see* AppleTalk Link Access Protocol)

Alert Burst field, 75

All The Facts Inc., FaxPac gateway network server, 56

Altair
    FCC license required, 30
    network consistent with Ethernet, 30

American National Standards Institute, 8
    SCSI-2 standard, 38
    SCSI-3 standard, 38
    SCSI drives, 37
    X3T.9 committee developes FDDI standard, 73
    X9.17 encryption standard, 145

American Standard Code for Information Interchange, PC LAN use, 11

American Wire Gauge (AMG), 19

amplitude modulation, 26

analog sine wave, 25f

analog transmission, 25–27
    over broadband coaxial cable, 26–27

Andrew, 802.5 LANs run on unshielded twisted-pair cabling, 71

ANSI (*see* American National Standards Institute)

antennas, radio LANs, 29

antiviral utilities, 143

APIs (*see* application programming interfaces)

APPC (*see* Advanced Program-to-Program Communications)

Apple Computer Corporation, 1
    AppleTalk, 65
    LaserWriter, 2
    LaserWriter printer, 99
    narrow-band radio wireless license proposed, 29–30

System 7.0 and networking, 99

AppleEvents, 99

Apple Filing Protocol, 83

AppleTalk
    LANs, 65
    Macintosh networks, 98–100
    and OSI model, 98f
    Phase, 1, 66
    specifications
        for LocalTalk hardware, Physical layer, 98
        for Token Ring hardware, Physical layer, 98

AppleTalk Filing Protocol, Protocol Manager, 93
AppleTalk Link Access Protocol, 98
AppleTalk Network layer, Datagram Delivery
    Protocol, 98
AppleTalk Session layer, 99
AppleTalk Transaction Protocol, 99
AppleTalk Transport layer, Name Binding Protocol,
    99
Application Program-to-Program communications, 90
applications
    Builder, 133
    layer software, 50
    programming interfaces, 91
        Communication Manager, 89
    programs, networks, 39
    software, network, 176
archive tape library management, 148
Arcnet
    frame
        fields, 75–76
        size, 76
    NIC, 76
    nodes configured as a bus, 76˜
    (see also Attached Resource Computer Network)
Arcnet Active/Passive Hub, 76
ArcnetPlus
    developed by Datapoint, NCR, and Standard
        Microsystems, 76–77
    supports IEEE 802 MAC interface, 76
    technology, 74
ARQ (see automatic repeat request)
ASCII (see American Standard Code for Information
    Interchange)
asynchronous communications
    serial printers, 8
    servers, 119
        selection criteria, 120
asynchronous devices, on MAP network, 71
asynchronous transmission, 15
AT&T
    LAN Manager version for NDIS, 94
    Network Access limit, 45
    Network Management Protocol, 132
    OSI compatible products, 48
    StarGroup, enterprise networking, 96–97
    Starlan 10 network, 63
    Starlan
        daisy-chanel network, 45
        MS-Net product, 81
    network, 61–62
    Unified Network Management Architecture, 131
Attached Resource Computer Network
    frame, 74f, 75
    specification, 74–75
    (see also Arcnet)
attachment unit interface, 52
audit trails, 138
AUI (see attachment unit interface)
automatic repeat request, error control, 54

B

backbone bridge topology, 104f
backup systems, 174–175
    for LANs, 148
backup technology, 147
bandwidth, broadband coaxial cabling, 18
Banyan
    Intelligent Communmications Adapter card, 96
    VINES has NetBios interface, 81
    VINES version, 36
baseband coaxial cable, 21
Basic Networking Utilities, provide NetBIOS inter-
    face for DOS, 96
Bell Labs, Unix development, 95
BERTs (see bit error rate testers)
bibliography, 179–180
binary data, encoded, 13f
Binary Synchronous Control, SNA layered architec-
    ture, 115–116
bit error rate testers, 134
BOB (see breakout boxes)
BPDUs (see bridge protocol data units)
breakout boxes, 134
bridge protocol data units, 105
bridges, 170
    advantages, 102–103
    communicate with STA, 105
    and routers, vendors, 189–190
    selection criteria, 109–110
    topologies, 103–104
    for uninterruptible power supplies, 147
Brighwork Development, QueueIT, 138
broadband cabling
    factories, 27
    LAN, 27f
broadband coaxial cable
    analog transmission, 26–27

bandwidth, 18
network structure, 26f, 27
broadband network
IEEE 802.3 10Broad36, 64
MAP, 70
Broderbund Software, For Comment network software, 4
brouters, 114
BSC (*see* Binary Synchronous Control)
bus
architecture, 34
network, 46f
and Ethernet, 59
specifications, 8
topology described, 46
Busy bit, 78

C

cables, 23
RJ octopus, 64
testers, 134
Token ring networks, 71
cabling, 18–22, 173
IBM system, 22
options for LANs, 22f
problems, 28
twisted pair, 18–19
cache memory, 35–36
CAD (*see* Computer-Aided Drawing)
call-back modems, 142
Call Request packet, 122
carrier sense multiple access with collision detection, 57–58
cartridge
drives, 147
tape backups, 147
cascaded bridge topology, 103f
CCITT (*see* International Consultative Com mittee for Telephone and Telegraph)
central processing unit, 24
CGA (*see* Color Graphics Adapter)
"Cheapernet," 61
checklists for network evaluation/selection, 167–178
Cheyenne Software, Monitrix, 138–139
Clearing phase, 122
client servers, 97–98
Closeup program, 3

CMIP (*see* Common Management Information Protocol)
CMOL (*see* Common Management Information Protocol, Over Logical Link Control)
CMOT (*see* Common Management Information Protocol, Over the Transmission Control Protocol)
CMS 8800 (*see* Communications Management Systems)
coaxial cable, 20f, 21
Colorado Memory Systems, 147
color coding twisted pair wire, 19f
Color Graphics Adapter, 41
3Com
Ethershare, MS-Net product, 81
LAN Manager version for NDIS, 94
NDIS, 129
Combine, Wireman, 134
Common Management Information Protocol
Over Logical Link Control, 128–129
Over the Transmission Control Protocol, 128
Communication Manager, application programming interfaces, 89
communications
basics, 11–30
system, data, 12f
Communications Management Systems, Racal-Milgo, 129
company priorities, cost effectiveness, 172
Compaq Computer Corporation
Intelligent Disk Array, 38
Static Column Page-Mode RAM, 36
Systempro EISA machines, 36
Computer-Aided Drawing, 2
Computer Associates, CA-NET-MAN/PC, 127
Computer Virus Industry Association, 144
Configuration Management, 126
configuring Ethernet LAN, 59–60
Connection-Oriented Service (Type 2), 53–54
connectivity, 24
Connectivity Manager, MHS program, 157–158
Conrad, Thomas (*see* Thomas Conrad Corporation)
contention networks, 57–78
controller chip, IDS, 38
Control Program for Microcomputers, 79
Coordinator
groupware, 4
software, scheduling meetings, 4f

corrugated metallic shielded cable, 32
cost of cabling, 18
cost effectiveness, company priorities, 172
Count field, indicates data field length, 76
CP/M (*see* Control Program for Microcomputers)
CPU (*see* central processing unit)
cross-platform gateways, E-Mail, 162
CSMA/CD (*see* carrier sense multiple access with
    collision detection)

D

daisy-chained PCs
    small network, 45
    with zero slot LAN, 16f
DAP (*see* directory access protocol)
DA (*see* Destination Address; Draft Addendum) data
    collection and analysis, specific conditions, 137
    collisions
        CSMA/CD networks, 58
        frame format, 48
    communications
        equipment, 11
        system, 12f
    encoding, 12
    formats
        ASCII, 11
        EBCDIC, 11
    representation, 11
    terminal
        communications equipment interface, 13
        equipment, 11
    traffic, 170
    transmission, 15–17
    unit, LLC, 55
database management software, network, 175
Database Manager
integrated with NetWare, 87
    Query Manager, 90
Data field
    size, 76
    Token Ring frame, 73
Data Flow Control field, 116
Data frame, Arcnet, 75
Datagram Delivery Protocol, AppleTalk network
    layer, 98
Data Link Controls layer, OS/2EE, 90
Data Link layer, 48–52
    ALAP, 98

SNA layered architecture, 115–116
Datapoint Corporation, ArcnetPlus development, 74,
    76–77
Data Stream Protocol, 99
dBASE IV, for networks, 2–3
DCE (*see* data communications equipment)
DDP (*see* Datagram Delivery Protocol)
DEC (*See* Digital Equipment Corporation)
Defense Department Encryption Standard (DES), 145
Destination Access, 69
Destination Address, 73
    Ethernet, 60
Destination Node ID field, 75
Destination Service Access Point, 55
DFT (*see* Distributed Function Terminal)
DID (*see* Destination Node ID; Direct Inward
    Dialing)
differential phase-shift keying, 65
Digital Equipment Corporation
    All-in-1,157
    EMA Enterprise network, 133
    and Ethernet, 59
    LAT protocol, 113
    network management, 132f
    OSI compatible products, 48
    STA development, 104
    VAX, IBM communications with OSI, 48
    VAX on MAP Network, 71
Direct Inward Dialing, 155
directory
    access protocol, 163
    hashing, 35, 82
    information tree, 163
    system agents, 163
    user agent, 163
disk
    caching, 35
    drives, file servers, 37–38
    duplexing, 150–151
    mirroring, 150
    servers, needed redundant software, 80
diskless microcomputer, network nodes, 40
Disk Operating System, IBM computers, 79–80
DIS (*see* Draft International Standard)
Distributed Function Terminal coaxial gateways,
    117–118
distributed processing, 1–9
distributed star topology, 47
DIT (*see* directory information tree)

LLs (*see* Dynamic Link Libraries)
omain management, LAN Server preference, 94
omains, 164
OS (*see* Disk Operating System)
P (*see* Draft Proposal)
PSK (*see* differential phase-shift keying)
raft Addendum, 9
raft International Standard, 9
raft Proposal, 9
SAP (*see* Destination Service Access Point)
SAs (*see* directory system agents)
TE (*see* data terminal equipment)
UA, (*see* directory, user agent)
ynamic Data Collection, 133
ynamic Link Libraries, 93

asyLAN, zero slot LANs, 17
BCDIC (*see* Extended Binary Coded Decimal
    Interchange Code)
CMA (*see* European Computer Manufacturers
    Association)
DI (*see* electronic data interchange)
D (*see* End Delimiter)
GA (*see* Extended Graphics Adapter)
HLLAPI (*see* Emmulator High Level Language
    Application Programming Interface)
IA (*see* Electronics Industry Association)
ISA, (*see* Extended Industry Standard Architecture)
LAP (*see* EtherTalk Link Access Protocol)
electronic data interchange, transmission over X.400,
    162
Electronic Industries Association
    DTE/DCE interface, 13
    RS-232C interface, 13–14
    RS-232D interface, 14
    RS-449 interface, 14
    RS-530 interface, 15
electronic mail (*see* E-Mail)
Electronics Industry Association, 8
Element Management Systems, 129, 131
elevator *see*king, 82
E-Mail
    CCITT X.400 recommendations, 158–162
    cross-platform gateways, 162
    on LANs, 157
    on networks, 153–165
    software, 175
    selection criteria, 164–165
    softwrare manufacturers, vendors, 190–191
    standardization of specifications, 3–4
    transmission by fax, 155
EMA (*see* EMA Enterprise network)
Emmulator High Level Language Application
    Programming Interface, 89–90
EMSs (*see* Element Management Systems)
emulators, Communication Manager, 89
encoding
    data, 12
    scheme, Non Return to Zero Inverted, 12
encryption, 144
End Delimiter, 69, 73
Enhanced Small Device Interface, 37
enterprise networking, 7–8
    AT&T StarGroup, 96–97
    features, 96
    with Macintosh, 100
    management systems, LAN link, 129
erasable disk drive, Sony, 38
erasable optical drives, 148
ergometric design, 174
error control function, LLC, 54
ESDI (*see* Enhanced Small Device Interface)
Ethernet 2.0, IEEE 802.3 competitor, 63
Ethernet, 17
    bridging LANs with FDDI backbones, 107
    and bus network, 59
    DEC VAX, 48
    Destination Address, 60
    frame, 60f
    linkage to networks, 106
    network, 27
        interface cards, vendors, 191
    outperforms token ring network, 72
Ethershare, 3Com product, 81
EtherTalk drivers, for Macintosh, 98
EtherTalk Link Access Protocol, 66
European Computer Manufacturers Associa-tion, 8
expanded memory, 39–40
Extended Binary Coded Decimal Interchange Code,
    IBM mainframe
    use, 11
extended distance MAU, 71
Extended Graphics Adapter/Array, 41
Extended Industry Standard Architecture, 33–34
    vs. Micro Channel Architecture, 35

F

factories, broadband cabling, 27
fan out device, 61
FATs (*see* file allocation tables)
fault management, 226
fax
    servers
        on networks, 153–165
        selection criteria, 156–157
    standards, CCITT, 154–157
    transmissions, E-Mail, 155
FaxPac gateway network server, All The Facts Inc.,
    156
FBE (*see* Free Buffer Enquiry)
FC (*see* Frame Control)
FCS (*see* Frame Check Sequence)
FDDI (*see* Fiber Distributed Data Interface)
Federal Communication Commission
    Altair requires license, 30
    IR transmission license not required, 28
    narrow-band radio wireless license required, 29
    radio LANs licenses not required, 29
Fiber Distributed Data Interface, 73–74
fields, in Arcnet frame, 75–76
files
    allocation tables, 80, 148–149
    caching, 82
file servers, 31–35
    allocation, 84
    AT class speed with bus mastering, 33
    disk drives, 37–38
    Intel 80386SX microprocessor, 32
    Intel 80486 microprocessor, 33
    memory use, 36
    multiprocessor, 36–37
    NetWare, 82
    optical disk drives, 38–39
    platform, 173
    RAM, 35–36
    standard Intel 80386 microprocessor, 32–33
    with zero slot LAN, 16f
File Transfer Access and Management protocol, 50
File Transfer Access Method, Open Systems
    Interconnect, 83
filing systems, PC network, 6
filtering, specific conditions, 136
fire-retardant teflon cable, 23
Flags field, 111
flexible topology of Arcnet, 76

floppy drives, control, 144
flow control, LLC layer, 54
focal point, host computer, 129
ForComment network software, Broderbund
    Software, 4
Fragment Offset field, 111
Frame Check Sequence, 66, 69, 73, 113
Frame Control, 68
    field, 73
frame format, data collisions, 48
Frame Status field, 73
Free Buffer Enquiry, Arcnet, 75
frequency
    modulation, 25–26
    radio wireless LANs, 29f
Frye Computer Systems, NetWare Early Warning
    System, 137
FS (*see* Frame Status field)
FTAM (*see* File Transfer Access and Management;
    File Transfer Access Method)
future growth, 169

G

gateways, 114–123, 171
General Motors
    first all-MAP plant, 71
    Saturn automibile built at all-MAP plant, 71
Government OSI Profile (GOSIP), 48
graphics standards, 41
groupware
    Coordinator, 4
    network software, 4–5
guardbands, 27

H

hardware
    current, 169
    resources, efficiency, 3
HDLC (*see* High Level Data Link Control)
Header Checksum field, 111
HELLO message, 114
Heterogeneous LAN Management architecture, 129
Hewlett-Packard
    LANProbe, 135
    LaserJet, 2
    OpenView, 133
        and SNMP use, 127

High Level Data Link Control, 112
High-level Data Link Control, protocol, LAPB, 122
High Level Data Link Control, supported by VINES, 96
High Performance File System, 92
High Sierra format, Microsoft, 38
high-speed file systems, 85
HLM (*see* Heterogeneous LAN Management)
host computer, focal point, 129
hot fix, 149
HPFS (*see* High Performance File System; high-speed file systems)
hubs, for uninterruptible power supplies, 147
HubTalk, out-or-band diagnostics, 77
Huffman, modified, 154

IBM (*see* International Business Machines)
ICA (*see* Interapplication Communication Architecture)
ICMP (*see* Internet Control Message Protocol)
IDS (*see* Intelligent Disk Array)
IEEE (*see* Institute of Electrical & Electronics Engineers)
IETF (*see* Internet Engineering Task Force)
improved information management, 5–6
improved security, 6–7
Industry Standard Architecture, 33
infrared
    systems
        Photolink device, 28
        Photonics Corporation, 28
    transmission, FCC licence not required, 28
Institute of Electrical and Electronic Engineers
    802.1 Committee STA standard, 104
    802.1D standard, 105
    802.2 Committee specifications, 52
    802.3 1Base5 standard, 61
    802.3 10Base2 standard, 61
    802.3 10BaseT, 63–64
    802.3 10Broad36 specification, 64–65
    802.5 Token Ring specification, 71
    802.6 Committee MAN specifications, 77–78
    802 Committee, 8
    802 Committee specifications, 55
    ArcnetPlus supports 802 MAC interface, 76
Integrated Services Digital Network, 154
Intel 80286 microprocessor, and PC AT, 32

Intel 80386SX microprocessor, file servers, 32
Intel 80486 microprocessor, 32
Intel, and Ethernet, 59
Intelligent Communmications Adapter card, supports VINES, 96
Intelligent Disk Array, Compaq Computer Corporation, 38
Interapplication Communication Architecture, 99
interleaved memory, 36
International Business Machines
    4341 mainframes on MAP network, 71
    8209 LAN Bridge, 106
    bridges gap between NetWare, 92
    cabling system, 22
    EBCDIC mainframe use, 11
    LAN Manager Program, 130–131
    LAN Manager version for NDIS, 94
    LAN Server, 81
        requirements, 94
    LU 6.2 SNA protocol, 129–130
    NetView, 129–131
    OS/2 Extended Edition, 88–90
    OSI compatible products, 48
    PC AT and Intel 80286 microprocessor, 32
    PC-DOS, 79
    PC LAN, 27, 81
    Presentation Manager for graphics interface, 91–92
    PS/2 using Token Ring Network, 48
    SNA introduced, 115
    SQL, 97
    STP originator, 20
    Token Ring Network, 47
    Type 5 Fiber Optics cable, 23
    XGA, 41
International Consultative Committee for Telephone and Telegraph, 8–9
    facsimile machine groups, 153f
    fax standards, 154–157
    X.25 standard, 121–123
    X.400 recommendations, 158–162
International Standards Organization, 9
    OSI model developed, 48
International Telecommunications Union, CCITT affiliated, 8
Internet Control Message Protocol, 111–112
Internet Engineering Task Force, PPP specifications development, 112
Internet Protocol Header Length, 110–111

interoperability, 170
Invisible Software, Netdiag, 137
Invitation to Transmit frame, 75
IP (*see* internet protocol)
IR (*see* infrared entries)
ISA (*see* Industry Standard Architecture)
ISDN (*see* Integrated Services Digital Network)
ISO (*see* International Standards Organization)

J

"jabber" defined, 46
Jobs, Steve, 1

K

L

LACE (*see* Laser Atmospheric Communications Equipment)
LANanalyzers, Novell, 136
LAN Manager
    AT&T StarGroup support, 96
    IBM support for NDIS, 94
    Microsoft, 92–94
    name service, 164
    operating systems, Microsoft, 81
    structure, 93f
    (*see also* Local Area Network)
LAN Network Manager, Token Ring LANs management, 130
LANProbe, Hewlett-Packard, 135
LAN Server
    IBM, 81
    integraged with NetWare, 87
    requirements, 94
LANSYSTEMS, LANspool, 138
LANtern Services manager, Novell, 127
LAN-to-SNA communications, 118
LAN Works, supports NDIS, 94
Laser Atmospheric Communications Equipment, 28
Laser Communications, Inc., LACE product, 28
LaserJet, Hewlett Packard, 2
laser transmission, 28
LaserWriter
    Apple Corporation, 2
    Apple printer, 99
LAT (*see* Local Area Transport)
LAWN (*see* Local Area Wireless Network)

layered architecture, OS/2 EE, 89
layered protocols, OSI model, 48–50
Link Access Procedure Balanced, HDLC protocol, 122
linking (*see* networking)
Link Support Layer, ODI, 84
Litton Industries, password protection, 142
LLC (*see* Logical Link Control sublayer)
load balancing, remote bridges, 107
Local Area Networks, 7
    backups, 147
    backup systems, 148
    for cabling options, 22f
    E-Mail, 157
    Ethernet bridged with FDDI backbones, 107
    gateway linkage to minicomputer/mainframe networks, 114
    hardware, 31–43
    link to enterprise network management systems, 129
    management hardware tools, 134
    Management software tools, 137–138
    network management, 133–134
    NIC for transmission, 42
    security programs, 145–146
    SNA gateways, 117
    Token Ring, 20
Local Area Transport, 113
Local Area Wireless Network, O'Neill Communications Inc., 29
LocalTalk interface, for Macintosh computer, 65
LocalTalk Link Access Protocol, 66
Logical Link Control sublayer, 52–53
Logical Unit 6.2, IBM SNA protocol, 129–130
logical units, 116
Lotus Notes, Sybase, 85
low-resolution color monitor, 41
LSL (*see* Link Support Layer)
LT Auditor program, 138
LUs (*see* logical units)

M

McGee, Network HQ, 126
Macintosh
    AppleTalk networks, 98–100
    EtherTalk drivers, 98
    NetWare, 84
    network nodes compatibility, 39

TokenTalk drivers, 98
uses StarGroup Server, 96–97
MAC (*see* Medium Access Control sublayer; message authentication code protection)
Magee, Network H.Q., 139
Mail Handling System
  gateway to X.400, 160f
  Novell, 157
  Seal program, 158
main distribution frame, 24
mainframes, 2
  IBM 4341 on MAP network, 71
maintenance, 172
  contracts, 176
management
  and control of networks, 176
  network tools, 176
Management Information Base, 127, 128
Manchester, encoded frame, transformed NRZ encoding, 65
Manchester coding, 59
Manchester Encoded Binary, 12
MANs (*see* Metropolitan Area Networks)
Manufacturing Automation Protocol, 70–71
Manufacturing Message Standard, 70
MAP(*see* Manufacturing Automation Protocol)
MAU (*see* medium attachment unit; Multistation Access Units)
386MAX, memory manager programs, 40
MCBs (*see* Message Control Blocks)
MDF (*see* main distribution frame)
MDI (*see* Medium Dependent Interface)
Media Access Control
  layer, 55
    contains token-passing protocols, 74
Media Access Unit (802.3), 10Base 5 specifications, 60–61
Medium Access Control, sublayer, 52, 55
Medium Attachment Unit, 52
  status, 64
Medium Dependent Interface, 52
Megadata, narrow-band system, 30
memory manager programs, 40
menu management, 137–138
MENU utility, NetWare, 137–138
message authentication code protection, 145
Message Control Blocks, 158
Message Handling System (*see* Mail Handling System)

Message Transfer Agent, 160
Metropolitan Area Networks, 7
  IEEE 802.6 committee specifications, 77–78
MHS (*see* Mail Handling System)
MIB (*see* Management Information Base)
Micro Channel Architecture, 33–35
  vs. Extended Industry Standard Architecture, 35
  XGA interface, 41
microcomputers
  DCE circuit card, 12
  manufacturers, EISA, 34
  on MAP network, 71
  networking, 2
microprocessing chip, file server, 32
microprocessors
  8088/80486,, 32
  80286 and PC AT, 32
  80386SX file servers, 32
Microsoft
  Disk Operating System, 79
  High Sierra format, 38
  LAN Manager, 92–93
    operating systems, 81
    packaging, 94
    version for NDIS, 94
  MS-DOS, 3.1, 80
  multiprocessor to LAN Manager software, 36–37
  Network Driver Interface Specification, 129
  Networks, "plain vanilla" network operating system, 80
  New Technology, 91
  OS/2 32-bit version, 90–91
  OS/2 Standard Edition, 88
  Windows, SNMP alarms, 127
minicomuters, DEC VAX on MAP network, 71
MIP (*see* Management Information Base)
mission/structure of firms, 167–168
Mitsubishi, Palm Recognition System, 141
MLIDs (*see* Multiple Link Interface Drivers)
MMS (*see* Manufacturing Message Standard)
modems, 25–26
  pooling, 119
modulation/demodulation (*see* modems)
Monitor bit, 73
Monitrix, Cheyenne Software, 138–139
monochrome monitor, 41
Motorola, narrow-cast LAN, 30
Mountain Computer, 147
MPI (*see* Multiple Protocol Interface)

MS-DOS (*see* Microsoft, Disk Operating System)
MS-NET (*see* Microsoft, Networks)
MTA (*see* Message Transfer Agent)
multimode fiber, 21
multiple file allocation tables, 148–149
Multiple Link Interface Drivers, ODI, 84
Multiple Protocol Interface, 84–85
Multiprocessing Server Pak, Microsoft, 36–37
multiprocessors, file servers, 36–37
Multistation Access Units, 47, 71

N

Name Binding Protocol, AppleTalk Transport layer,
    99
Name Binding Service, 99
Named Mailslots, OS/2 support, 88
Named Pipes, 85, 88
Name Service
    Lan Manager, 164
    NetWare, 164
narrow-band radio wireless, FCC license required, 29
National Computer Security Association Bulletin
        Board, 144
National Institute of Standards and Technology
        Computer
    Security Bulletin Board, 144
NAU (*see* Network Access Unit)
NCR Corporation
    ArcnetPlus development, 76–77
    WaveLAN limited distance, 29
NDIS (*see* Network Driver Interface Specification)
needs analysis, 167–173
Negative Acknowledgment frame, declines FBE, 75
NetBIOS
    interface, needed for opeating systems, 81
    interprocess communication routine, Protocol
        Manager, 93
    program, 80–81
    Protocol Manager, 93
    served by NetWare, 87
NetBIOS Extended User Interface, Protocol Manager,
    93
NetCommander, zero slot LANs, 17
NETCON utility program, 164
Netdiag, Invisible Software, 137
NetFrame Corporation, NetFrame machine, 37
Net Room, networkwide memory management
        program, 40

NetView
    IBM network management, 90, 129–131
    network loadable module, 87
NetWare, 2.2, 82
    3.11 structure, 83
    3270 LAN Workstation program, 86
    accounting management, 126
    enterprise networking, 86–87
    file servers, 82
        Novell software, 35
    future open architecture, 87f
    has NetBios interface, 81
    integrated with Database Manager, 87
    integrated with LAN Server, 87
    integrated with OS/2 Communication Manager, 87
    LAN, SNMP alarms, 127
    Macintosh, 84
    MENU utility, 137–138
    Name Service, 82, 164
    NetFrame bridge to LAN Manager, 37
    Novell, 81–87
    open architecture, 87
    optical disk drives, 38
    and OS/2, 85–86
    password protection, 142
    PCONSOLE, 155
    run on Systempro, 36
    Sequenced Packet Exchange protocol, 86
    Streams, 87
    to serve NetBIOS and SMB, 87
    user access restrictions, 5
    X.400 gateway, 161
NetWare Access Server, Novell, 87, 119–120
NetWare Connection, 0, 84
NetWare Loadable Module, 83
    runs on NetWare 3.11 server, 120
NetWare Requester
    Novell program, 83
    for OS/2, 85, 86f
network, fax servers security, 156
Network Access
    limit, AT&T, 45
    unauthorized, 141–152
Network Access Unit, 62
Network Addressable Units, Systems Network
        Architecture, 116
Network Archivist, Palindrome, 148
Network Driver Interface Specification
    Microsoft/3Com development, 93–94

Microsoft, 129
etwork File System, Sun Micro system, 83
etwork HQ, McGee, 126
etwork Hub Unit, 62
tworking, 1–9
  PCs, 2
  trends, 1
twork interface card, 42–43, 174
  LAN-specific, 42
  in nodes, 46
  specifications, 52
  support EISA, 77
etwork Management Protocol
  AT&T, 132
  for NMS, 127
etwork Management Station, 127
etwork Management Vector Transport, 129
etwork Node Manager, OpenView, 133
etwork Operating System, 80–81, 174, 192
etworks
  application programs, 39
  application software, 176
  architecture, 45–46
  components selection, 173–175
  database management software, 175
  directory services, and CCITT X.500 standard,
    162–162
  E-Mail, 3–4
  Ethernet linkage, 106
  fax server selection, 154–155
  file server functions, 31–32
  filing systems, 6
  growth, 2
  layer, 51
  management
    and control, 176–177
    DEC, 132f
NetView, 90
NOS by AT&T, 96
  simplification, 82
  system, 125–139
    tools and vendors, 192
  Monitor, nodes, 72
  monitoring, 135–136, 137
  nodes
    diskless microcomputer, 40
memory, 39
  for PCs, 39–42
    selection, 41–42

overall design, 169–170
physical danger protection, 146
procurement process, 177–178
routing faxes, 155–156
security, 141–152
software, 2, 79–100, 175–177
  groupware, 4–5
  as threat, 143
speed, 18
standards, 8–9
system fault tolerance, 152
topology, 45, 171
types, 7–8
users
  access, 5f
  training, 177
  workstations, 174
vendors, 189–193
word processing software, 175–176
networkwide memory management program, Net
  Room, 40
NEWS (see NetWare Early Warning System)
New Technology, Microsoft, 91
NFS (see Network File System)
NHU (see Network Hub Unit)
NIC (see network interface card)
NLM (see NetView network loadable module;
  NetWare Loadable Modules)
NMS (see Network Management Station; network
  management system)
NMVT (see Network Management Vector Transport)
NNS (see NetWare, Name Service)
nodes, network Monitor, 72
noncontention networks, 57–78, 67
Non Return to Zero Inverted, encoding scheme, 12
NOS (see Network Operating System)
Novell
  AS/400 support, 86
  enhanced CICS support, 86
  LANanalyzers, 136
  LANtern Services manager, 127
  Mail Handling System, 157
  MHS gateway to X.400, 160f
  NetWare, 81–87
    file server software, 35
    has NetBios interface, 81
    optical disk drives, 38
  NetWare Access Server, 87, 119–120
  NetWare Requester program, 83

Open Data-Link Interface, 84–85
pricing policies, 84
Service Advertising Protocol, 86
SNA Gateway, 86
venture with IBM, 87
NZRI (*see* Non Return to Zero Inverted)

O

ODLI (*see* Open Data-Link Interface)
OEM (*see* original equipment manufacturers)
OnGuard, file access restricted, 145
on-line sources of virus information, 144
on-line UPS, 146
on-site spares, 176
open architecture, NetWare, 87
Open Data-Link Interface
    LSL, 84
    MLIDs, 84
    Novell, 84–85
open network architecture, vs. proprietary network
    architecture, 171
Open Shortest Path First protocol, 112
OpenSystems Interconnect Model, 9
    and AppleTalk, 98f
    File Transfer Access Method, 83
    ISO development, 48
    Protocol Manager, 93
OpenView
    Hewlett-Packard, 133
    Network Node Manager, 133
Operating System/2 (*see* OS/2)
Operating System for PS/2 microcomputers, OS/2,
    88–94
operating systems, 79–80
optical disk drives, 147–148
    file servers, 38–39
    Netware, 38
optic fiber cable, 21
Options field, 111
original equipment manufacturers, 80
OS/2
    Communication Manager, integrated with
        NetWare, 87
    Kernel, 86
    Operating System for PS/2 microcomputers,
        88–94
OS/2 Extended Edition (OS/2 EE), 88

OSI *see* OpenSystems Interconnection Model)
OSPF (*see* Open Shortest Path First protocol)
out-of-band diagnostics, HubTalk, 77
overall network design, 169–170

P

Pacerlink, supports NDIS, 94
Packet Level, X.25 Recommendation, 122
Palindrome, Network Archivist, 148
paper trail, 168
Passive Hubs
    Arcnet, 76
    ProNET-10 LAN, 77
password protection, 142
Path Control field, 116
PBX (*see* private branch exchange)
PC-DOS (*see* International Business Machines)
PC LAN, International Business Machines, 81
PDUs (*see* Protocol Data Units)
performance, 170
    analysis, 138–139
    management, 125–126
personal identification number, 156
phase modulation, 26
Photolink device, infrared systems, 28
Photonics Corporation, infrared systems, 28
PHY (*see* Physical Layer Protocol)
physical environment, 169
Physical layer, 52, 55
    AppleTalk specifications
        for LocalTalk hardware, 98
        for Token Ring hardware, 98
    FDDI, 73
    SNA layered architecture, 115–116
Physical Layer Protocol, in FDDI Physical layer, 73
physical level interface, X.21,, 122
physical medium attachment, 52
Physical Medium Dependent Layer, 74
Physical Signaling sublayer, 52
physical units, 116
PIN (*see* personal identification number)
pipes, program channels, 88
pixels defined, 41
"plain vanilla" network operatng system, Microsoft
    Networks, 80–81
PMA (*see* physical medium attachment)
PMD (*see* Physical Medium Dependent Layer)

oint-to-Point Protocol, 112
    encapsulation format, 113f
OS (*see* Program Option Select)
ostScript Protocol, 99
PC (*see* Program-to-Program Communication)
PP (*see* Point-to-Point Protocol)
reamble/Postamble, 65–66
resentation layer
    AppleTalk Filing Protocol, 99
    protocol, 50
resentation Manager
    graphics interface for IBM, 91–92
    OS/2 EE graphics interface, 89
resentation Services layer, 116
ricing policies, Novell, 84
rinter Access Protocol, 99
rinters
    LaserJet, 2
    LaserWriter, 2
    on MAP network, 71
    spooling software, 17
    utility programs, 138
rinting management, 138
riority field, 73
rivate branch exchange, 24
rivate E-Mail, X.400 gateways, 161–162
rocurement process, network, 177–178
Program Option Select, Micro Channel Architecture,
    34
programs limitations, running under MS-NET, 81
Program-to-Program Communication, 99
ProNET-10 LAN, by Proteon, 77
proprietary networks, 74–78
    operating systems, 81–97
    vs. open network architecture, 171
protected mode, OS/2 support, 88
Proteon, ProNET-10 LAN, 77
Protocol
    analyzers, 135, 136
    field, 111
    layer, SDLC and SNA support, 90
Protocol Data Units, 127
Protocol Manager
    retains active NDIS driver list, 94
    support, 93
protocols, Open Data-Link Interface, 84
public E-Mail, X.400 gateways, 161–162
PU (*see* physical units)

Q

QPSX (*see* Queued Packet and Synchronous Switch)
QUEMM, memory manager programs, 40
Query Manager, Database Manager, 90
Queued Packet and Synchronous Switch, 78
queues, interprocess communicatinons, 88
Quiescent phase, 122

R

Racal-Milgo, Communications Management
    Systems, 129
radio LANs, 29–30
    FCC licenses not required, 29
RAM (*see* Random Access Memory)
Random Access Memory, 35–36
Read-Only Memory, 40
Receive Not Ready, 54
record locking, not in early DOS, 80
Redirect message, 112
Redirector program, 80–81
reliability, 18, 172
    criteria, 152
remote bridges, 107–109
remote corrections, 3
remote SNA gateways, 118
repeaters, 101–102
Request Counter bit, 78
Requests for Comments, 128
resequencing with Network layer, 51
Reservation field, 73
resource management, 126–127, 139
Revelation, application programs, 39
Revset-Shamir-Adelman encryption system, 145
RFCs (*see* Requests for Comments)
ring
    network, MAU, 70f
    topology, 47–48
Ring In, MAU connection, 71
Ring Out, MAU connection, 71
RIP (*see* routing information protocol)
RI (*see* Ring In)
RJ octopus cable, RJ-45 connectors, 64
RNR (*see* Receive Not Ready)
robots, on MAP network, 71
ROM (*see* Read-Only Memory)
RO (*see* Ring Out)

routers, 110, 171
  limitations, 113
  selection criteria, 113–114
    for unterruptible power supplies, 147
routing faxes to network users, 155–156
routing information protocol, 112
Routing Table Maintenance Protocol, 99
RS-232C interface, 13–14
RS-232 standard, 8
RS-422 used in LocalTalk bus network, 65
RSA (*see* Revset-Shamir-Adelman)
RTMP (*see* Routing Table Maintenance Protocol)

S

SAA (*see* Systems Application Architecture)
Saber, Menu System, 137–138
SAP (*see* service access point; Service Advertising
  Protocol)
SA (*see* Source Address)
scheduling meetings, Coordinator software, 4f
SCSI (*see* Small Computer System Interface)
SDLC (*see* synchronous data link control protocol)
SD (*see* Start Delimiter)
Seal program, Mail Handling System, 158
security, 18, 172
  criteria, 152
  management, 126, 138
  measures for PC LANS, 144–145
  for network fax servers, 156
Security Guardian, file access restricted, 145
See d field, 65
semaphores (flags), 88
Sequenced Packet Exchange protocol, NetWare, 86
Serial Line Internet Protocol, 112
serial printers, asynchronous communications, 8
Server Message Block, served by NetWare, 81, 87
service access point, 55
Service Advertising Protocol, Novell, 86
Session layer
  OSI model, 81
  protocol, 51
Session Protocol, 99
shared hardware resources, 2
shared information, 3
shared software resources, 2–3
shielded twister pair, 20
Sid Kick, accessory program, 39
SID (*see* Source Node ID)

signal quality error, 64
simple network management protocol, 127
  TCP/IP, 127
single-mode optic fiber, 21–22
Single View Management, 133
Sitelock
  program, 6
  user control, 138
SLIP (*see* Serial Line Internet Protocol)
Small Computer System Interface-2 standard, ANSI
  committee debate, 38
Small Computer System Interface-3 standard, ANSI
  committee debate, 38
Small Computer System Interface, 37-38
small network, daisy-channel PCs, 45
SMB (*see* Server Message Block)
SMC (*see* Standard Microsystems Corporation)
SMF (*see* Standard Message Format)
SMI (*see* structure of management information)
SMP (*see* Symmetric Multiprocessing)
SNA (*see* system network architecture)
SNMP (*see* simple network management protocol)
software, 79–100
  analysis of need, 168–169
  current, 169
  E-Mail, 175
  for networks, 2
  networks, 175–177
  resources, efficiency, 3
  threats to networks, 143
SOH (*see* Start of Header field)
Sony, erasable disk drive, 38
Source Address, 69, 73
  node transmitting Ethernet frrame, 60
Source Node ID field, 75
Source Quench message, 112
source routing transparent bridge, 106–107
Source Service Access Point, 55
Spanning Tree Algorithm, 104–105
  redundancy for remote bridge, 109f
specifications
  bus, 8
  IEEE 802.2 committee, 42
  MANs, 8
  network interface card, 52
  voice/data integration, 8
speed, networks, 18
spread spectrum defined, 29
SPX (*see* Sequenced Packet Exchange)

QE (*see* signal quality error)
QL (*see* Structured Query Language)
RT (*see* source routing transparent bridge)
SAP (*see* Source Service Access Point)
SCPs (*see* system service control points)
tandard Message Format, 159
tandard Microsystems Corporation
    Arcnet license, 74
    ArcnetPlus development, 76–77
    ArcnetPlus turbo driver, 76
tandards development, networks, 9
tandby UPS, 146
tarGroup Computer Manager, Accumaster
    Integrator links, 132
tarGroup Network Manager, Accumaster Integrator
    links, 132
tarGroup Server, for Macintosh, 96–97
tarlan
    daisy-chanel network, AT&T, 45
    standard, 61–63
    star topology, 62f
Start Delimiter, 68
    field, 73
Start of Header field, 75
star topology, 46–47
    Starlan, 62f
STA (*see* Spanning Tree Algorithm)
Static Column Page-Mode RAM, Compaq, 36
STDA (*see* StreetTalk Directory Assistance)
STP (*see* shielded twister pair)
StreetTalk
    Directory Assistance, 95
    VINES database, 95–96
Structured Query Language, 90
    IBM, 97
Structured Query Language Server, Sybase, 85
structure of management information, 128
Sun Micro system
    Network File System, 83
    SunNet Manager and SNMP use, 127
superservers, vendors, 193
Sybase
    Lotus Notes, 85
    SQL Server, 85
Symmetric Multiprocessing, VINES, 36
Synchronous Data Link Control
    protocol, 90
    SNA layered architecture, 115–116

supported by VINES, 96
synchronous transmission, 17
system fault tolerance, 148, 172
system network architecture, Gateway by Novell, 86
Systempro
    runs NetWare, 36
    runs VINES, 36
    synchronization, 38
systems
    integrators, Arcnet low cost, 76
    service control points, 116
Systems Application Architecture, 86, 89
Systems Network Architecture, 83
    devices, 90, 129
    gateway selection criteria, 118–119
    layered, 115f
    network addressable units, 116
        in operation, 116–117

T

T-1 service, 108
TCNS (*see* Thomas Conrad Networks Systems)
TCP/IP (*see* Transmission (Transport) Control
    Protocol/Internet Protocol)
terminals
    data communications equipment interface, 13
    on MAP network, 71
terminate and stay resident programs, 39–40, 139,
    144
Thin Ethernet (*see* "Cheapernet")
Thomas Conrad Corporation
    Arcnet license, 74
    ArcnetPlus turbo driver, 76
    Networks Systems, 77
thread process, 88
Time-Domain Reflectometers, 134
TLAP(*see* TokenTalk Link Access Protocol)
Token Bus
    802.4 specification, 67–68
    Arcnet, 75
    frame control panels, 68f
    LAN, 70
    network, Arcnet, 75
    operation, 69
Token Ring
    basic operation, 72–73
    frame, 73

token formats, 72f
interface coupler gateway, 118
Local Area Network, 20
packets, 106
Token Ring Network
    cables, 71
    IBM, 47
    IBM PS/2, 48
    interface cards, 193
TokenTalk drivers, Macintosh, 98
TokenTalk Link Access Protocol, 66–67
topologies
    bridges, 103–104
    network structure, 45
Total Length field, 111
transaction tracking, 151
transformed NRZ encoding, Manchester encoded
        frame, 65
Transmission Control field, 116
Transmission Control Protocol/Internet Protocol, 60
    Protocol Manager, 93
    SNMP, 127
transmitting EDI, over X.400, 162
Transport Control Protocol/Internet Protocol, 83
Transport layer, 51
    mechanism, Protocol Manager, 93
Trojan horses programs, 143
troubleshooting with 10BaseT, 64
TSR (*see* terminate and stay resident programs)
twisted pair, 18–19
    cables, 23
Type 1 data cable, 22
Type 1 Outdoor data cable, 23
Type 1 Plenum data cable, 23
Type 2 Data/Telephone cable, 23
Type 5 Fiber Optics cable, 23
Type 6 Data cable, 23
Type 8 Under Carpet cable, 23
Type 9 Plenum Data cable, 23
Type of Service field, 111

U

UAs (*see* User Agents)
UDP (*see* User Datagram Protocol)
UMD (*see* Unscrambled Mode Delimiter)
Unacknowledged Connectionless Service (Type 1),
        53

Ungermann-Bass, 802.5 LANs run on unshielded
        twisted-pair
        cabling, 71
Unified Network Management Architecture, 96
    AT&T, 131
uninterruptible power supplies, 146, 147, 175
    workstations, 147
United Nations, CCITT affiliated, 8
universal wiring systems, 23–25
Unix
    API effects, 91
    operating system, 94–95
    VINES operates as process, 95
UNMA (*see* Unified Network Management
        Architecture)
Unscrambled Mode Delimiter, 65
unshielded twisted pair, 20–21
UPDATE message, 114
UPSs (*see* uninterruptible power supplies)
U.S. Department of State, CCITT affiliated, 8–9
user access, networks, 5f
User Agents, 159
User Datagram Protocol, 127
User-Defined Threshold, 133
user training, networks, 177
UTP (*see* unshielded twisted pair)

V

Value Added Processes (VAPs), 82
VAX, minicomputers, MAP network, 71
vendors
    new network architecture preparations, 97
    products on MAP network, 71
Video Graphics Array (VGA), 41
VINES
    Banyan Systems, 95
    has NetBios interface, 81
    packaging, 96
    run on Systempro, 36
    StreetTalk, 82
        and network directory servics, 163
    supports HDLC, 96
    supports NDIS, 94
    supports SDLC, 96
    supports X.25 protocol, 96
virtual memory, OS/2 support, 89
Virtual Networking Systems (*see* VINES)

tual terminal protocol, 40
uses, 143
  protection, 144
  scanning/removal, 143–144
rus Information Bulletin Board, 144
talink, STA development, 104
ice/data integration, specifications, 8
ice/data transmission cables, 23
T (*see* virtual terminal protocol)

W

ait state defined, 35
ANs (*see* Wide Area Networks)
atchdog, file access restricted, 145
aveLAN limited distance, NCR Corporation, 29
C (*see* wiring closet)
D (*see* Working Draft)
ide Area Networks, 7
indows, API effects, 91
ireless-in-Building Network (WIN), Motorola, 30
ireless LAN transmission, 28–30
iring closet, 25
ordPerfect
  application programs, 39
  E-Mail use, 3
  for networks, 2–3
ord processing software, network, 175–176
orking Draft, 9
orkstations
  network users, 174
  UPS, 147
rite-Once Read-Many drivers (WORM), 143, 147

X

X.25
  gateways, 120–121
  packet switch, selection criteria, 123
  protocol, supported by VINES, 96
  standard, 121–123
  WAN, connects LANs, 121f
X.75 Recommendation, 122
X.400
  features, 161
  gateways, private/public E-Mail, 161–162
Xerox, and Ethernet, 59
Xerox Networking System, 83
XGA (*see* Extended Graphics Array)
XNS (*see* Xerox Networking System)

Y

Z

ZeroNet, zero slot LANs, 17
zero slot LAN, RS-232 interface, 15–16
Zone Information Protocol, 99